Survivor's Guide to Computer Viruses

Virus Bulletin '93

Virus Bulletin Ltd • 21 The Quadrant • Abingdon • OX14 3YS • England

Tel (0235) 555139 • Fax (0235) 559935 • EMail VIRUSBTN@VAX.OX.AC.UK

ISBN 0 9522114 0 8

9 8 7 6 5 4 3 2 1

DOSETUP.EXE   SCATEMM.SYS   SCATEMM.TXT   SPEED.COM   DISCHRGE.C

DOSKEY.COM   DOSSHELL.VID   DOSSHELL.INI   DOSSHELL.COM   DOSSHELL.E

DOSSHELL.GRB   DOSSWAP.EXE   PACKING.LST   PRINT.EXE   APPNOTES.T

DOSSHELL.HLP   EDIT.HLP   RECOVER.EXE   DOSHELP.HLP   HELP.EXE

QBASIC.HLP   EDIT.COM   MONEY.BAS   MSHERC.COM   QBASIC.EXE

GORILLA.BAS   4201.CPI   4208.CPI   5202.CPI   APPEND.EXE

ASSIGN.COM   ATTRIB.EXE   BACKUP.EXE   CHKDSK.EXE   COMP.EXE

DISKCOMP.COM   DISKCOPY.COM   DRIVER.SYS   FC.EXE   FIND.EXE

GRAFTABL.COM   GRAP✶✶✶✶✶✶✶✶≍HICS.COM   GRAPHICS.PRO   LABEL.EXE

E.COM   NIBBLES.BAS   REMLINE.BAS   RESTORE

ZBIN.EXE   EXPAND.EXE   JOIN.EXE

NTER.SYS   README.TXT   REPLACE.EXE   SUBST.EXE   TREE.COM

FUNC.EXE   DISPLAY.SYS   EGA.CPI   SMARTDRV.SYS   EMM386.EXE

IN.EXE   MEM.EXE   FASTOPEN.EXE   COMMAND.COM

89 file(s)   2098733 bytes

18311168 bytes free

Contents

Go, litel book, go litel myn tragedie

G. Chaucer, Troilus and Criseyde

computer vir'|us [...] virus, or a computer virus, a program which infects other programs by modifying them to include a copy of itself; can act as a carrier of malicious code e.g. destroying data; may spread through a system or network; viruses can infect parts of the operating system and/or application programs [L, = slimy liquid, poison]

Introduction

Are you sitting comfortably? Then I'll begin...

The aim of this book is simple: to help computer users combat the virus problem. If the reader uses the advice and information provided, he should be able to limit the spread of viruses on machines under his control drastically. Note that I have chosen the words of the preceding sentence with care - even with all the expertise and attention to detail in the world, a virus-proof IBM-compatible PC is a contradiction in terms.

The book addresses the subjects which are central to the problem of virus control, namely:

- What are computer viruses?

- How can they 'infect' other objects?

- How to prevent virus infection?

- What should one look for in an anti-virus package?

- Where do viruses come from?

In order to defend yourself against viruses, you must gain an understanding of how viruses function: without this knowledge, the result will be rather like building a house on sand.

This volume is designed to supplement the information published in *Virus Bulletin* every month. Anti-virus software and techniques need to be updated whenever a radically new virus is discovered, and one volume cannot hope to prepare the reader for the many twists and turns that viruses may (will) take in the future. This book allows the fundamentals of good practice to be laid down - it should be considered the foundation upon which a solid security policy can be constructed.

The book contains technical analyses of the most important computer viruses, either for reasons of prevalence, or complexity. This is supplied in order that the reader may understand the foe he is likely to encounter. Included in this rogues' gallery are some viruses which have forced the anti-virus industry to change the way it operates. The onset of polymorphic viruses has led to a gradual decrease in scanner speed and accuracy - a discussion of the infamous Mutation Engine, which greatly contributed to this, is included.

World-class anti-virus research tends to be done by a handful of people who are usually employed by anti-virus companies and often *VB* contributors. A 'Who's Who' chapter identifies some of the more prominent figures in the anti-virus community.

Several people have been involved in the preparation of this book, especially Victoria Lammer, who spent many hours editing various contributions, Edward Wilding, founding *VB* editor, who wrote much of the text and is largely responsible for the success of *Virus Bulletin*, Jan Hruska, Peter Lammer, Keith Jackson, Mark Hamilton, Jim Bates, James Beckett, Richard Jacobs, Tim Twaits and Fridrik Skulason. Finally, my thanks go to Isobel Wilson, for putting up with the continual grousing, late nights, and bad tempers which preparing the book caused. I hope that the reader will judge the results worth it.

Richard Ford
Editor, *Virus Bulletin*

Oxford, September 1993

History of viruses

History does not repeat itself. Historians repeat each other.

A. Balfour

```
0000   fa e9 4a 01 34 12 00 05    08 00 01 00 00 00 00 20    ..J.4...  .......
0010   20 20 20 20 20 20 57 65    6c 63 6f 6d 65 20 74 6f         We lcome to
0020   20 74 68 65 20 44 75 6e    67 65 6f 6e 20 20 20 20    the Dun geon
0030   20 20 20 20 20 20 20 20    20 20 20 20 20 20 20 20
0040   20 20 20 20 20 20 20 20    20 20 20 20 20 20 20 20
0050   20 28 63 29 20 31 39 38    36 20 42 61 73 69 74 20    (c) 198 6 Basit
0060   26 20 41 6d 6a 61 64 20    28 70 76 74 29 20 4c 74    & Amjad  (pvt) Lt
0070   64 2e 20 20 20 20 20 20    20 20 20 20 20 20 20 20    d.
0080   20 42 52 41 49 4e 20 43    4f 4d 50 55 54 45 52 20     BRAIN C OMPUTER
0090   53 45 52 56 49 43 45 53    2e 2e 37 33 30 20 4e 49    SERVICES ..730 NI
00a0   5a 41 4d 20 42 4c 4f 43    4b 20 41 4c 4c 41 4d 41    ZAM BLOC K ALLAMA
00b0   20 49 51 42 41 4c 20 54    4f 57 4e 20 20 20 20 20     IQBAL T OWN
00c0   20 20 20 20 20 20 20 20    20 20 20 4c 41 48 4f 52              LAHOR
00d0   45 2d 50 41 4b 49 53 54    41 4e 2e 2e 50 48 4f 4e    E-PAKIST AN..PHON
00e0   45 20 3a 34 33 30 37 39    31 2c 34 34 33 32 34 38    E :43079 1,443248
00f0   2c 32 38 30 35 33 30 2e    20 20 20 20 20 20 20 20    ,280530.
0100   20 20 42 65 77 61 72 65    20 6f 66 20 74 68 69 73      Beware  of this
0110   20 56 49 52 55 53 2e 2e    2e 2e 2e 43 6f 6e 74 61     VIRUS.. ...Conta
0120   63 74 20 75 73 20 66 6f    72 20 76 61 63 63 69 6e    ct us fo r vaccin
0130   61 74 69 6f 6e 2e 2e 2e    2e                         ation...
0140   2e 2e 2e 2e 20 24 23 40    25                         ...  $#@ %
0150   8e d8 8e d0 bc 00 f0 fb    a0 06 7c a2 09 7c 8b 0e    ......... ..|..|..
0160   07 7c 89 0e 0a 7c e8 57    00 b9 05 00 bb 00 7e e8    .|...|.W .....~.
0170   2a 00 e8 4b 00 81 c3 00    02 e2 f4 a1 13 04 2d 07    *..K..... ....-.
0180   00 a3 13 04 b1 06 d3 e0    8e c0 be 00 7c bf 00 00    ........ ....|...
0190   b9 04 10 fc f3 a4 06 b8    00 02 50 cb 51 53 b9 04    ........ ..P.QS..
01a0   00 51 8a 36 09 7c b2 00    8b 0e 0a 7c b8 01 02 cd    .Q.6.|.. ...|....
01b0   13 73 09 b4 00 cd 13 59    e2 e7 cd 18 59 5b 59 c3    .s.....Y ....Y[Y.
01c0   a0 0a 7c fe c0 a2 0a 7c    3c 0a 75 1a c6 06 0a 7c    ..|....| <.u....|
01d0   01 a0 09 7c fe c0 a2 09    7c 3c 02 75 09 c6 06 09    ...|.... |<.u....
01e0   7c 00 fe 06 0b 7c c3 00    00 00 00 32 e3 23 4d 59    |....|.. ...2.#MY
01f0   f4 a1 82 bc c3 12 00 7e    12 cd 21 a2 3c 5f 0c 05    .......~ ..!.<_..
```

Pervading Animal

In the 1960s and 1970s when giant mainframes roamed the world and computers were the preserve of a technocratic elite, there existed a phenomenon known as 'the rabbit'. A 'rabbit', which usually happened by accident, much to the chagrin of the technicians, was a computer program written in an interpreted command language which replicated or cloned itself thus causing severe and often crippling system degradation. Not all 'rabbits' were unintentional - the 'Pervading Animal', for instance, was a malicious program which ran on the Univac 1108 system. 'Pervading Animal' appended itself to executable code and marked these contaminated files with its own self-recognition signature. In this respect, 'Pervading Animal' was the exact forebear of today's computer viruses, many of which utilise precisely the same *modus operandi.*

Harlie

Computing and science fiction are two domains which share a symbiotic relationship - nowhere is this more true than with computer viruses. David Gerrold's *When Harlie Was One*, published in 1972, referred to a computer program which manipulated auto-dial modems in order to upgrade or communicate with remote systems. In the plot, a bug in the code causes this program to spread itself uncontrollably across the telephone network. For no obvious reason, this sub-plot was removed from later editions of Gerrold's book.

Bolt Beranek and Newman

Concurrent with the publication of '*Harlie*', two programmers, Beranek and Newman, were hard at work developing 'The Creeper'. As life copies art, so 'The Creeper' copied science fiction. Written to spread under the now antiquated Tenex operating system, 'The Creeper' was functionally identical to the program described in Gerrold's book, except that it contained no lethal bug. 'The Creeper' copied itself from the host system to remote systems, deleting all previous versions of itself. A subsequent development was 'The Reaper', a 'search and destroy' program which stalked the hapless 'Creeper' across the same network eliminating it from all its hiding places. It has been postulated that 'The Reaper' was thus the first anti-virus program.

Brunner

John Brunner, the English science fiction writer, wrote an even more prescient prediction in his famous story *The Shockwave Rider*, published in 1975. The book is about a disgruntled manager within a multi-national corporation who decides to inflict mayhem upon his masters' networks with the aid of the 'Tapeworm', a highly sophisticated program which could circumvent access control by referencing stored user IDs, passwords and access codes. The 'Tapeworm' was self-replicating and capable of monitoring the status of all its counterparts - thus any attempt to destroy one of its segments resulted in the activation of a stored segment elsewhere. This 'Tapeworm' as described by Brunner has obvious parallels with the real life worm programs which were later to afflict the Internet and DECNet. It is also interesting to note the underlying theme within Brunner's book of the concept of the downtrodden individual fighting back against the authoritarian power elite. Eulogising the 'oppressed' in this way has become a prerequisite of hacker culture.

Xerox

Actual experimentation with worm programs was being undertaken at this time in California at the Xerox research facility at Palo Alto. Xerox's research centred around the concept of employing 'benign' worm code to conduct diagnostic and fault repair in distributed systems. Communication between worm segments, much as described by Brunner, was also central to the research.

At about the same time, Motorola was also engaged in experimentation, most notably with its processes 'Friar Tuck' and 'Robin Hood' which utilised Xerox CP-V timesharing. This experiment was essentially an exercise in survivability - 'Robin' protected 'Tuck' from deletion and vice versa. In much the same way, 'survivability', the process by which a modern day virus avoids detection, is heavily dependent on such code self-recognition, both in memory and on disk.

Elk Cloner

The first verified report of a computer virus was issued in 1981. 'Elk Cloner' infected the boot sector of disks on Apple II PCs and copied itself to the boot sectors of diskettes as they were accessed. The virus contained a number of 'payloads', it inverted the screen, caused text to flash and even displayed a poetic inclination describing itself as 'the program with personality' which 'will stick to you like glue/will modify RAM too'.

Trusting Trust

The cat was well and truly set amongst the pigeons a year later with the delivery of an award winning speech at the Association of Computing Machinery by the Unix 'guru' Ken Thompson. Thompson described a Unix 'C' compiler which had been trojanised in such a way that any subsequently compiled software (including 'C' compilers) contained the Trojan horse. The paper was entitled

'Reflections on Trusting Trust' and correctly asserted that no compiled software, whatever its origin, could be trusted inherently.

Cohen

In November 1983, Dr Frederick Cohen demonstrated self-replicating code in a series of VAX and Unix experiments conducted at Lehigh University in Pennsylvania. A colleague of Cohen's, one Len Adleman, is reputed to have coined the phrase 'virus' in reference to this self-replicating code. The experiments were subsequently published in the *Computers & Security* journal and caused something of an uproar within the computer security fraternity. Cohen subsequently demonstrated virus propagation on a UNIVAC machine configured to the much revered Bell-LaPadula security model which dictates that less privileged users may write to but not read information from a more privileged level. Cohen demonstrated that a virus can propagate on such a system.

Gibson

1984 also saw the publication of another work of science fiction which was to have a profound influence upon the 'hacker' psyche. *Neuromancer* by William Gibson introduced the concept of 'Cyberspace' whereby all computers were inextricably linked in a network which could be navigated. Gibson is widely accredited with predicting the arrival of virtual reality and is classed as a demi-god by most hackers. A predictable theme within Cyberpunk, as the genre came to be known, is that of the lone hacker fighting the large corporates and conglomerates. Not surprisingly, Robert Morris, later convicted for releasing the Internet Worm, was an addicted fan of Gibson's books.

The Dirty Dozen

1985 was a relatively quiet year, during which the most significant development was the creation of the 'Dirty Dozen'. This is a list of the most common trojan horse programs to be found on bulletin boards.

Brain

The big year in IBM PC virus 'history' was 1986. Reports started to appear in newspapers worldwide of the 'Brain' virus. In fact, this boot sector virus, which only infected 360 K floppy disks, quickly spread worldwide with reports being received from Asia, the Middle East, Europe and the United States. Examination of the virus revealed that it purports to have been developed in Lahore, Pakistan in January 1986. What amazing piece of deduction led the community to this conclusion? Was it a brilliant piece of forensic science? Well, not exactly - the developers, Basit and Amjad Farooq Alvi had left their names, address and telephone numbers in ASCII text within the boot sector of every infected disk.

The brothers ran a software house in Lahore and were reportedly annoyed at the extent of software piracy and theft taking place in their country. The virus was a clumsy attempt to define the extent of such copying. It is interesting that the Brain virus introduced the concept of 'stealth': any attempt to read logical sector 0 of the infected diskette while the virus was memory-resident was intercepted and redirected to clean boot sector code stored elsewhere on disk. In 1992, Virus Bulletin was sent a very polite letter by Amjad Alvi requesting information about the Second International *Virus Bulletin* Conference. The letterhead upon which the letter was written suggests that the brothers' computer business is flourishing!

The Brain virus became something of a collector's item with self-appointed 'experts' refusing interested and legitimate parties any access to the code. In the United Kingdom, Dr Alan Solomon, who ran a data recovery company and managed to obtain a sample, persistently refused to let outside parties examine the virus while simultaneously making an enormous issue of the virus within the popular press. Needless to say, the early disassemblies of the virus were execrable. In October 1987 the University of Delaware campus suffered an infestation of the Brain virus. The subsequent technical reports and active code, made available to responsible organisations by Anne Webster of the University's Academic Computing Center, helped to remove the veil of mystery surrounding the virus.

Chaos

December 1986 also heralded the convening of a computer virus forum held by the Chaos Computer Club in Hamburg, Germany. The CCC is a loose alliance of underground hackers and phreakers, best known for its association with a group known as the 'VAX busters' which specialised in hacking into VAX/VMS systems worldwide. In a television interview shown on British television in 1989, a member of the group claimed that the club had written a virus construction set in which any semi-competent programmer could create a functioning virus with any one of a number of different payloads and activation conditions.

Burger

The following year saw the publication of *Computer Viruses: A High Tech Disease*. This book, which contained source code to the Vienna (aka DOS 62) virus as well as listings in Basic and Pascal is widely accredited as inciting the subsequent explosion in the number of PC viruses. An English language edition of the book published in the United States by Abacus Press fanned the flames and resulted in widespread condemnation. 'There is no doubt,' concluded British researcher Jim Bates, 'that some damage will result from attempted copies of the Vienna virus listing, which is to be deplored.' Burger himself attended the Hamburg Congress at which he distributed copies of his demonstration virus VIRDEM.COM, a simple non-resident COM file infecting virus. This 'demonstration' virus coupled with the Vienna virus are now the most hacked computer viruses in the world - at the time of writing the latter specimen has no fewer than 104 uniquely identifiable known variants. Mark Washburn, author of the self-mutating 1260 virus which appeared in 1991, readily admitted that he had used Burger's book as a template for his experimentation.

It was also in 1987 that viruses started to afflict other microcomputers including the Apple Macintosh, the Commodore Amiga and the Atari ST. The ubiquitous nVIR virus first appeared in Germany, was modified and subsequently re-released in this year. The two strains of nVIR are arguably the most prevalent Mac virus in the world.

Brandow

Also afflicting the Apple Macintosh in this year was the Peace virus which was developed by a contract programmer at the behest of Richard Brandow, who at the time published MacMAG magazine. The virus contained the following message, which the virus was designed to display on the 2nd March, 1988:

```
RICHARD BRANDOW, publisher of MacMag, and
its entire staff would like to take this
opportunity to convey their UNIVERSAL
MESSAGE OF PEACE to all Macintosh users
around the world.
```

Once the message was displayed, the virus removed itself from the system file in which it hid and thus eliminated itself from all infected machines. Consequently, the virus is now believed to be extinct except for a few 'laboratory' examples in the hands of researchers. The Peace virus had been uploaded to the CompuServe bulletin board and is believed to have been widely circulated. In an interview with the Chicago Tribune in 1988, Brandow accepted responsibility for the virus and described it as a 'message'. 'We look at it as something that's really positive.'

In fact, Brandow's virus subsequently infected a master disk at the Aldus Corporation's main duplication facility in March 1988. Some 5,000 copies of the Freehand illustration program were destroyed while a further 5,000 copies were recalled. The incident cost Aldus an estimated $7,000.

On August 20th 1992 Brandow, now 28 years old and living in Canada, was formally charged with 'malicious mischief' by prosecutors in King County, Washington State, USA and faces 10 years imprisonment if convicted. 'What are they going to do? It happened four years ago and I am here in Montreal...', was his immediate reaction upon hearing of his imminent extradition.

1987 also witnessed the first virus aimed specifically at the Commodore Amiga machine. Written by the self-styled 'Swiss Cracker's Association', the virus was detected in November of that year. It infects the boot sector of disks and displays the following message to screen:

```
Something wonderful has happened Your AMIGA
is alive !!! and, even better... Some of
your disks are infected with a VIRUS!!!
Another masterpiece of The Mega-Mighty SCA.
```

Similarly, viruses started to appear on Atari PCs, two of which (Aladdin and Frankie) were specifically written to execute under Mac emulation on the ST.

The Lehigh Virus and Other PC Examples

However, it was on IBM PCs that the burgeoning virus threat was becoming most apparent. The 405 virus, a crude overwriting specimen culled from Burger's book appeared 'in the wild' in Austria but failed to cause much panic as it crippled its host program - thus it could not replicate without being detected almost immediately. Intriguingly, a somewhat primitive virus which only infected COMMAND.COM caused several infections at Lehigh

University in November 1987, giving rise to speculation that one of
Dr Cohen's former students or associates may have been responsible.
The incident had a beneficial side effect: Ken van Wyk, who worked
at the University's computer center at the time and who formed part
of the team that tackled the outbreak, went on to join the Computer
Emergency Response Team and now moderates the hugely popular
and informative electronic conference known as Virus-L which
provides a wealth of detailed information and discussion about virus
threats and anti-virus measures.

More significant threats were viruses such as Jerusalem which was
discovered in Israel and spread with relative ease, and Cascade
which caused a striking screen effect in the Autumn of 1988. The
latter virus is renowned due to its well known falling letters display.
From a technical point of view it was particularly interesting as it
was the first virus to introduce code encryption which limited the
choice of a detection pattern to the decryption routine.

The Bitnet Chain Letter

In December 1987, the first major network attack occurred. The
Christmas Tree chain letter spread from a node at the University of
Klausthal Zellerfield in West Germany onto Bitnet, via a gateway to
the European Academic Research Network (EARN) and thence onto
IBM's internal network known as VNet. It was launched on 9th
December 1987 and had various effects, one of which was to
paralyse the IBM worldwide network on 11th December 1987.

The Christmas Tree chain letter is written in REXX and spreads on
VM/CMS installations. The program is a combination of a trojan
horse and a chain letter which invites recipients to execute its code.
When run, it draws a Christmas tree on screen, sends a copy of itself
to all the user's correspondents in the user files NAMES and
NETLOG and then deletes itself. The chain letter can thus spread to
every user account on the system.

Significantly, the source code of this program appeared in Burger's *Computer Viruses: A High Tech Disease*. The program has since reappeared a number of times in both its original and modified forms.

Disbelievers

On 10th February 1988, a posting was sent to CompuServe which expressed doubt about the existence of computer viruses: it specifically cited the general reluctance of 'researchers' to produce working copies of virus code. This cynicism was later echoed by a Professor Brunvard of Utah who contemptuously dismissed computer viruses as a myth. Adding fuel to the fire was one Peter Norton, developer of the world acclaimed *Norton Utilities* and well known PC guru. In an interview with Insight magazine he dismissed the phenomenon as an 'urban myth', akin to the alligators said to frequent the sewers of New York. Ironically, Mr Norton's company, the Peter Norton Group, was destined to be absorbed by the Symantec Corporation, a heavyweight vendor of anti-virus software for both the Mac and the PC.

On 22nd April 1988, the aforementioned Virus-L electronic conference was established and quickly built a huge following of enthusiastic 'virologists'. Virus-L now has over twenty thousand subscribers worldwide.

Friday The Thirteenth

On Friday 13th May 1988, the Jerusalem virus activated worldwide. Sites affected in the UK included City University in London, Glasgow's Royal Infirmary and at British Rail's computer centre in Derby. The virus simply deletes any program which is run on its trigger date and thus causes inconvenience rather than extensive damage. At the time there was some debate about virus naming conventions which has remained unresolved to this day - the Jerusalem virus was variously reported as the 1813 virus, the 1808 virus, the Israeli virus and even the PLO virus, all of which served to confuse the uninitiated thoroughly.

CVIA

In June 1988, the Computer Virus Industry Association was launched by John McAfee, then president of the Interpath Corporation of Santa Clara, California. The Homebase bulletin board administered by Jim Goodwin was the hub of the CVIA's virus monitoring activity worldwide. Computer viruses were to prove profitable for Mr McAfee - five years after the establishment of the CVIA, he was to float his company on the US stock exchange, offering 2,100,000 shares of common stock. The flotation is believed to have realised $30,000,000.

Burleson

On the 11th July 1988, a programmer from Fort Worth in Texas was charged with computer sabotage for single-handedly destroying 168,000 database records belonging to his former employee, the IRA Insurance company of Fort Worth. Donald Burleson introduced a program routine, described by the Tarrant attorney as being 'just like a human virus'. Burleson had in fact exploited a back door in the system, deleted audit and log files and manually erased the records. He was found guilty of committing computer sabotage on 20th September 1988 and forced to pay $12,000 in compensation. In this instance, no virus program had been introduced into the system, but the level of destruction caused by Burleson indicated the potential danger presented by malicious program code.

Mike RoChenle

The subject of computer viruses attracts hoaxers, probably because there is so much public ignorance about the phenomenon. This ignorance coupled with a certain morbid fascination has caused grossly exaggerated and even unfounded virus reports to gain short-lived credibility. One of the earliest hoaxes was perpetrated by one Mike RoChenle (Microchannel). In June 1988 he posted a seemingly earnest warning to numerous bulletin boards in the United States which described a 'really nasty virus' which migrated across the subcarrier frequencies on 2400 baud modems. An 'infected' modem would then transmit the virus to other modems by attaching itself to incoming binary data!

Warnings about the (technically impossible) 2400 baud modem virus quickly spread across the networks causing panic-stricken users to switch temporarily to 1200 or lower baud rates. NASA's Jet Propulsion Laboratory issued an official warning about the 'virus' which demonstrated that gullibility and paranoia existed at all levels.

The Internet Worm

One of the most widely reported attacks was the Internet worm which struck the US DARPA Internet computer network on 2nd November 1988. The worm was released by Robert Morris, a Cornell University student, on a public access machine at the Massachusetts Institute of Technology. The worm replicated by exploiting a number of bugs in the Unix operating system on VAX and Sun Microsystems hardware, including a bug in *sendmail* (an electronic mailing program) and in *fingerd* (a program for obtaining details of who is logged on to the system). Stanford University, MIT, the University of Maryland and Berkeley University in California were infected within 5 hours of the worm being released. The NASA Research Institute at Ames and the Lawrence Livermore national laboratory were also infected as well as some 6,000 other computer systems. Computers in the UK were unaffected.

The worm consisted of some 4000 lines of 'C' code and once it was analysed, the specialists distributed bug fixes to *sendmail* and *fingerd* which prevented the worm from propagating further. Decompilation proved that the worm was not deliberately malicious. It did, however, cause the overloading of infected systems.

HI.COM

The worm season continued into December 1988. The Bitnet chain letter was re-released on December 8th while a further attack program known as HI.COM was released on 22nd December from a European Hepnet node, probably originating at the Institute of Physics at the University of Neuchatel in Switzerland. This worm spread rapidly across DECNet onto the US Space Physics analysis Network (SPAN) and the High Energy Physics Network. The program displayed a Christmas tree and advised the user to 'stop computing and have a good time at home!!!!'

CERT

The Internet worm prompted the establishment of the Computer Emergency Response Team with headquarters at Carnegie Mellon University, Pittsburgh, USA (<cert@sei.cmu.edu>, Tel +1 412 268 7090) in December 1988. The team comprises computer experts on the Internet whose intention is to combat all threats to networks connected to the DARPA Internet, including providing patches, bug fixes and advisories about known security loopholes.

CoTRA

The dissemination of the Jerusalem virus was later to prompt the creation of the UK's Computer Threat Research Organisation under the auspices of Joe Hirst, an independent virus researcher based in Brighton, and Mark Gibbs of Novell UK. The aims of the association included the investigation of all threats to computer systems including trojans, viruses and security loopholes, and to provide impartial information and advice to concerned end-users. Many industry representatives, journalists and interested parties attended an inaugural meeting of CoTRA in February 1989 in London, but the organisation gradually disintegrated. CoTRA was intended from its inception to be a non-profit making body. It was soon to become evident that tackling the technical problem was best left in the hands of a commercially minded anti-virus 'industry'.

Cornell Provost's Commission

In April 1989 the Cornell Provost's Commission of Enquiry into the Internet worm incident concluded that Robert Morris, son of the departmental chief of the National Computer Security Center (a division of the NSA), had indeed released the worm program. On the advice of his attorney, Morris himself refused to cooperate with the commission. The commission concluded that Morris had violated the university's computer misuse policy but that he did not intend the worm to destroy data or to propagate widely. The number of infected systems was in the thousands, although the widely believed total of 6,000 computers could not be confirmed. Interestingly, the commission rebuked John McAfee and his CVIA which had estimated the financial losses accruing to be in the region of $96 million - a figure which the commission dismissed as 'grossly exaggerated and self-serving'.

Virus Bulletin

In July 1989, Virus Bulletin Ltd was launched as a sister company of Sophos Ltd, by then heavily engaged in anti-virus software. A monthly publication, *Virus Bulletin* rapidly gained a worldwide readership; it continues to offer highly detailed technical information on virus development, anti-virus techniques, software product reviews and up to date industry news. The first edition of *VB* listed 14 IBM PC viruses and 10 Macintosh viruses.

The Editor of *VB* was then Edward Wilding, succeeded by Richard Ford in January 1993; the Technical Editor was Joe Hirst, who simultaneously announced the creation of the British Computer Virus Research Centre based in Brighton.

Virus News International

In response to the launch of *Virus Bulletin*, S&S Enterprises (now S&S International) set up a rival information service known as *Virus Fax International* in late 1989. Between ten and twenty sheets of virus-related news were faxed to subscribers on a regular basis. Early in 1990, the format changed to an A5 monthly publication renamed *Virus News International*. In January 1993 the format changed again, to A4. *VNI* now includes general security news and anti-virus product reviews.

The Modified Disassembly

Concurrent with the establishment of *VB*, an incident occurred which demonstrated the dangers in distributing virus code even within the research community. The 'Icelandic' virus was disassembled by Fridrik Skulason (who replaced Joe Hirst as Technical Editor of *VB* in January 1990), who at the time was working at the University of Iceland. Before distributing his disassembly to interested researchers, Skulason slightly modified the virus in order to detect any reassembly from it by converting a number in hexadecimal to decimal. This modified virus subsequently turned up 'in the wild' in the United States (as the 'Saratoga' virus) proving a leak in the research community. A prolonged ethical debate commenced about whether research modifications to virus code were justifiable.

Datacrime

The Datacrime virus was discovered in Holland in the spring or early summer of 1989 (Alan Solomon claims to have spoken directly with its author). It caused immediate concern to researchers due to its intentionally destructive trigger routine, the like of which had not been seen in any existing computer virus. The virus activates between October 13th and December 31st (any year). It low level formats track 0 of the hard disk, destroying critical disk information.

The first public announcement about the virus in the UK was made by Dr. Jan Hruska at a computer security seminar at RAF Brampton.

The Datacrime virus was due to trigger on Friday, October 13th 1989 which happened to coincide with the trigger date of the Jerusalem virus, as well as being the final date of the annual COMPSEC computer security gathering in London. Alarm spread worldwide - the United States Department of Defense issued an internal security advisory, while the National Institute of Standards & Technology issued a public warning about Datacrime which was known in the US as the 'Columbus day' virus.

If the situation neared panic in the United States, it was approaching levels of mass hysteria in The Netherlands where Dutch police handed out thousands of detection software programs developed locally by Jan Terpstra of IBM. 'Britain On the Blink' was the headline of the Sun newspaper as the trigger date approached. The paper went on to describe a doomsday scenario predicting that vital air traffic control computers and air defence systems would crash as the virus triggered worldwide.

In fact there was only one publicly announced virus outbreak on Friday 13th October 1989. The Royal National Institute for the Blind's central office in London was hit by the Jerusalem virus. No substantial damage occurred although the incident received widescale television and radio news coverage. Datacrime itself is understood to have triggered only on a few computers worldwide. The Datacrime fiasco, as the scare story came to be known, engendered prolonged scepticism within press associations and agencies.

IBM

Immediately prior to the imminent Datacrime trigger date, IBM announced the availability of its Virscan virus scanning software for MS-DOS. The software, developed at IBM's T J Watson Research Center, was made available on October 4th 1989 for $35.00 and included longer search strings than those published in the *Virus Bulletin* in order to minimise the risk of false positives.

WANK Worm

On 16th October 1989 VAX/VMS computers on the SPAN network were attacked once again by a worm program. The worm propagated using DECNet protocols and if it discovered that it was running with system privileges, it changed the system announcement messages to display a screen banner declaring 'WORMS AGAINST NUCLEAR KILLERS', with the sub-texts:

```
Your System Has Been Officially WANKed
```

and

```
You talk of times of peace for all, and
then prepare for war.
```

The worm also changed the DECNet account password to a random string and mailed information on the password to the user GEMPAK on SPAN node 6.59. If the worm had system privileges, it disabled the mail to the SYSTEM account and modified the system login command procedure to appear to delete all files (it didn't actually do so). The worm then proceeded to access other systems by picking node numbers at random using the PHONE command to get a list of active users on the remote system. After accessing the RIGHTSLIST file, it attempted to access the remote system using the list of users found, to which it added a list of 81 standard users coded into the worm itself. It penetrated accounts where passwords were the same as the name of the account or were null.

The worm then looked for an account which had access to SYSUAF.DAT. If such an account was found, the worm copied itself to that account and started executing.

Within a very short time, CERT issued a warning and a corrective response which reiterated the advice which had been posted during the HI.COM incident. Had this advice been followed in the first place, the opportunity for the latter worm to propagate would have been hugely reduced. This revealed a general tendency towards slackness and a refusal to comply with security recommendations and to implement patches.

AIDS Diskette

At the end of 1989, an incident occurred which sent shockwaves through the computing establishment in the UK and Europe and eventually precipitated the successful drafting of the UK's Computer Misuse Act which became legislation in August 1990.

Between the 8th and 12th December 1989, some twenty thousand envelopes containing a 5.25 inch floppy disk were bulk mailed from postal districts in west and south-west London to computer users in the UK, Europe, Africa, Scandinavia and Australia. The disks, which were DOS compatible, were marked 'AIDS Information Diskette Version 2.0' and encouraged the recipient to insert the disk and install its contents on the computer. A blue leaflet accompanied the disk, on the reverse of which and in very small print, was the 'License Agreement' which urged the user to send $189 or $378 to a post office box number in Panama for using the software. The 'Agreement' threatened unspecified action if the appropriate fee was not paid:

```
Most serious consequences of your failure
to abide by the terms of the license
agreement: your conscience may haunt you
for the rest of your life; you will owe
compensation...
```

The disk contained an interactive questionnaire to assess the user's exposure to the biological HIV/AIDS virus. Once installed, the program printed an invoice giving the address in Panama to which payment should be sent: 'The PC Cyborg Corporation, P.O. Box 87-17-44, Panama 7, Panama'.

However, the installation procedure made modifications to the AUTOEXEC.BAT file with the result that every time AUTOEXEC.BAT executed, a counter in a hidden file was incremented. When this had happened a random number of times (around 90), the trigger activated. The user was instructed to wait, while the file names in the root directory of the hard disk were encrypted and marked 'hidden'. The only plaintext file remaining contained the following message:

```
If you are reading this message, then your
software lease from PC Cyborg has expired.
Renew the software lease before using this
computer again. Warning: do not attempt to
use this computer until you have renewed
your software lease. Use the information
below for renewal.

Dear Customer:

It is time to pay your software lease
from PC Cyborg Corporation. Complete the
INVOICE and attach payment for the lease
option of your choice. If you don't use
the printed INVOICE, then be sure to refer
to the all important reference numbers
below in all correspondence. In return you
will receive: - a renewal software package
with easy-to-follow, complete
instructions; -an automatic, self-
installing diskette that anyone can apply
in minutes.
Important reference numbers: A302980-
1887436

The price of 365 user applications is
US$189. The price of a lease for the
```

```
lifetime of your hard disk is US$378. You
must enclose a bankers draft, cashier's
check or international money order payable
to PC CYBORG CORPORATION for the full
amount of $189 or $378 with your order .
Include your name, company, address, city,
state, country, zip or postal code. Mail
your order to PC Cyborg Corporation, P.O.
Box 87-17-44, Panama 7, Panama.
```

New Scotland Yard's Computer Crime Unit immediately commenced what eventually became the most extensive computer crime investigation ever launched in the United Kingdom. It soon became clear that the perpetrator of the scam had obtained mailing labels from the *PC Business World* circulation department in October 1989. Other recipients had been selected from World Health organisation databases.

The case was eventually solved by a lucky break, when Dr Joseph Popp began behaving erratically while in transit at Schiphol Airport, Amsterdam. He was stopped by a security guard there, who searched his luggage in an attempt to find out who he was. He found a rubber stamp marked 'PC Cyborg Corporation', and alerted the authorities. Popp was later extradited to the UK to await trial. During his stay at Her Majesty's pleasure, he was reported to be wearing hair curlers in his beard, and a condom on his nose, apparently 'in order to ward off radiation'. Not surprisingly, he was found unfit to be tried and returned to the United States.

An interesting epilogue to Popp's story is that he has since been found guilty of 'attempted extortion' by a court in Rome. Popp was tried in absentia, and therefore has not been jailed, but it is understood that the Italian authorities are investigating the possibility of extraditing him.

New Zealand

In 1990, the number of known computer viruses began to increase. The New Zealand virus was the first virus to infect the DOS Boot Sector of the hard drive. It was apparently written by a student in Wellington, New Zealand, who claims that the virus was never intended to be released in the wild. The virus has a trigger routine which displays the message

```
Your PC is now Stoned!
```

every eighth time the machine is booted from an infected disk.

The virus was written in early 1988 - by mid 1990 it had spread all over the world, although it was still quite rare in Europe. The New Zealand virus is still the second most common virus seen at the time of writing - September 1993. The complexity of viruses continued to increase, and in early 1990 the 4K virus was distributed among the research community. 4K was the most complex virus to date, and took the concept of 'stealth' to previously unimaginable levels, hiding its presence in infected files by a number of different mechanisms.

PC Today

In July 1990, UK computer magazine *PC Today* distributed a cover disk which was apparently infected with the Disk Killer virus. The publisher, Database Publications, claimed that a total of 56,500 such disks had been released. Fortunately, it transpired that the virus was inactive, due to a bug within the virus code. However, the incident was 'the luckiest escape to date'. Other magazine distributors were not to be so lucky...

The Bulgarian Virus Factory

In November 1990, Bryan Clough travelled to Bulgaria to investigate the notorious Bulgarian 'Virus factory'. What he found was a country about to go bankrupt, besieged with many problems - all of them more pressing than the virus problem. While in Bulgaria, Clough met Vesselin Bontchev (then a leading virus researcher in the Bulgarian Academy of Sciences, now one of the best known figures in the anti-virus community), who was receiving new viruses written locally at the rate of one per week.

The so-called 'Dark Avenger' was just beginning his virus writing career around this time. He is reported to have begun virus writing in September 1988, but allowed his first virus into the wild in March of the following year. At the time he had written only a handful of viruses, but by mid 1993 he had written at least fifteen viruses, with many different known variants, causing untold damage to the computing industry.

Polymorphism: The Washburn Legacy

Mark Washburn, a self-styled 'virus researcher' from the United States, catapulted himself into fame by writing the V2P? series of polymorphic viruses. This meant that every time the virus infected a host file, the infected file appeared to be different, making it impossible to detect with a simple hexadecimal search pattern.

At the time, this caused something of a shockwave throughout the industry, as scanner manufacturers scrambled to catch up with this latest technical development. Washburn justified his efforts under the auspices of 'research', although what he managed to prove is unclear. None of these viruses are known to be in the wild in the UK. If they were, it would be an interesting test case to see if Washburn could be held legally responsible for the consequences of his creations.

The First International *Virus Bulletin* Conference

The first ever *Virus Bulletin* conference, was held in St. Helier, Jersey in September 1989 and was attended by over 150 delegates and 20 speakers. The conference is now firmly established as the major annual conference on computer viruses in the world.

Michelangelo

March 6th, 1992, was announced as Michelangelo day by the anti-virus community, and was, users were told, the day that computing as we knew it would end. The Michelangelo virus had been in the wild for some time, (accounting for about 4% of all reports) and by then, several companies had had rather embarrassing slip-ups by distributing the virus (most notably Leading Edge Products and the aptly named DaVinci Systems). The general air of panic and chaos was aggravated by television and radio bulletins, and Vesselin Bontchev's announcement that the University of Hamburg had received 28 mailbags containing requests for the Virus Test Centre's free Michelangelo cure program.

The level of incompetence and understanding was never more apparent than when self-appointed 'experts' proclaimed that the best way to detect whether the virus was present was to set the clock forward to the trigger date of the virus and reboot the machine. *Virus Bulletin* received three reports from anguished users who had caused the virus to trigger by doing exactly this.

When the big day came the world held its breath and nothing happened... well certainly not much. Those who had been predicting the coming of the apocalypse were not disappointed however. John McAfee, one of the most vocal prophets of doom, (who in February 1992 predicted that 'up to 5 million PCs worldwide are infected') claimed that the mad scanning frenzy which preceded the big day had averted the catastrophe.

The big winners of Michelangelo day were the anti-virus software manufacturers and vendors. Central Point announced that its sales of anti-virus software had increased 700% in February, while Egghead software announced a 3000% increase in sales of anti-virus software in the week leading up to March 6th.

The story was not all hype however, as an unnamed UK company found out on the fateful day, when the virus triggered on more than 100 machines on one site! This particular semi-governmental company (which shall not be named at their request) was well aware of the virus' trigger date, but had been using anti-virus software which was more than 12 months out of date. Up to date anti-virus software had to be couriered to the site before the remaining machines could be cleaned.

The Little Black Book

Another Mark up to no good in America at this time was Mark Ludwig, author of *The Little Black Book of Computer Viruses*. The book claims to be written to help users understand more about computer viruses and how they work, but in fact turned out to be more of a virus writer's course, containing source code and hex dumps of virus code. For those readers incapable of typing in these code fragments, a disk containing the four viruses described in the book could be obtained for an additional $15.

Rather unsurprisingly, the publishing of the book caused a furore in the anti-virus community and the user community at large. Ludwig then proceeded to make himself look increasingly ridiculous by protesting that the virus code in his book was protected by copyright, and that publication of any parts of the virus code was both illegal and a violation of his copyright. Ludwig's veiled threats of litigation were never carried out, even though *Virus Bulletin* had already published search strings for these viruses.

A Peach of a Virus

By the spring of 1992, the number of computer viruses had risen drastically from the handful which were known at this time in the preceding year. Viruses were no longer the simple beasts they had been several months earlier. Two techniques which were to become increasingly common were being developed: increased polymorphism and the targeting of anti-virus software.

The most famous example of polymorphism is without doubt the Mutation Engine. Washburn's techniques used in the 1260 virus had been extended in terms of complexity by orders of magnitude, to produce not a polymorphic virus, but a polymorphic engine which could be incorporated into other viruses.

The Mutation Engine (also known as MtE or DAME) was the work of the Dark Avenger, and was distributed as an object module, complete with documentation and ready to be linked in to other virus code. At the time, the Mutation Engine caused something of a stir within the research community, and it was not until several months later that the majority of scanners were capable of detecting it reliably. Even at the time of writing, there are still a number of scanners which cannot detect all variants of MtE viruses.

The other increasingly used technique was the targeting of anti-virus software. A prime example is the Peach virus, which deletes the checksum database of Central Point's anti-virus product, *CPAV*. Insufficient cautionary measures by the developers of *CPAV* meant that if the checksum database was deleted, the program assumed it was being run for the first time, and simply recompiled the checksum database without alerting the user. This security hole led to the infamous quote by Jim Bates, who commented 'that the author of the virus [was] presumably acting under the assumption that having had their knickers deleted the integrity checker will not feel the draught.' Though hard to believe, the fact is that this technique works: *CPAV* (now devoid of underwear) was successfully spoofed by this trick.

The Computer Underground

By mid 1992 the computer underground was prospering. During the previous year, these 'digital desperados' had grouped together into tighter and more cohesive groups, with childish names such as 'Phalcon/Skism'. Each of these groups had its own magazine, like *40Hex* or *Phrack!* which contained source code listings for viruses, hacking information, or various other little titbits of information which members of the computer underground might wish to acquire. Not content with this, the computer underground (now all with their own 'handles' like Dark Avenger or Nowhere Man) set up virus exchange bulletin board systems, where they could gather and exchange virus code and ideas.

Britain was not without its share of such virus writing groups. The most well known was the so-called ARCV (Association for Really Cruel Viruses), which managed to publish one edition of its typo-ridden newsletter before earning the attention of New Scotland Yard's Computer Crime Unit. As members of the ARCV claimed to have written several viruses, the CCU mounted an operation to bring them to justice. At the time of writing, the outcome of this case is yet to be decided, but all known ARCV machines are currently impounded by New Scotland Yard, and to all practical purposes the ARCV is no more.

The work carried out by the CCU has been one of the reasons why there are comparatively few organised hacking and virus writing groups in the UK at this time. Its staff have every intention of keeping things that way. In the event of your computer being infected by a computer virus, the CCU would like to hear from you. Their telephone number is 071 230 1177.

Shattered Glass

The last quarter of 1992 brought with it a new type of virus: the first *Windows* virus. The sample, named WinVir_1.4 was capable of infecting executables in the NE (New Executable) format, but although it executed and ran in the *Windows* environment, it did not utilise any of the additional functionality within *Windows* itself.

The first real *Windows* virus was not far away though: the Twitch, virus used various different *Windows* calls to infect files under *Windows*. These trends may make those who produce *Windows* scanners rather uncomfortable...

Imageline v. McAfee

Ever since the start of the anti-virus industry, the law concerning false positives, false negatives and liability had yet to be tried in court. If a virus scanner identifies a perfectly inoffensive file as infected what steps does the scanner manufacturer take?

This thorny question rose its head in January 1993, when Imageline, a small start-up US company, attempted to sue McAfee Associates for tarnishing the name of its product. Imageline won the first rounds of the fight, and the anti-virus vendors were waiting with bated breath for the result of the case. The case was settled out of court, and neither side was prepared to comment on the final agreement.

MSAV

The long awaited launch of the Microsoft anti-virus product marked the launch of a new era in virus prevention (or so users were told). By including anti-virus software in the operating system, Microsoft hoped to provide minimum protection for all its users.

MSAV was finally launched in the spring of 1993, and turned out to be a subset of Central Point's product, *CPAV*. The reviews received by the product were lukewarm at best, although the product was capable of defending users from most viruses known to be in the wild. [*For the Virus Bulletin review of MSAV, see VB, May 1993, p.17. Ed.*]

What Next?

What does the future hold? Fortune telling (especially in print) is a dangerous game, and given the youth of the industry, most experts refuse to be drawn on this subject. However, one thing is for certain: the problem is not simply going to disappear.

The future will probably see more virus construction sets produced by the computer underworld. Rather than the current offerings, the next generation of virus construction toolkits are likely to use complex polymorphism, in order to make generic detection much more difficult. As the number of users who are protecting their machines grows (particularly with the advent of *MSAV*), anti-virus software will be increasingly targeted. The virus writers *are* organised, and are working with the intention of causing as many problems as they can.

Not everything is doom and gloom, however. Computer users are gaining an increased awareness of the issues, and their habits are gradually changing. One of the best defences against computer viruses is free: good computing practice. In addition, the long hand of the law is catching up with the computer criminals. Dr Popp and the ARCV (currently awaiting trial) have been brought to heel, and new offenders will be treated harshly: computer crime is becoming too expensive to tolerate. The laws concerning computers will be rewritten many times over before they are workable - it is very early days, and the action taken now will change how the industry grows and flourishes, or wilts and dies.

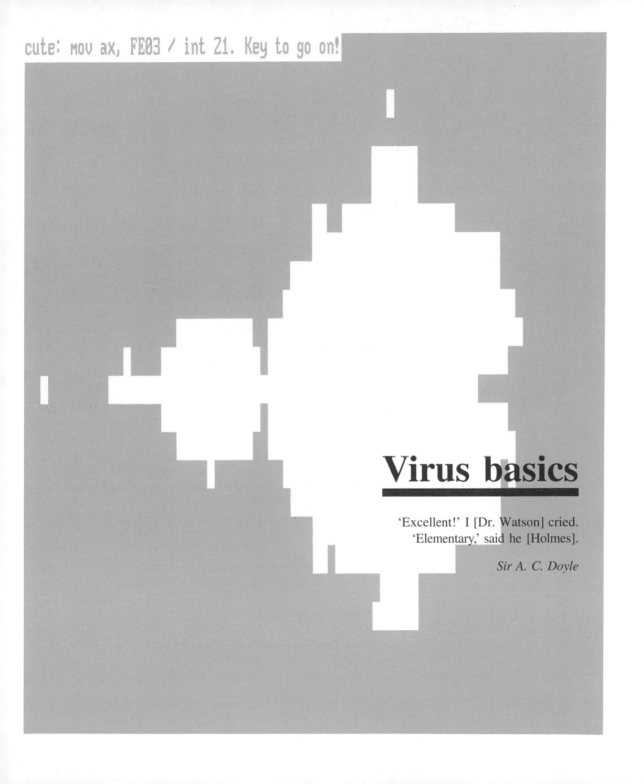

Virus basics

'Excellent!' I [Dr. Watson] cried.
'Elementary,' said he [Holmes].

Sir A. C. Doyle

To the overworked IT Manager, the precise differences between trojan horses, computer viruses and logic bombs is an area of distinction for which he cares little: each in its turn can seriously affect system performance and usability. However, by gaining a better feel for the nature of each class of malicious code, it is well worth taking the time to learn how such programs operate. Know thine enemy, for by gaining a sound understanding of the principles involved, it becomes easy to spot his Achilles' heel.

Animal, Mineral or Vegetable?

Malicious software can be thought of in one of three different (but closely linked) categories: trojan horses, logic bombs and computer viruses. A logic bomb is defined as any program which takes some action when triggered by some condition, such as the date, or the absence of data from an application. The action does not have to be malicious in its intent: the necessary criterion is simply that the program's operation is altered by a change in the environment in which it operates.

A trojan horse is, as the name suggests, a program which is allowed onto the user's PC under false pretences, whereupon it has undesirable side effects. Perhaps the best known example of a trojan horse program is the infamous Aids Diskette.

A computer virus is a piece of self-replicating code, that is, code which can make copies of itself in such a way as to 'infect' parts of the operating system or environment. As the name implies, the biological analogy is relatively good at describing the action of computer viruses in the real world.

Virus Types

Computer viruses can be divided into five different types: Bootstrap sector viruses (or Boot Sector viruses), Parasitic viruses, Multi-partite viruses, Companion viruses and Link viruses. These classifications take into account the different ways in which the virus can infect different parts of the system. The manner in which each of these types operates has one thing in common: any virus has to be executed in order to operate. Each class, in effect, is simply a different way of ensuring that the virus code is executed.

Bootstrap Sector Viruses

When an IBM-compatible computer is first switched on, a routine known as the POST (or Power On Self Test) checks the hardware of the machine. This program is stored in the Read-Only Memory of the computer, and cannot be infected by a virus. In ATs and 386/486 machines, this process collects information from the CMOS such as the time, date and passwords prior to loading the Master Boot Sector followed by the DOS Boot Sector. Boot Sector viruses alter the code stored either in the Master Boot Sector or the DOS Boot Sector. This can be done in one of several different ways. Usually, the original contents of the boot sector is replaced by the virus code. When the machine is turned on, the ROM blindly loads the contents of the boot sector, allowing the virus to be executed. Once loaded, the virus code generally loads the original boot code into memory and executes it, so that, as far as the user is concerned, nothing is amiss.

The above begs the question of how boot sector viruses spread. Clearly, the most common way of a machine becoming infected with a boot sector virus is for it to be booted with an infected diskette in the floppy disk drive.

Note: A disk does not have to be bootable in order to be infected with a boot sector virus. Almost every user has, at some time or another, seen the message

```
Non-System disk or disk error..
Replace and strike any key when ready
```

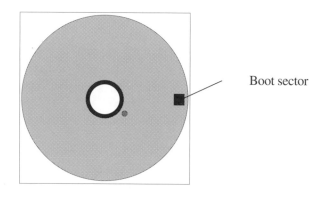

Boot sector

Uninfected disk

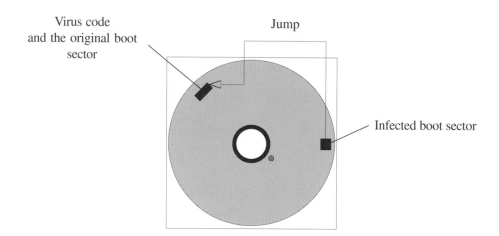

Virus code and the original boot sector

Jump

Infected boot sector

Disk infected with a bootstrap sector virus

This message is displayed by code stored within the boot sector of the floppy disk - and therefore if the disk has been infected by a boot sector virus, by the time this message has been displayed, the hard drive may have been infected.

Boot sector viruses usually spread through exchange of any media which can be used to boot the computer and can only infect when an attempt is made to boot from this media. This might lead one to believe that boot sector viruses would be an extremely inefficient method of distributing virus code. However nothing could be further from the truth: out of the seven most common viruses reported in the wild, six are capable of infecting disk boot sectors.

Due to the need for exchange of bootable media for boot sector infection, boot sector viruses are often distributed by means of trojan horse (or 'dropper') programs whose sole purpose is to infect the boot sector of the machines on which they are run. This allows the deliberate distribution of boot sector viruses via bulletin board systems, thereby vastly increasing the potential for the virus to spread.

When dealing with floppy disks infected with boot sector viruses, it is useful to remember that it is perfectly safe to copy the files off the disk, as the virus can only spread when the disk boot sector is executed. Warning: Do not use the DISKCOPY utility to copy the files. DISKCOPY operates on a sector by sector basis, and will therefore copy across the contents of the host diskette, boot sector virus and all - effectively infecting the new diskette. For this reason, a simple file by file copy (using COPY or XCOPY) should be used.

Boot sector viruses are usually stored on the disk in three different parts. These are:

1. The boot sector. This consists of code which loads the rest of the virus into memory.

2. One other sector. This sector is used to store the contents of the 'original' boot sector, so that once the virus has become

memory-resident, it can continue the boot process as it would before infection.

3. A number of other sectors, where the bulk of the virus code is stored.

Only the first of these sectors actually needs to be used, and there are a few boot sector viruses which are either only one sector long or do not store the contents of the original boot sector (e.g. SVC 6.0).

The method of allocating extra storage space for the virus varies from sample to sample. Some viruses (such as Form and Disk Killer) search the File Allocation Table (FAT) for unused sectors on the disk. The virus code is then stored in these sectors, which are subsequently marked as 'bad' meaning that DOS will not attempt to store data in them. Several different boot sector viruses use parts of the disk which are normally unused by those systems running MS-DOS (such as the area immediately after the Master Boot Sector). This technique is rather risky if the computer is configured in a non-standard way, or has third-party security software running on it.

Other methods of allocating space include using Track 40 on 360K floppy disks (this is an area which DOS does not use for data storage, as not all disk drives recognise this track) or decreasing the size of the first partition on the hard disk.

By definition, all boot sector viruses modify the contents of the boot sector in some way. The changes to the original boot sector do not always have to be large: some of the newer boot sector viruses are capable of infecting the hard drive by modifying only ten bytes of the boot sector!

Parasitic Viruses

By far the largest number of viruses are parasitic viruses which infect executable files stored on the computer. They generally leave the contents of the host program relatively unchanged, but append or prepend their code to the host, and divert execution flow so that the virus code is executed first. Once the virus code has finished its task, control is passed to the original program which, in most cases, executes normally. The extra execution time added by the virus is usually not perceptible, and the virus remains hidden to the user.

As parasitic viruses infect executable files, they can spread through any media which can be used to store files, including disks, modems and networks. Infection usually spreads when an infected file is executed.

The class of parasitic viruses can be further broken down to those which become memory-resident after execution and those which do

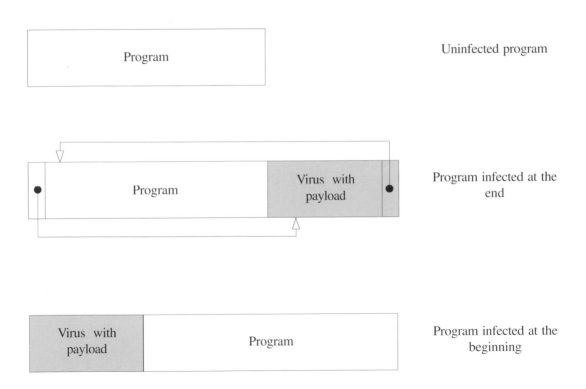

Program infection with a parasitic virus

not. Memory-resident viruses tend to infect other files as they are accessed, opened or run. Viruses which do not become memory-resident, such as Vienna, generally find an uninfected file and infect it before returning control to the host program.

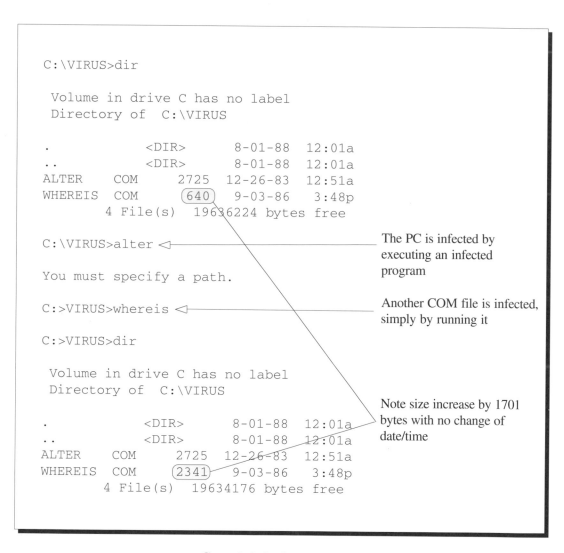

```
C:\VIRUS>dir

 Volume in drive C has no label
 Directory of  C:\VIRUS

 .              <DIR>       8-01-88  12:01a
 ..             <DIR>       8-01-88  12:01a
 ALTER   COM     2725    12-26-83  12:51a
 WHEREIS COM      640     9-03-86   3:48p
        4 File(s)  19636224 bytes free

C:\VIRUS>alter

You must specify a path.

C:>VIRUS>whereis

C:>VIRUS>dir

 Volume in drive C has no label
 Directory of  C:\VIRUS

 .              <DIR>       8-01-88  12:01a
 ..             <DIR>       8-01-88  12:01a
 ALTER   COM     2725    12-26-83  12:51a
 WHEREIS COM     2341     9-03-86   3:48p
        4 File(s)  19634176 bytes free
```

The PC is infected by executing an infected program

Another COM file is infected, simply by running it

Note size increase by 1701 bytes with no change of date/time

Cascade infecting a program

Parasitic viruses need to be able to distinguish between uninfected files and those which are already infected. If the virus does not have this capability (eg Jerusalem), it will repeatedly reinfect programs until they become either too large to fit on disk or in memory, thus revealing its presence. Methods of marking infection include examining the first instructions of the program code, or looking for a special infection marker which the virus uses to designate infected files. One common marker is the seconds field of the file's date/time stamp set to 62. This is not noticeable by the user (as the DIR command only shows hours and minutes), but allows the virus to prevent multiple infections in the same file.

Multi-Partite Viruses

A multi-partite virus is one which is capable of infecting both boot sectors and executable files, which has the advantages of both boot sector virus and parasitic virus infectious behaviour. An example of this type of virus is Flip, which infects not only COM and EXE files, but also the Master Boot Sector. By adopting this 'best of both worlds' technique, the virus has far more opportunities to spread. It is therefore no surprise that the small number of multi-partite viruses account for a disproportionately large number of infections.

This class of virus shares its infection mechanism with both of the preceding types, and therefore can spread by both infected media and infected files. The virus will become active if an infected file is executed or if the PC is booted from an infected disk.

Most multi-partite viruses are fully multi-partite. This means that starting with just an infected boot sector, the virus will attempt to infect files, and vice versa. However, some multi-partite viruses (e.g. Spanish Telecom) cannot do this; for example, the boot sector part of the virus may only be capable of infecting other boot sectors, whereas the file infecting part of the virus can infect both boot sectors and files.

Companion Viruses

Perhaps the simplest type of virus are companion viruses which take advantage of the fact that DOS allows files to share the same first name (eg WS.EXE and WS.COM) in the same directory. When the user attempts to run a program, he will type the name of the file that he wishes to execute. The operating system then examines files in the current directory for files with the same name. If there are two files with the same name, but different extension, the operating system will choose which file to execute by examining the file's extension. For example, DOS (actually, COMMAND.COM) will execute a COM file in preference to an EXE file, so in the case above, typing WS would execute the file WS.COM, not WS.EXE.

A companion virus infects EXE files by creating a COM file containing the virus code with the same name. When the user then attempts to run the infected program, the COM file (containing the virus code) is executed, not the intended application. This allows the virus to carry out whatever operation its author intended. Once the virus has completed its activity, it usually loads and executes the EXE file of the same name. Consequently, the virus infects EXE files without making any changes whatsoever to their contents.

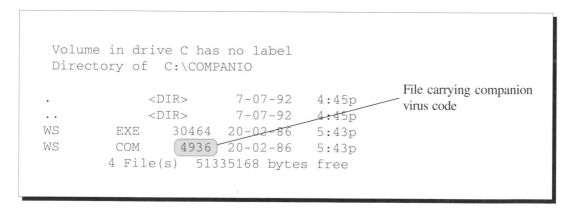

```
Volume in drive C has no label
Directory of  C:\COMPANIO

.              <DIR>        7-07-92    4:45p
..             <DIR>        7-07-92    4:45p
WS      EXE    30464    20-02-86      5:43p
WS      COM     4936    20-02-86      5:43p
     4 File(s)    51335168 bytes free
```

File carrying companion virus code

Companion virus infection

The directory listing shows how an unsophisticated companion virus has infected WS.EXE by creating a file with the same name but different extension in the same directory. A slightly more subtle technique is to set the attributes of the companion file to hidden, so that the user is not alerted to the presence of the virus. The disadvantage of this technique is that the virus can no longer propagate by using the DOS COPY command, as this command does not copy hidden files.

Companion viruses are spread via any media which can be used to exchange executable code. However, out of the viruses in the wild, only a handful are companion viruses, and none of these are widespread. It is not thought that companion viruses pose a major threat in practice.

Link Viruses

Using one of the most unusual infection techniques, link viruses are extremely virulent and once released on a system, can spread extremely quickly.

Like companion viruses, they do not change the contents of the executable code itself, but alterations are made to the directory structure, linking the first cluster pointer of the directory entry of executable files to a single cluster containing the virus code. Once the virus code has executed, it loads the executable file by reading the correct starting cluster value which is stored elsewhere.

The first such virus to use this technique was the much-hyped DIR-II virus, which (like so many other developments in the virus field) was believed to herald a new age of virus writing. Surprisingly, there have been no other link viruses discovered in the wild.

Viruses of this type can spread through any media which can be used for storage or transmission of executable code.

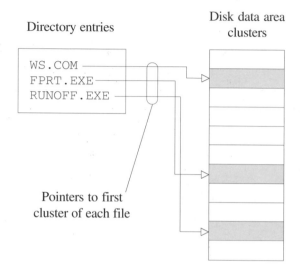

Directory entries in an uninfected system

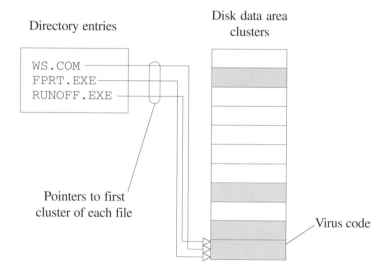

Directory entries in a system infected with a link virus

Executable Code

The one factor which all these virus types have in common is that they make alterations to the way in which the computer handles executable code. The golden rule of virus protection is very simple: any exchange of executable code is a potential source of infection. Therefore it follows that it is the executable code on the system which needs to be protected. This sounds relatively easy until one begins to examine the question of what exactly constitutes executable code, as applied to virus prevention.

Virus Behaviour

Non memory-resident viruses

As the name implies, non memory-resident viruses do not remain active in memory after an infected application is executed. The virus operates on a single shot mechanism, and only infects other executables when an infected program is executed.

Typical behaviour of this class of virus is to search for a suitable host file when an infected program is run, infect it, and then return control to the host program. Examples of viruses which operate using this technique are Vienna and Datacrime.

As is common in all classes of viruses, non memory-resident viruses may still contain a trigger (or payload) routine which has undesirable consequences for the user. For a discussion of trigger routines, see below.

Memory-resident viruses

Unlike their simpler brothers, memory-resident viruses install themselves in memory, so that long after an infected program has been executed, they can still infect files, invoke a trigger routine, or monitor system activity.

Exceptions to the Rules

Some viruses do not really fall into either category. For example, the Typo virus infects files only when an infected file is executed (as one would expect for a non memory-resident virus) but also leaves a small TSR element active in memory. This TSR carries the trigger of the virus, while the main body of the virus contains the replication code.

Hide and Seek

If a virus can remain undetected on a system for a long time, it is much more likely to spread to a large number of machines. Virus authors are aware of this, and therefore have expended a great deal of energy attempting to hide the presence of their viruses or to make them more difficult to detect. There are two principal techniques used: encryption and stealth. We will examine each in turn.

Encryption

Encryption is a technique of hiding the original information by transforming it in some way. This is precisely what an encrypted virus does. The idea is that every different infection of the virus will appear to be different to the last, making it impossible to detect the presence of the virus by searching for a single fixed string. However, encrypted viruses have one weakness, which (to date) has meant that there is no such thing as an undetectable virus: they are required to decrypt themselves before executing, and this decryption routine cannot be encrypted. The reasons for this are simple: the body of the virus must be unencrypted when it is executed, or it will not operate. Therefore the virus must start with a decryption routine which must (*a priori*) also be unencrypted. The anti-virus vendors search for this decryption routine to find the virus. One of the first viruses to use encryption was the Cascade virus, which had a simple XOR-type 35-byte long encryption routine.

It is worth noting that the encryption used by current viruses is extremely primitive, and is nowhere near secure enough to be used for preserving data confidentiality. In practice, it does not need to be complex, as its only purpose is to make data appear different. Unfortunately, the possibilites of introducing complications to this process are endless. To take a simple example, a virus could use two stages of encryption, where the key for the second stage is stored in an encrypted form within the first. Such 'refinements' make the process of disassembling the virus more difficult; they have no other effect.

One of the more common techniques employed by the virus writers to make virus detection difficult, is to change the decryption routine from infection to infection. This means that two identical host files infected by the same virus will appear completely different when infected by the same virus. This is known as polymorphism. Since little or no code remains the same between infections, it is impossible to determine a fixed hexadecimal detection pattern for viruses which are encrypted in this way.

This makes detection of polymorphic viruses something of a problem, although not an insurmountable one. Even for highly polymorphic viruses, there are certain characteristics which do not change - after all, the end result of the decryption routine must be the virus body, so although the code changes, its purpose does not. The scanner manufacturers use traits within the decryption routine (such as the presence of JMP instructions to specific offsets etc.) in order to identify viruses disguised in this manner.

The first truly polymorphic viruses were written by a self-appointed 'virus researcher', Mark Washburn, who wrote the 'experimental' virus 1260. This was followed by a number of other creations in the V2Pn series (V2P2, V2P6 etc.), all of which presented a challenge to anti-virus software manufacturers. V2P6 is still a cause of problems for some anti-virus vendors.

Probably the most significant advance in polymorphic virus writing occurred when the Bulgarian virus writer Dark Avenger released his polymorphic virus engine, the Mutation Engine (also known as MtE or DAME). This virus construction tool allows novice programmers to produce complex polymorphic viruses without having to understand the complicated techniques necessary to write polymorphic code.

The Dark Avenger distributed the Mutation Engine as an object module - that is, a compiled 'sub-routine' which could be called from within a virus, complete with detailed instructions on how it should be used and an example virus (Dedicated). The Dark Avenger even offers technical support on his 'product' via various virus exchange BBSs in Bulgaria. The documentation supplied with the Mutation Engine states that it is copyright 1991 CrazySoft, Inc.

In early 1993 two more polymorphic engines appeared: The Trident Polymorphic Engine and the NuKE encryption device. As these polymorphic engines become more common, the problems for the virus scanner manufacturers grow, with search routines becoming increasingly processor-intensive.

Stealth: Hiding From the Hunters

A stealth virus is one which attempts to 'trick' other software running on the machine into believing that it is not present anywhere on the machine. Stealth functions range from the simple, such as subverting the DIR command, so that infected files appear to have the same size, to complex interception of various DOS services. Some of the more advanced stealth viruses attempt to intercept direct sector reads in an attempt to remain hidden.

Stealth viruses usually take advantage of the way MS-DOS handles communication between the software and the hardware of the machine itself. This technique is known as interrupt interception, and in order to understand the properties of stealth viruses more fully, we shall consider this in more depth.

The hardware of most IBM-PCs and compatibles differs in several ways, for example different graphics cards or different hard drives. Clearly, software designed to run on the PC cannot take all these different hardware configurations into account. Therefore standard functions, such as disk accesses or screen writes are provided by DOS or the BIOS, ensuring a standard communication interface.

This interface is handled by interrupts. An interrupt request consists of executing an INT instruction with the appropriate values held in different registers. The standard DOS interrupt, which handles most DOS input/output functions is INT 21h, and the low-level disk interrupt is INT 13h.

When an interrupt is generated, the *Intel* microprocessor searches a particular area of RAM for the address of the code which the interrupt routine should execute. This area of memory is known as the interrupt table, and the memory addresses which it contains are known as interrupt vectors, because they point to the code which handles the interrupt request.

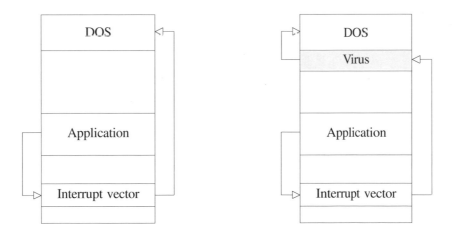

Interrupt routing before and after the virus gains control

A virus can take advantage of this system by altering the interrupt vector so that it points not to DOS code, but to the virus code. This means that the virus can monitor certain activities. Let us consider the process which occurs when a user types the DIR command with a stealth virus in memory.

The DIR command uses two DOS interrupts in order to access the disk to determine the directory contents. The virus code is activated whenever the DOS interrupt, Int 21h is called and if this call is a request which will return the size of a file on disk, the virus ensures that if a file is infected, it subtracts the length of the virus from it. Therefore, infected files do not appear to have grown longer.

The technique of pointing an interrupt vector to a different area of the code is known as 'hooking' the interrupt. Most stealth viruses only hook interrupt, 21h, while many boot sector viruses hook Int 13h instead. Most interrupts have a number of subfunctions. In the case of the 4K virus, 18 different subfunctions are intercepted , including Find First Matching File (11h), Find Next Matching File (12h), Open File (3Dh) and Close File (3Eh). As well as the obvious simple stealth features, the 4K virus will actually 'disinfect' any infected file if an application tries to read from it, only to reinfect it on closing the file.

As it is impossible to trust the values returned from these interrupts if the PC is infected with a virus, it is essential that the PC is booted from a clean system disk before the hard drive is checked for viruses. A scanner or a checksummer which uses the ordinary DOS services cannot discover the 4K virus on disk if it is active in memory.

The Unscannable Virus

There has been much discussion over whether it is possible to write a computer virus which is impossible to detect with a scanner. A highly polymorphic virus which uses sparse infection techniques seems to fit the bill.

Such a virus would be so polymorphic that although a detection routine would be possible, it would be incredibly processor-intensive, making scanning for the virus impractical for most files on the system. If the virus infected sparsely, for example by only infecting files whose time stamp had a seconds' value of greater than 30, only 50% of all files would be infected... but the anti-virus vendor would not be able to use the virus' self-recognition routine to eliminate most uninfected files. Of course, if someone then wrote a virus which infected files with a time stamp of less than 30 seconds...

High-level Language Viruses

Although most viruses are written in assembly language, several are written in high-level languages (such as C or Pascal). The main advantage of assembly language is that high-level languages frequently do not provide the necessary functionality which viruses require. Furthermore, the assembly code is smaller and more efficient for the task at hand.

The biggest problems which high-level language viruses pose to anti-virus software vendors is the increased risk of false positives. If, for example, a virus is written in Borland C++, and the vendor simply extracts a hexadecimal search pattern for the virus, there is a very real danger that this pattern will simply detect all executables compiled using the same version of the compiler.

The Anatomy of an Infection

Now that we have discussed the way in which a virus is capable of infecting objects on a PC, and the different actions it can take when memory-resident, let us examine how a typical infection may spread and develop over time.

Once important distinction to make before examining this topic is the difference between a virus being active in RAM and being stored on disk.

A virus becomes active in RAM when it is executed. Once resident, this active state can generally only be cleared when either the virus itself unloads itself from memory or when the PC is switched off. However, most media which is infected by a virus will carry this infection even after the power has been cut off from the machine. The different properties of infected media and infected machines are illustrated in the first four blocks of the diagram on the next page.

Let us consider the case of a PC which is infected by the Form virus by bootstrapping from an infected diskette. When the power is switched on, the machine is booted from the infected disk, the virus becomes memory-resident and infects the hard disk. If the power is now switched off, the virus is destroyed in memory, but not from the hard disk. This means that the next time the machine is booted up from the hard drive, the virus will once again become active in memory.

The last four parts of the diagram illustrate how the virus spreads on to other floppy disks and how it is possible to remove the virus from memory by resetting the PC. It is important to ensure that no viruses are memory-resident when checking for computer viruses, as a memory-resident virus could 'stealth' the anti-virus software, making its results invalid.

Executable Path

The basic rule of virus infection is that in order for a virus to infect a computer it must be executed. Therefore by ensuring that the system only executes legitimate virus-free code, it is possible to protect it from infection. Note that this does not simply mean that only COM and EXE files are potential sources of infection - life is slightly more complicated than this.

Any file which contains executable code has to be treated as a potential virus carrier. This includes files with interpreted basic commands, spreadsheet macros etc.

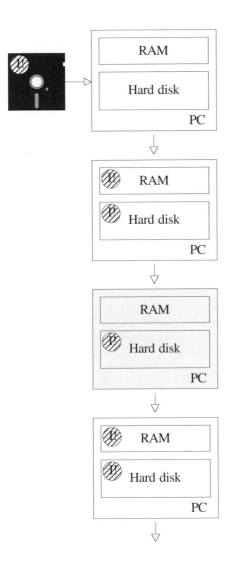

1. In an uninfected PC both the RAM and the hard disk are free from infection. An infected floppy disk is introduced into the floppy disk drive.

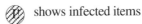 shows infected items

2. When an infected program from the floppy disk is run, the hard disk becomes infected and the virus becomes active in RAM.

3. If power is now switched off, the hard disk remains infected while the contents of RAM (including the virus) are lost.

4. When the PC is switched back on and bootstrapped from the (infected) hard disk, the virus becomes active in RAM once again.

Infecting a PC and disks (1)

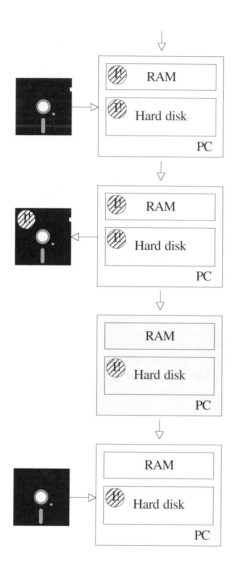

5. If an unprotected, clean floppy disk is then used...

6. ...it immediately becomes infected. Any unprotected floppy disk which is used in this PC while the virus is active becomes infected.

7. If power is now switched off, the hard disk once again remains infected, while the contents of the RAM (including the virus) are lost.

8. The virus can be kept inactive by switching the PC back on with a clean write-protected system disk in the floppy disk drive. Despite the fact that the hard disk remains infected, the virus is not active in RAM. Anti-virus actions can commence.

Infecting a PC and disks (2)

On a PC, the following items are most at risk from a virus attack:

1. Master Boot Sector on hard disks - this area is infected by viruses such as New Zealand and Joshi.

2. DOS Boot Sector on hard and floppy disks - several viruses use the DBS as their host (eg Form, Michelangelo etc.).

3. The DOS Files IO.SYS and MSDOS.SYS.

4. CONFIG.SYS - although CONFIG.SYS is a text file, it acts as a pointer to executable code, and therefore could be used to load an infected object. DOS does not require device drivers loaded through CONFIG.SYS to have any particular extension (eg the file README.TXT could be loaded as a device driver, as long as the contents of the file were executable), and therefore should be treated as an infectable object.

5. Device drivers - several viruses exist which attempt to infect device drivers.

6. COMMAND.COM - this file is infected by many of the standard file-infecting viruses.

7. AUTOEXEC.BAT - this is a possible attack point, but is normally targeted by trojan horses, rather than viruses.

8. Application files - the most frequently targeted object. Note that overlay files (which usually have extensions OVL or OVR etc.) are also subject to attack.

9. Files with macros - no viruses (other than purely experimental ones) have been shown to attack these files.

The reader should be aware that this list is incomplete. The definition of executable code on the IBM PC is vague, and with the advent of *Windows* has become more so. At least one virus is known to infect batch files, and compiler libraries and Dynamic Link Libraries (DLLs) could also be the target of infection. For a full discussion of this complex subject the reader is referred to *VB* July 1993, pp. 9-11.

To keep the system free from viruses, the user must make sure that all the code executed during the steps described above is virus-free. Unfortunately this is much harder than it seems, as some of the objects which could be infected by viruses alter their contents in the normal day-to-day running of the machine, making virus detection and prevention a troublesome task.

Virus Infiltration: How viruses get through the door

Just like with biological viruses, subject behaviour has a significant effect on the probability of infection. By altering the habits of users, and examining how most virus infections occur, it is possible to educate staff on the risk which their different actions carry, and thus minimise the risk of virus infection. The following list of infection routes and methods has been assembled by studying real-life cases in which organisations or individuals have introduced viruses to their PCs.

Pirated Software

Software piracy (the illegal copying and distribution of computer software) provides an excellent channel for virus distribution. Games are probably the most commonly pirated software and they tend to be exchanged between PC users at a far greater rate than 'serious' software. For this reason, they are also most prone to becoming infected.

Avoiding pirated software is good computing practice. Ignoring the moral obligation of the user to pay for the service he is receiving, computer software should always be obtained from a traceable, reputable source - from a security standpoint alone, pirated software is a definite no.

Bulletin Boards

Bulletin boards usually provide the means of downloading software which is classified either as 'public domain' (free) or 'shareware' (free to copy and try, but those who use it should pay). Most of the reputable boards have a SYSOP (SYStem OPerator) who takes great pains to ensure the integrity of the files available on his BBS, though this is unfortunately not always the case. In addition, due to the large number of files uploaded and downloaded to BBSs, there is a chance that executable code obtained from BBSs might be infected. It is also not unheard of for virus writers to infect a program deliberately with a new virus and upload it to a BBS, allowing the new virus to propagate widely.

Shareware

The concept of shareware is a very attractive one: computer users are allowed to make unlimited copies of a particular piece of software and pass it on to others who may be interested in using it. If a user finds the software useful, he is under moral obligation to send a small sum of money (frequently of the order to $20-25 US) to the author of the software.

Unfortunately shareware distribution has the same problems associated with it as software obtained from BBS: the user is unable to trace the origins of the software. The actual code being passed on may well have been obtained from a copy of a copy of a copy and by the time ity reaches the end-user, the software has had the chance to become infected many times on any one of the many computers it has passed through *en route*.

Magazine Cover Disks

It is becoming increasingly difficult to buy a computer magazine without a 'free' cover disk attached to the front cover. Such disks generally contain shareware or demonstration programs of larger packages. Although the manufacturers are now (after a number of accidents) aware of the risks of virus infection, this method of software distribution is not to be trusted despite the 'virus checked' lable on the floppies.

On a number of occasions the disks have been found to be virus infected:

- *Personal Computing* Vol. 3 No.1, Database Publications, March 1990, New Zealand mutation.

- *PC Today* Vol. 4 No 4, Database Publications, August 1990, Disk Killer (inactive), 40,000 copies.

- *PC-World,* Benelux, 9th November 1990, IDG Communications, Cascade, 16,000 copies.

- *Soft & Micro*, France, May 1991, 4K, unknown number of copies.

Such *faux pas* are not limited to IBM PC software: viruses have often been shipped on the cover disk of the more home oriented computers (eg *ST Format*, October 1992, Ghost virus). The examples given clearly highlight the potential dangers with this method of software distribution.

Public Domain Software

Public Domain software is completely free for anyone to use. Unfortunately it suffers from all the disadvantages of shareware distribution, with the added disadvantage that there is frequently nobody to supply the 'latest' version.

PCs at Home

One of the most common routes of infection in businesses is via the home PC. Consider the (true) scenario of the executive who used a home PC for company work. Unbeknown to him, his 14 year old son was also using the PC to play games on. These games obtained from friends at school turned out to be infected with a computer virus. The executive then unwittingly introduced the virus to his company. This can happen even if a company virus-checks all disks which arrive by normal means such as post.

Service Engineers

As a service engineer frequently has to examine several PCs in one day, his diagnostic software disks are an ideal transmission media for computer viruses.

Customers should insist that the engineers' disks are scanned before before being used on a company PC, and also check that the disks are write-protected. In addition, employees should not trade software with the engineer - a habit which is not only dangerous but often illegal.

Due to the increasing prevalence of computer viruses, a standard operation when examining a recalcitrant PC is to check for viruses, and it is not uncommon for engineers to carry their own anti-virus software. When dealing with reputable firms, the danger of infection via this route is reduced drastically.

Shrink-wrapped software

The term 'shrink-wrapped software' normally applies to commercial software which has been purchased pre-packaged. The disks are usually shipped in sealed (or shrink-wrapped) packages, although this is normally done for legislative purposes rather than anti-virus measures. By breaking the seal, the user implicitly agrees to abide by the manufacturers terms and conditions - hence the small print which generally covers the cardboard wrapping the disks. An additional benefit of this system is that there is a good chance that the disks have not been tampered with since they were produced.

Even though shrink-wrapped software is probably the safest way to obtain software, there have still been a few cases of viruses distributed in this way:

- Zinc Software, Utah, USA, 20th November 1991, Zinc Interface Library, Form.

- Focus, Taiwan, December 1991, 2theMAX VGA cards, Michelangelo.

- Novell, Utah, USA, 11th December 1991, *NetWare* Encyclopedia, 3800 copies, NoInt.

- Da Vinci Systems, North Carolina, USA, 1st February 1992, 900 copies, Michelangelo.

Due to the rise in user awareness of computer viruses, most major companies now have stringent Quality Assurance (QA) procedures in order to prevent virus propagation via commercial software. Although there is a chance of infection from shrink-wrapped software, the risk is small. However, a useful prophylactic, regardless of the source, is that any software is scanned for viruses before being used on a 'clean' machine.

Viruses and *Windows*

Life for the virus hunters is rapidly becoming more complicated as the PC operating system gets increasingly complex. One large bone of contention at this time is the security of *Windows*, and whether it is possible to use anti-virus software from within the program.

Windows viruses

At the time of writing (September 1993), there are two known *Windows* viruses, WinVir_1.4 and Twitch. The former is a very simple virus which is capable of infecting files in the Microsoft 'NE' format. When a user attempts to execute an infected file by double clicking on its icon, the virus infects every file in the current directory and disinfects its current host program before returning control to the operating system. The user incorrectly assumes that the double click has not registered, and tries to run the program again. This operation is successful (as the host file is no longer infected with the virus) and the user is therefore unaware of the presence of the virus. [*For more details on the WinVir_1.4 virus see VB, November 1992, p.19. Ed.*]

Twitch is one of the most complex viruses in existence. It is a fully-fledged *Windows* executable and is capable of becoming memory-resident under *Windows*. The virus causes an irritating screen shake (or twitch) periodically [*see VB, September 1993, p.13. Ed.*].

Anti-virus software under *Windows*

The danger of relying on *Windows*-based virus detection is that it is impossible to boot the system in a manner which can guarantee that the PCs memory is not infected. Unlike DOS, *Windows* cannot be installed on a write-protected bootable floppy diskette, and therefore has to be executed from the hard drive. This leaves the possibility that some part of the code needed to run the anti-virus software is infected, and that a stealth virus could evade detection. To be fair to the manufacturers of *Windows*-based scanners, the user is (in most cases) warned of this possibility, but how many users will really grasp the issues involved, prefering pretty pictures to secure operation?

In short, just about the only secure use of *Windows*-based scanners is to check floppy disks for the presence of viruses.

Viruses and PC Networks

As has already been discussed, computer viruses spread by the exchange of executable code. With an increasing number of systems networked together, there is no more effective way for a virus to spread than by taking advantage of this channel. PC networks allow high speed exchange of both executables and data, and, combining this with a large number of users sharing executables can provide the ideal breeding ground for viruses.

However, all is not lost, as the danger of a large-scale virus attack on a networked system can be reduced dramatically simply by using some of the security features which most network operating systems provide. The following discussion describes virus behaviour under *NetWare* 3.11 and *NetWare* 286, although many of the countermeasures are applicable to other network operating systems.

Virus Infection under *NetWare*

Many of the simple file-infecting viruses are capable of operating under *NetWare* due to the operating system's excellent emulation of logical DOS disks.

The main difference between local drives and *NetWare* is that *NetWare* does not allow software to access the remote disk on a sector by sector basis either through the DOS interrupts INT 25h or the BIOS interrupt Bh. This precludes any infection of the boot sector of the server by boot sector viruses from a workstation (although if the server itself were booted from an infected diskette, a virus would certainly infect its boot sector).

The situation is very different for parasitic viruses, most of which operate on a file by file basis, rather than by accessing individual sectors. This means that if the user accessing a file has full read-write privileges for that file, the file could become infected.

The point of entry of a virus onto a network is usually the user workstation. A typical scenario would be that a user infects his workstation either by executing an infected file or booting from a disk which is infected with a multi-partite virus. The virus becomes memory-resident and will attempt to infect files as they are executed or accessed.

When the user logs on to the network, he executes LOGIN.EXE which is stored in the LOGIN directory of the file-server, which will allow access to the allotted file areas on the file server. The worst case is if LOGIN.EXE is unprotected, as it will then become infected.

On a typical active network, an infection can spread to almost every workstation within minutes of the LOGIN program becoming infected - whenever a new user logs on to the network, his machine will be infected by the virus.

Infected workstation ...

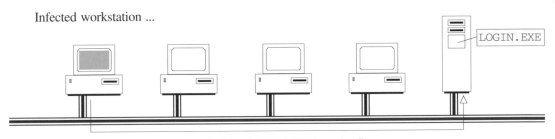

... infects LOGIN.EXE on the file server

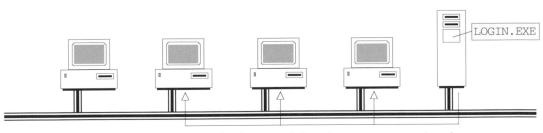

after which every workstation becomes infected as soon as a user logs in

Large scale network infection through LOGIN.EXE

Fortunately, it is easy to set up a network in such a way as to minimise the way in which a virus can spread. In order to see how this can be achieved, we must first examine the different security mechanisms built into *NetWare* 3.11.

Locking The Door

NetWare 3.11 provides access control in four different ways: the login procedure, trustee rights, directory rights and file attributes.

1. The login procedure requires all users to identify themselves to the network by means of a username and password.

2. Trustee rights are granted to each user by the 'network supervisor' and allow the network manager to specify which actions a user is allowed to take in specific directories. For example, a user may have permission to read files in a shared directory, but not to write to them. Note that these rights are set by *NetWare* at the file server, and therefore cannot be subverted by a virus executing on a workstation.

3. Directory rights (read, write, open etc.) are set separately and can be used to limit the access to certain directories, such as those containing executables. Just like trustee rights, they are set by the file server (but see warning of 'Execute Only' right later).

4. File attributes (such as the DOS read-only attribute) are handled by the workstation and behave in exactly the same way as those on local hard drives. These therefore provide no protection against virus attack.

It can be seen that by properly applying these different mechanisms, the spread of a virus infection can be limited. It is important to note that the virus accesses the file server with the same rights as the user who is running an infected worksation - therefore if the system supervisor logs on from an infected workstation, it is likely that considerable damage will result.

Practical Anti-virus Measures

Diskless Workstations

Diskless workstations are PCs in their own right, sometimes equipped with a hard drive, but with no floppy disk drive. The reasoning behind this measure is clear: if the user does not have the means of introducing a floppy disk into the machine it should be impossible for him to infect the workstation.

This 'no floppy, no virus' mentality only holds up to a certain extent. It is quite true that the introduction of diskless workstations limits the number of ways in which viruses can infiltrate the system, as well as providing additional security benefits (such as preventing users stealing data on a diskette). Unfortunately diskless workstations do not stop deliberate introduction of malicious code (for example, code can still be entered using the keyboard or DEBUG) - several techniques which can be used are described in Burger's book *Computer Viruses - A High Tech Disease*. It is also still possible for a virus to enter the system via modem or Email links: any route by which executable code can be loaded onto the system is a potential source of infection.

Before embarking on a project of removing floppy disk drives from all PCs installed in the office, it is worth considering the substantial impact which such a measure may have on productivity, as the transfer of legitimate data by users will be made much more difficult. The decision to adopt such draconian measures is a major one, and should not be taken lightly - especially as there are other lines of defence which offer good protection against virus infection.

Remote bootstrap ROMs

As has been discussed earlier, PCs use the contents of the boot sector to load in the operating system. This boot process is a potential source of infection, and by utilising special hardware, it is possible to minimise the chances of infection occurring.

Most network cards can be fitted with a special chip which contains code to allow the PC to boot from code stored on the file server instead of from the local disk. Note that the PC will still attempt to boot locally, and only in the event of no disk being in the floppy drive will the boot be performed using the code stored on the file server.

This process has several advantages. Firstly, as the PC is not usually booted locally, the effects of boot sector viruses are greatly reduced. Secondly, any updates to the operating system can be carried out centrally, without the need for the system manager to tend to each machine individually. If an organisation has decided to use diskless workstations, the use of remote bootstrap ROMs is recommended.

NetWare Loadable anti-virus software

In the last year, several of the larger anti-virus software houses have released *NetWare* Loadable Modules (NLMs) which run anti-virus software. This software is designed to be run on the file server, rather than a workstation, and has considerable advantages over ordinary DOS-based virus scanning.

The most obvious advantage of the server-based strategy is that it is impossible for a DOS virus to 'stealth' the server software, as the virus will not be memory-resident on the server. In addition to this, several of the NLMs have code which allows files to be scanned as they are written to the file server. This means that rather than waiting for an infected file to be scanned before the alarm can be raised, the system manager can be notified of problems as soon as a virus attempts to infect any executable on the server. This allows a proactive stance to be taken toward virus detection.

The second advantage to this system is that the system manager can set the anti-virus software to be run continuously as a background process on the file server. This greatly reduces the risks of a virus spreading rapidly over the network, as well as centralising virus reporting and detection.

The use of virus non-specific software on critical areas of the file server is also recommended. This can either be done using NLMs or by using a simple checksumming program from a workstation attached to the server. It is vital that the workstation from which these checks are conducted is securely booted.

Two IDs for network supervisors

The weak link in many multi-user computing environments is that one or more users must be given higher privileges for system administration. Unfortunately, these higher privileges are also assigned to a virus if the system manager logs on to the file server from an infected workstation. Onc virus (GP1) attempts to exploit exactly this weak link by capturing the network supervisor's password.

One excellent method of reducing the risk of infiltration by such techniques is the use of two different passwords for the network manager: one identity has privileges for all operations on the server, and one which just has read access to all areas. This allows the use of the former ID to be used solely for system administration functions.

NetWare Boot Disk

As stealth viruses have become more common, the dangers of accessing the server from an infected workstation have increased dramatically, and the need to access the server from a virus-free workstation when performing system-related tasks is paramount.

To access *NetWare* 3.11 securely, a normal DOS disk should be prepared (using the DOS format with the /S option), which in addition to the normal DOS system files and COMMAND.COM also contains the following *NetWare* 3.11 files:

```
IPX.COM
NETx.EXE
```

```
LOGIN.EXE
MAP.EXE
```

This disk should then be write-protected.

To access the network, switch off the workstation, and then boot it from this write-protected diskette. Note that using the Ctrl-Alt-Del sequence is not sufficient, as several viruses can survive this. Once the machine has booted, run IPX, followed by NETx. Next, log on to the server by running LOGIN from the floppy diskette using the command line qualifier '/S NUL'. This prevents the contents of the login script being executed, ensuring that no software is run from the server.

Execute Only

One setting of the *NetWare* file attributes which has been heralded as a very useful way of preventing virus infection is the execute-only attribute. The attribute is intended to prevent files specified as execute-only from being modified or even read - the only allowed operation is the execute function.

Setting the execute-only attribute is a mixed blessing. On the one hand, it prevents the modification of executables, but on the other it makes them unreadable to DOS based anti-virus software and impossible to back up.

This attribute offers **no protection against companion viruses** which do not modify the 'infected' EXE file in any way. Also, as the execute-only attribute is controlled (at least in part) at the workstation end (as clearly a file must be read into memory in order to execute it), it is not completely secure to being subverted by a virus on the workstation. Files marked as execute-only can still be deleted or renamed, and therefore it is possible for these files to be attacked by viruses - although the virus would have to target this attribute specifically.

It is recommended that this attribute is used together with marking the directory rights as read only. In this way a reasonable level of protection can be achieved under *NetWare*.

```
Volume Serial Number is 1 FF-866
Direc ry  f C: DO
                    \  S              4
[.]   to      [..]      A      COUNTRY.SYS    EGA.SYS       FORMAT.COM
KEYB.COM      KEYBOARD.S S   HIMEM.SYS      MODE.COM      SETVER.EXE
ANSI.SYS      DEBUG.E E      FDISK.EXE      MIRROR.COM    RAMDRIVE.S S
SHARE.EXE     SYS.COMX  Y    UNDELETE.EXE   UNFORMAT.CO   XCOPY.EXE
DISPLAY.COMo  DOSETUP.EX     SCATEMM.SYS    SCATEMM.TXTM  SPEED.COM Y
DISCHRGE.COM  DOSKEY.COME    DOSSHELL.VID   DOSSHELL.IN   DOSSHELL.C M
DOSSHELL.EXE  DOSSHELL.GR    DOSSWAP. XE    PACKING.LST   PRINT.EXE O
APPNOTES TX   DOSSHELL.H     EDIT.HLP       RECOVER.E E   DOSHELP.HL
HELP.EXE.     QBASIC.HLPL    EDIT.COM       MONEY.BA      MSHERC.C
QBASIC.EXE    GORILLA.BA B   4201.CPIE      4208.CPISX    5202.CPIO
APPEND.E E    ASSIGN.COMS    ATTRIB.EXE     BACKUP.EXE    CHKDSK
COMP.EXE      DISKCOMP.CO    DISKCOPY.COM   DRIVER.SYS I  FC.EXE.E
FIND.EXE      GRA TABL.CO
MORE.COMX     NIB LES.B      REMLINE.  U    RE IORES.     U I EXEX P
EXE2BIN EXE   EXP  D. XA     JOIN:E EBA     LC :P.ER       D IA  E
 RINTER SYS   RE  NE.E ES    REP  CX  S     U S.   XEO          M
  L   C EX      F AYTX        G L P.EX        R D  S
        . ET   B XE S SP               E     S
P      .    e(s  AM2  T3M bytE  APE        D C I         S R
N SFUN .       D ADL  . Y M bytFA .C I     S B T EXE     L A F   E
EDLIN.EXE     MISPE 0987 3   esATO E   E   SMA T RV. Y   TREE.CO CO
C:\HSG>89 fil  )EM.18319360  esSfreeN.EX   COMMAND.COMS  EMM386.EXEM
```

Anti-virus procedures

The only way to be absolutely safe is never to try anything
for the first time.

Magnus Pyke

Anti-virus procedures can be divided into five parts:

- Preparation
- Prevention
- Detection
- Containment
- Recovery

Preparation

An organisation has to prepare itself for a potential virus attack before it occurs.

Regular and sound backups

Backups are especially important in case of an attack by a destructive virus. In case of data loss, the system can be efficiently restored. As part of the backup procedure, the master disks for all software (including the operating system) should be write-protected and stored in a safe place. This will enable a speedy restoration of any infected executables.

Important! The backups should be sound, which means that there is little point in doing them unless the data can actually be restored. They should be tested from time to time by performing complete restorations of the system.

Write-protected system floppy disk

A write-protected system floppy disk should be prepared in advance and should contain all system files. These are automatically transferred to the floppy disk when it is formatted with the command

```
FORMAT A:/S
```

This disk should also contain AUTOEXEC.BAT, CONFIG.SYS and any other system files or device drivers which are necessary to access the hard disk. Note that CONFIG.SYS normally refers to other files which are loaded into memory before the system is started, using statements such as 'DEVICE=filename'. All these files should be copied onto the floppy disk, and CONFIG.SYS on the floppy should be modified, if necessary, to ensure that it refers to the files on the floppy disk, rather than the original copies on the hard disk.

After all these files have been copied, **the floppy disk should be write-protected**. This is a hardware protection against the modification of any information on the disk. No virus, or for that matter, any software, can write to a write-protected floppy disk (provided that the floppy disk drive recognises write-protect tabs correctly!).

If a computer becomes infected, this disk will be used to bootstrap the computer. This will ensure that various items on the computer can be examined through a 'clean' operating system, giving the virus no chance to employ hiding techniques.

Contingency plan

This plan, which can be put into action in case of a virus attack, is usually part a point-by-point checklist and should include information on the following topics:

- The person within the organisation responsible for dealing with the attack and his deputy

- The consultant(s) outside the organisation who can be called in to help deal with the attack

- Exact procedure for isolating infected disks and PCs

- Public Relations procedure to prevent unauthorised leaks about the attack spreading outside the organisation

Prevention

Preventing a virus attack involves not allowing the virus code to reach any of the company's PCs. The need to communicate, however, introduces a potential virus entry path into any environment. Application software has to be purchased or updated, new operating systems installed, disks interchanged. The higher the volume of inbound traffic, the more opportunity a virus has to enter the environment.

Five techniques are widely recognised in being effective in practice: creating user awareness, implementing hygiene rules, using disk authorisation software, providing a 'dirty' PC and providing a quarantine PC.

Creating user awareness

Creating user awareness is the most important factor in establishing an effective virus prevention policy. A virus will in most cases penetrate an organisation due to one or more users' actions. Users must be made aware what actions can lead to virus penetration, consequent losses to the organisation and, in the end, a threat to their own jobs.

Strengthening awareness is a matter of common sense and measures include the use of leaflets, posters, presentations, showing educational virus videos and so on.

Hygiene rules

The observance of 'hygiene' is by far the most effective way of preventing a virus attack. A virus program has little chance of reaching a computer which is not networked, has a limited number of users (preferably only one), and is never used with disks from other sources.

The list of rules is straightforward and it essentially boils down to the fact that every executable item which is to run on a computer should be treated with suspicion. This includes demonstration disks, shareware, public domain and bulletin board software.

A simple example set of rules is:

- Do not use software 'pulled down' from bulletin boards
- Do not use shareware
- Use only programs from reputable manufacturers

Disk authorisation software

Disk authorisation software can be used very effectively to enforce anti-virus procedures, thereby decreasing the likelihood of virus penetration. Any disks from outside the organisation are unusable on the PCs inside the organisation until they have been virus-checked and converted into the company format.

The use of disk authorisation software is a very effective way of enforcing the company anti-virus policies, while not requiring the administrative overheads of a full access-control package.

Dirty PC

A dirty PC is a physically isolated machine without a hard disk, not connected to networks, which can be used for playing games and essentially doing anything which would be dangerous to do on a machine used for day-to-day work. Employees should be encouraged to use it to try out any software coming from outside, including demo disks and games. No company work should ever be done on that machine, and no disks used on the dirty PC should ever be used in any other computer.

This concept is a useful tool against viruses, if carefully controlled, although it is not recommend in more rigorously structured organisations such as the Government.

Quarantine PC

A quarantine PC is a stand-alone machine not connected to networks. Apart from having permanently installed virus-specific anti-virus software, this PC is kept completely clean and is used to check incoming disks for viruses. Only disks and programs which have been cleared are allowed through.

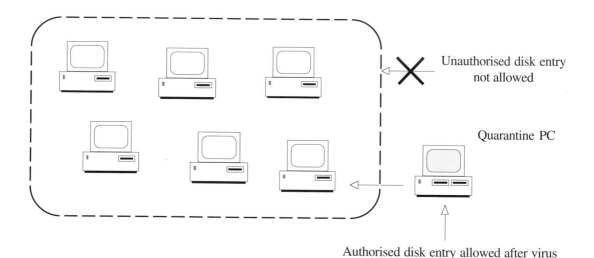

Unauthorised disk entry not allowed

Quarantine PC

Authorised disk entry allowed after virus check

Quarantine PC used for checking all incoming disks

The quarantine function is often linked with the gateway function when using disk authorisation software.

Detection

Should a virus penetrate the initial obstacles placed in its way, its presence must be detected as soon as possible. Although there are several 'classic' indicators of a virus attack listed below, in practice it is very difficult to distinguish between a physical fault and a virus. Furthermore, as virus awareness spreads, users are more likely to attribute faults to viruses instead of the machine malfunction. It is normally up to the support desk to recognise the symptoms and act accordingly.

'Strange' occurrences

Sometimes users will notice 'strange' things happening, such as programs taking longer to load than usual, a disk light flashing when it should not be, program size varying or free memory size decreasing. All these occurrences could be symptoms of a virus attack, but they should not be relied upon for detecting virus presence. They rely too much on the subjective powers of observation of an individual to be usable in a reliable way.

Anti-virus software

Anti-virus software should always be used on a 'clean' (virus-free) PC. You can ensure that your PC is clean by switching it off and then bootstrapping it from a clean, write-protected system disk before running anti-virus software. If a virus is active in memory, it can 'fool' the anti-virus program by hiding its presence.

Various types of anti-virus software are analysed in a separate section in this chapter.

Containment

When a virus is detected, infected PCs and disks have to be identified and isolated. A contingency plan prepared in advance will be extremely valuable at the moment of virus discovery. A point-by-point checklist makes it more difficult to forget an important item in the panic which often follows a virus attack.

Network access

Viruses can spread very rapidly over networks. If the exact nature of the attack is unknown, the safest measure may be to disconnect infected PCs physically from the network.

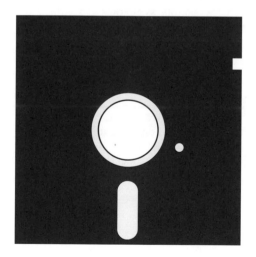

Write-unprotected 5-1/4" disk

Write-protected 5-1/4" disk

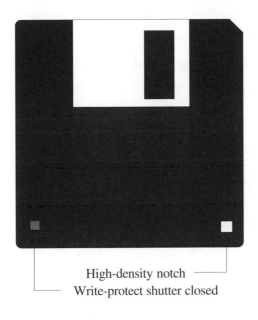

High-density notch
Write-protect shutter closed

Write-unprotected 3-1/2" disk

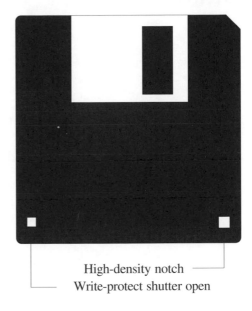

High-density notch
Write-protect shutter open

Write-protected 3-1/2" disk

Disk interchange

Any disk interchange between PCs should be temporarily suspended. Masking tape placed over disk drives is a good physical indicator that the drives should not be used.

Write-protect tabs

All floppy disks which are not purposefully intended to be infected, should be write-protected. On 5.25" disks the application of the write-protect tab means that nothing can be written to that disk. 3.5" disks are write-protected when the write-protect shutter is open.

Write-protection on disks is a hardware function and cannot be overridden in software.

Recovery

Recovery from a virus attack involves:

1. Elimination of the virus from the infected PC hard and floppy disks

and

2. Recovery from any virus side-effects

Elimination of the virus from infected PCs

To eliminate the virus from the infected hard disk, each PC should be switched off and then bootstrapped from a write-protected clean system floppy disk. Infected objects (bootstrap sectors, executables) should be identified and replaced with clean copies.

Replacing infected executables is best done by deleting the old copy using the DOS command 'DEL' and 'COPY' the originals from the manufacturers' delivery disks. Using 'DEL' first is not really necessary, but it can help avoid mistakes. Most anti-virus software offers the capability of 'disinfecting' the executables, but this practice has been shown to be very unreliable.

Replacing infected bootstrap sectors can be done with disk editing tools or disinfecting anti-virus software (it is generally a much safer practice than disinfecting executables), but if the worst comes to the worst, the 'brute force' approach is possible. All data files on the hard disk should be backed up first and the disk reformatted. For disks infected with DOS boot sector viruses such as Form, a DOS

```
FORMAT
```

is sufficient, while for Master Boot Sector viruses (e.g. New Zealand and Joshi), a low level format should be performed. Data files should then be restored from the backups and the executables restored from the manufacturers' original disks. The replacement of the DOS boot sector can also be performed by the 'SYS' command (which transfers the whole operating system), while the command

```
FDISK /MBR
```

replaces the Master Boot Sector code in DOS 3.31 and later.

To clear infected floppy disks, a virus scanner should be run on each floppy, in order to discover whether it contains any virus code. After any valuable data has been backed up, infected floppies should be reformatted under clean system conditions. Use the command

```
FORMAT A:
```

Before eliminating a virus, do not forget to preserve a copy in a safe place, on a clearly marked disk, for detailed analysis. This is best done by one of the organisations involved in virus research such as *Virus Bulletin*.

Recovery from virus side-effects

Recovery from virus side-effects depends on the virus. In the case of innocuous viruses such as Cascade, recovery from side-effects is not necessary, while in the case of a virus such as Michelangelo, recovery will involve the restoration of a complete hard disk.

Other points

There are a few other things worth bearing in mind during recovery from a virus attack:

- Discover and close loopholes which allowed the virus to enter the organisation

- Inform any possible recipients of the infected disks outside the organisation that they may be affected by the virus

- Consider the implications to the organisation of the bad publicity

- In the UK, inform the *Computer Crime Unit* of *New Scotland Yard* in London about the attack (Tel 071 230 1177, Fax 071 831 8845)

Anti-virus software

Anti-virus software can be divided into two categories: Virus-specific and Virus-non-specific. Virus-specific software relies on the knowledge of particular viruses in order to detect them, while virus-non-specific software should (in theory) detect all viruses, past, present and future. Each category can, in turn, be divided into sub-categories.

Scanning software

Virus scanning software is the most popular type of anti-virus software today. It relies on the knowledge of specific viruses. When a new virus appears in the wild, it is analysed, and its characteristics recorded. The virus-scanning program will scan all executables on a disk, including the operating system and the bootstrap sector(s), and compare their contents with the known virus characteristics.

This type of software can only discover viruses that it 'knows' about, and as such must continually be updated with new virus intelligence as new viruses appear. This is the main problem with this type of software. Scanning software is especially useful for checking incoming floppy disks for the presence of known viruses.

Checksumming software

Checksumming software relies on the calculation of a checksum of any executable on the system followed by periodic recalculations in order to verify that the checksum has not changed. If a virus attacks an executable, it will change it, which will result in a completely different checksum.

This type of software is reactive rather than proactive, in that a virus attack will be detected after it happens. Checksumming software also relies on the fact that the executables are 'clean' (i.e. virus-free) before the initial checksumming is applied. This can be ensured by using virus-specific scanning software to check the system for the presence of any known viruses.

The checksumming approach is the only known method which will detect all viruses with absolute certainty. This makes it inherently desirable as a long-term anti-virus strategy in any organisation. The method of performing the checksumming process (the checksumming algorithm) is very important. Three general approaches are possible: simple checksums, cyclic redundancy checks (CRCs) and cryptographic checksums. Cryptographic checksums are the most secure approach.

Virus monitoring software

Monitoring software packages (also called on-line packages) install themselves as memory-resident TSR (Terminate-but-Stay-Resident). They intercept and monitor disk I/O, trying either to monitor system integrity or to detect 'virus activity'.

The main problem with such packages is that there is no defined list of what constitutes virus activity and virus authors are not obliged to follow a particular set of rules when producing their creations. Any widely used virus monitor is an open invitation to virus authors to produce a virus which is not recognised by the monitor.

False alarms can also result from legitimate program activity which is misinterpreted by the anti-virus software (this in turn usually leads to users ignoring all warnings!).

Integrity shells

The idea behind integrity shells is that a layer is added above the DOS command level, so that the shell 'filters through' any request to execute a program. Before executing the program, the anti-virus part of the shell will perform an on-line checksum of the executable and compare it with a previously computed value. If the values do not agree, execution of the program will not commence.

'Inoculation' software

'Inoculation' software which labels disks or executables in such a way that a particular virus will not infect them is **not to be trusted**. This software introduces a virus signature into objects it wants to protect, leading the virus to believe that the object is already infected. Apart from the fact that such 'protection' can only be done against one, or at most a few viruses, it is not a long-term solution and can introduce a false sense of security as well as false virus alarms when scanning software is run.

Virus removal software

The simplest form of virus removal software are the DOS DEL, SYS, FDISK and FORMAT commands. The DEL command deletes infected programs and the FORMAT command re-initialises infected disks. SYS and FDISK commands are convenient ways of replacing boot sectors.

Virus scanning software often provides automatic file deletion which enables a quick and automatic removal of infected files. Once infected files have been removed, they can be replaced with manufacturers' originals.

Disinfection software

Disinfection software attempts to remove viruses from infected disks and infected programs in such a way as to restore the infected item to its previous state. Since viruses are often mutated (changed) in subtle ways making them look the same to virus detection software, disinfection software can (and often does) make mistakes, taking off a few bytes too many or too few. Unfortunately, this can have catastrophic consequences potentially leading to data corruption much worse than that produced by most viruses. Disinfection of boot sector viruses is more feasible than the disinfection of executables, although generic tools (DEL, SYS, FDISK and FORMAT) are still a preferable solution.

Summary of anti-virus software

In summary, the recommended long-term approach is to use checksumming software in conjunction with virus scanning software, provided its limitations are clearly understood. Virus monitoring software is not recommended. 'Inoculation' software should not be used, while disinfection software must be used with great care. Integrity shells are an attractive concept, though often difficult to use in practice.

Options   View   **Info**   Help

┌─────────────────────────────────────┐
│ Search criteria   ▶   │
│ **Do search**   │
│ Clear criteria...   │
│ Count matches   │
│ Print...   │
│ Specify print file...   │
└─────────────────────────────────────┘

Virus name: Form
Infects: DOS bo
Memory resident
Trigger conditi
Infected hard d

Next   Mo

A boot sector virus from Switzerland infecting
hard disks and floppy disks. On the 18th of
every month the virus produces a noise when keys
are pressed. The original boot sector is stored in
the last physical sector of the hard disk. (VB Nov
91).

Anti-virus products

Well, now, there's a remedy for everything except death.

Miguel de Cervantes

Esc quits

Reviewing Anti-virus Products

Dr. Keith Jackson

Reviewing anti-virus software products is fraught, with many contradictions and obstacles. It is ridiculously easy to test how well a scanning program checks a test set of virus infected files and knock up a quick review, as is evidenced by the many so-called 'reviews' written by computer journalists. Paradoxically, writing a fair, objective, review of an anti-virus product is somewhat more difficult. This section discusses what sorts of anti-virus software are currently available, how anti-virus products should be tested before publication of a review, and what features a user of anti-virus software should consider when contemplating purchase.

Although many manufacturers of anti-virus products dress things up in different disguises, underneath layers of often impenetrable jargon there are only really a few key techniques which are used. Virus detection is usually achieved by looking for evidence of the presence of a particular virus, or by detecting that a file has been altered (which may or may not have been caused by a virus). These two techniques are known by the jargon terms 'scanning' and 'checksumming', and are offered in various configurations by different manufacturers. Once a virus has been identified, anti-virus products often provide facilities which can remove a named virus from an infected file, or from the boot sector of a disk. This process is often called 'cleaning' or 'disinfecting'. Removal of a virus leaving the original bytes intact is not always possible as some viruses do not preserve all parts of the infected object. In such cases all infected components must be deleted to ensure that the virus infection is completely eradicated.

Scanners look for a distinct pattern, or a distinct feature, to identify the presence of a virus. Obviously scanning can only detect known viruses, as for it to succeed, someone has to have previously detected the virus, spent some time analysing how it works, extracted a signature, and added it to the existing anti-virus product. Finding a pattern that is contained within a particular virus, but not present in any other file is quite a difficult task, and given the current known total number of PC viruses (about 3,000 in September 1993; depending on whom you believe) the total amount of effort that must be applied to signature extraction is very large. If a signature is not unique then it can cause false alarms by wrongly detecting a virus in files which are uninfected (see below).

Not all viruses can be detected by searching for a particular sequence of bytes. In particular those viruses which encrypt themselves with a unique key every time they replicate, and viruses that change themselves every time that they replicate (a property known as polymorphism), both require that a scanning program uses techniques beyond mere pattern matching. The capability of detecting such viruses is often quoted as one of the main distinctions between a scanning program which is 'good', and one that is merely 'ordinary'.

As the number of viruses can only increase, it is probable that scanning programs are ultimately doomed. At some point in time manufacturers will be swamped by the amount of work required to extract signatures, by the size of the data files that will need to be maintained, and by a slowdown in the scanning speed caused by the number of signatures. The last problem has been addressed with some success, and various manufacturers claim that their products are not 'unduly affected' (whatever that means) by wholesale increases in the number of virus signatures which have to be searched for. Even though these problems have affected scanning programs for many years now, it must be admitted that their popularity is showing no signs of waning as yet, though what they will do when there are 20,000 known PC viruses is anybody's guess. Would-be purchasers of a scanning program should be aware that many current products are beginning to show signs of falling behind in this never-ending game of catch-up, a fact that often gets pointed out by reviewers of anti-virus software, and always vehemently denied by the manufacturer at whom the charge is levelled.

A checksumming anti-virus program calculates checksums across the content of a file by applying the rules of a specific algorithm to the file under study, and as a result calculates a unique number which will always vary if the content of the file is altered in any way. A checksum is verified by recalculating its value, and comparing it with the original value. The whole process of verifying checksums relies on the simple fact that a virus must alter a file to infect it. Therefore if a virus infection occurs, the checksum associated with the infected file must be different from the checksum calculated for the uninfected file. Verification of a checksum can never say what sort of virus infection has occurred - it can only detect that the content of a file has altered.

One of the most important features about a checksumming program is the algorithm which is used to calculate the checksums. The checksumming algorithm should be of some cryptographic merit to prevent a virus author from studying a particular checksum program, figuring out how it creates/stores its checksums, and then writing a virus which will change a file, recalculate the correct checksum, and update the stored checksums. If a trivial algorithm is used to calculate the checksums, then such reverse-engineering is eminently possible. If a very secure encryption algorithm is used to calculate the checksums, then the speed of operation will be impossibly slow. Obviously a balance has to be struck between these two extremes. The best checksumming programs offer a choice of algorithm, and leave the selection between speed of operation and algorithm complexity in the hands of the end-user. Any checksumming product which will not release any details of the algorithm(s) used, and merely say that such information is 'proprietary' should be avoided. Their claims cannot be verified.

Several manufacturers of anti-virus software offer a feature termed 'immunization' (or some similar phrase), whereby self-verifying checksumming software is added to an executing program such that the checksum is verified before the program is allowed to execute. Any change that has been made to the program can therefore be detected, and execution refused. This technique causes many problems: it often interferes with the execution of the program that it is trying to protect, the executable image of a file is often changed as a program's configuration is changed, and updating in such a manner often writes to a location which is a fixed distance away from the start of a file - thereby inducing chaos when immunization software is added. If immunization is to be used, it should be inserted by the developers of a particular piece of software, and any attempt to tag it on at a later stage should be avoided like the plague.

All of the anti-virus features described so far can be provided as memory-resident programs, as well as stand alone programs. A user must take a conscious decision to execute a stand-alone program, and after an initial burst of activity they often fall into disuse. Memory-resident programs offer dynamic virus detection at all times, and require no further action on the part of the user. This is at the expense of introducing an overhead on program execution (see below), and the possible introduction of incompatibilities. There are some computer programs that will not co-exist with memory-resident anti-virus programs, and when contemplating purchase of such a product, users should take great care to test out the proposed product with all versions of the computer programs that will be used. If the manufacturer will not permit such a test, then act sensibly and walk away.

From the user's point of view, the only real source of unbiased information about an anti-virus product will come from a review of the product. It is very difficult to decide whom to believe and whom to dismiss when considering the volume of words that are written on this subject. A few golden rules should help.

Firstly treat anything provided by the manufacturer or vendor with heavy doses of disbelief. They have a vested interest in altering the meaning of words, to the point of almost lying, in order to increase the sales of a particular product. A second source of information to avoid is from a journalist writing a short piece about the product. By its very nature such an article will have been written after a very cursory inspection of the product, and will not spot any problems other than the most blatantly obvious. The best source of reliable information about anti-virus software comes from reviews written by experts on the subject. Such reviews are regularly published by specialist anti-virus publications (*Virus Bulletin* and *Virus News International* are probably the two best known), and intermittently one of the general purpose computer magazines will publish a comparative review of anti-virus products written by a respectable research organisation. These are sometimes (note the words of caution) quite good.

When considering reviews of an anti-virus product, it is often difficult to try and separate objective measurement from opinions about the product. To say that a scanning program detected 92% of viruses in a given test-set can be confirmed by anybody who has a copy of the test-set. It is (hopefully!) repeatable, and therefore objective. To say that detecting 92% of this test set is very good, and is grounds for purchasing the product, is an opinion and such statements should always be treated with due caution. A good reviewer will always be quite careful to separate fact from opinion, will point out problems honestly and fairly, and will try to ensure that the manufacturer of the product being reviewed sees the content of the review before publication with the aim of correcting anything that is obviously erroneous. Unfortunately, there is no simple way of ensuring that a particular reviewer is any good, or is just hacking off the text as fast as possible. Only experience can provide such information. If you've found a regular reviewer that you trust (maybe by word of mouth recommendation from a trusted friend), then stick with him. Nothing else really works.

When writing a review, it is important to take a long look at the documentation which accompanies a product, make notes on anything which appears to be misleading, idiotic, or just plainly wrong. Poor documentation on its own is not a reason to reject a product - yet anybody considering purchase has a right to know what help they will receive from the documentation. Access to information is very important. It is highly unlikely that anybody will read a manual from cover to cover, but when a problem occurs, an index, for example, is essential. Many vendors seem to think that pretty presentation can be used as an excuse for a lack of content in the documentation, and react vociferously to this being pointed out in reviews. With the exception of pointing out factual errors, writing about documentation will always be only one person's opinion, and should be treated with due scepticism.

Recently there has been a trend towards providing magnificently implemented user interfaces with anti-virus software products. Although ease of use is undoubtedly necessary, such efforts are somewhat missing the point. Anti-virus products are after all only utility software; their greatest contribution occurs when they carry out their task quietly, and a user interface similar to those on offer from a word processor or spreadsheet seems somewhat superfluous. This trend has been taken to greater heights by the introduction of Windows based anti-virus products. Several scanning programs which were capable of being executed as a DOS program under *Microsoft Windows* have been raised to higher levels by the introduction of beautifully sculpted Windows versions. To avoid missing stealth viruses, it is important to ensure that a virus is not already present in memory when an anti-virus program executes. The only way to **guarantee** this is to boot the computer from a floppy disk that is known to be virus-free. If anybody knows how to boot a Windows based system using only a floppy disk, then I for one am waiting to hear from them.

The next thing to look at is the installation program. Is it easy to use? Does it permit a wide variety of installation options? Can the anti-virus program be installed in any desired subdirectory? Does the installation program fail to operate correctly when seldom used options are selected? (It's amazing how many fail this test). How much hard disk space does a complete installation require? Is a floppy disk installation possible and/or viable? How much RAM do the memory-resident programs require? These and other similar questions should always be discussed honestly in any review.

Now the difficult bit. Measuring how well an anti-virus program actually carries out its designed tasks is the source of most arguments between reviewers and developers of anti-virus products. Consider the case of a scanning program which has been tested against the set of test viruses available to the reviewer. It is likely, and also very desirable, that the test set is not the same as that available to the developer. If the two test sets were the same, then barring incompetence, a score of 100% would be guaranteed every time, making the test pointless. Therefore the person who gets to construct the test set (and maintain it) is in a position of great power.

This simple point has dogged attempts to provide a standardised testing protocol for anti-virus scanning software. Who is going to decide which viruses are included in the test set? Does the test set contain non-viruses (i.e. non-replicating code)? If the test set is made readily available then unless the parties to which it is sent are **always** trustworthy, this action may itself help in spreading viruses to far-flung corners of the world. In the end a 'standard' test set of viruses would probably lead to the development of anti-virus software which scored highly against this test set, but reacted poorly when used in the real world, which would undoubtedly be counter-productive. Probably the best solution to this dilemma is that test sets have to be continuously updated, should reflect which viruses are actually known to be 'in the wild', and that all anti-virus products should be tested against various sets of test viruses. This means that any serious would-be purchaser may need to consult reviews from several trusted reviewers. Such is life.

One thing that is apparently easy to measure is the speed at which a scanning program can inspect a disk. This ease of measurement conceals the fact that a simple measurement of scan time is only useful for one particular computer and hard disk combination. It's useless for any other combination. The only way of making a measurement of scanning speed useful is to compare the product under test with two (or more) other well-known scanning programs, and report comparative timings. This complicates matters.

Many anti-virus products have a checksumming facility which attempts to detect alterations by verifying checksums calculated across the executable files. It is usually quite difficult to test the efficiency of checksumming programs. The developers often keep secret the actual algorithm used, and will not divulge details to reviewers (especially to reviewers?). This makes it impossible to comment meaningfully on the checksum algorithm. In several cases, products which claim to calculate checksums for files have been found not actually to be monitoring the entire file (which speeds things up considerably!). Such omissions are easy to test by making single bit changes to a test file, and testing that the checksumming program detects these changes. Not all products perform as well as they claim to do.

It is common for anti-virus products to include memory-resident software which monitors dynamically for virus activity. The efficacy of such products is quite difficult to measure, and it is common to find *ad hoc* tests used for each specific product. One thing which stands out in all products is that the overhead introduced by memory-resident software is **always** glossed over in the documentation provided by the developers. Products that slow down file loading and execution quite severely (up to a factor of three increase in loading time), have been known to claim in the documentation that the memory-resident software introduces only a 'slight degradation'. Users who intend to implement memory-resident software should insist upon a trial run before purchase.

It is likely that false alarms actually waste more money than viruses do. Herein lies a problem - the only way to test for false alarms is to test exhaustively the anti-virus product against all known software packages, on all types of computer, which is a task of Herculean proportions. Several developers of scanning programs maintain hard disks full of Gigabytes of installed software packages in a manful attempt to prevent false alarms. Even when precautions are taken to this extent, false alarms still occur, and as the number of viruses and their polymorphic characteristics increases, the chances of a false alarm likewise increase.

When considering purchase of any anti-virus products a few compromises inevitably have to be made. A scanning program should detect **all** viruses that are known to be 'in the wild', most viruses from the test sets used by reviewers, and should measure up favourably in comparative reviews. Scanning speed is of slightly lesser importance, but any product should be capable of scanning the entire hard disk of the system on which it is to be used in a time that is quick enough to permit it to be used frequently without undue interruption. Such timings are inevitably a matter of personal judgment.

It is always worth bearing in mind what a writer has to gain when writing about anti-virus software. Marketing types are taught always to present everything in a positive light, to gloss over problems, and to reply 'We're looking into this report' when faced with an objective measurement of something that cannot be glossed over. All of this should be treated with the contempt that it deserves, and duly ignored. It is after all merely meant to create more sales rather than to help anybody. The only independent source of information is from reviewers writing without an axe to grind. Even though they may separate out fact and opinion, their report is bound to be coloured by personal opinions (to do otherwise is impossible). Therefore, find more than one review about a product, extract all the factual information you can, compare and contrast the reviewers opinions, and make your decision. After all it's your money.

1993 Scanner Shoot-out

Mark Hamilton, VB January 1993

Virus Bulletin last pitted the ever-increasing number of virus scanners against the *VB* test-sets six months ago, in June 1992. This comparative review has proved to be the biggest ever, with 20 products tested.

The essential criteria which all products should meet are:

- Their ability to detect viruses known to be in the wild

- Their ability to detect self-mutating strains

- Their concordance with each other

Any well maintained scanner should score 100% against the 'In The Wild' test-set, as these are the viruses which it is likely to encounter. Another telling result is Mutation Engine detection. Even though the Mutation Engine has been known about since last March (see *VB* April 1992, p.11), many scanners fail to detect it. In that edition *VB's* Technical Editor wrote: 'Perhaps the appearance of the Mutation Engine should be considered a torture test for the R&D departments of all the anti-virus companies - if they are not able to detect it in a couple of months they would be well advised to redirect their efforts to other pursuits.' Far more than a couple of months have passed, and all scanners should get full marks.

The ability of the different packages to co-exist is measured in the concordance test. This test is of particular interest to anyone who wishes to use more than one scanner, as much time could be lost due to false alarms.

Two products submitted failed very early on in the testing process: the disks supplied with Fifth Generation's *Untouchable* product were unreadable, and Leprechaun's *Virus Buster* insisted on aborting with run time errors.

Allsafe Version 4.1

In The Wild   81.25%
Standard   94.51%
Enlarged   87.48%
Mutation Engine 0%

Xtree's *Allsafe* had file dates of June 1992, and it showed its age by performing poorly in all the virus detection tests. Particularly worrying is its failure to detect several viruses known to be at large. It also missed *all* the Mutation Engine infections and its false-positive identification of Anarkia in a text file provides an eye-opening insight to Xtree's detection strategy. A better result than last year, but still woefully inadequate.

Norton Antivirus Version 2.1

In The Wild   95.31%
Standard   98.63%
Enlarged   93.49%
Mutation Engine 94.14%

Symantec's *Norton Antivirus* proudly displays a sticker affixed to its packaging that proclaims 'Detects 100% of all viruses in the NCSA Library'. I have no information as to the precise contents of this library, but *Norton Antivirus* certainly does not detect all the viruses in the various test-sets used here. Its Mutation Engine detection algorithm needs tightening, as it detected only 1,446 of the 1,536 samples. Although the product did not fare too badly in any of the test-sets, its results were not outstanding. Most seriously, it missed viruses from the 'In The Wild' test-set.

Virex-PC Version 2.3

In The Wild	99.22%
Standard	98.90%
Enlarged	96.42%
Mutation Engine	99.93%

Virex-PC missed one virus, SBC, from the 'In The Wild' test set, but fared better in the Mutation Engine test-set, detecting all but one of the samples. However, *Virex* does have a problem with the concordance test: *AVScan* detected the signature for the 570 virus in this scanner, *Sweep* found signatures for Filedate 11-537, VCL-3 and Ryazan and *PC-Eye* reported an infection by USSR-1594.

Sweep Version 2.44

In The Wild	100%
Standard	100%
Enlarged	96.42%
Mutation Engine	100%

Another healthy result for Sophos' *Sweep*. Its recently overhauled scanning engine has helped make this one of the faster products tested.

AVScan Version 0.98H

In The Wild	100%
Standard	100%

Enlarged   98.47%
Mutation Engine 100%

AVScan is a freeware scanner by H+BEDV Datentechnik Gmbh, a
German software house. *AVScan's* scanning engine performed
extremely well against all the test-sets, and was also one of the
fastest scanners tested. *AVScan* is currently available on CompuServe
where it can be downloaded from the Virus Help forum.

HT-Scan Version 1.19

In The Wild   94.53%
Standard   97.25%
Enlarged   87.23%
Mutation Engine   94.14%

HT-Scan is now in its 19th release and needs to be able to detect
more common viruses, as it failed to find Father, PcVrsDs, Spanz
and SBC from the 'In The Wild' test-set. *HT-Scan* uses an external
module to detect Mutation Engine-encrypted viruses and this
obviously needs further development - it missed 90 of the 1,536
infections.

Dr Solomon's Anti-Virus Toolkit Version 6.02

In The Wild   100%
Standard   99.45%
Enlarged   99.11%
Mutation Engine   100%

Problems were encountered with the *Windows* version of Doctor
Solomon's *Anti-Virus Toolkit* when it came to detecting the Mutation
Engine-encrypted samples. The first time I ran the test, the program
reported that it had detected 1,474 files infected with viruses and that
it had checked the same number of files. However, this test-set
contains 1,536 infected files so I re-ran the test: again only 1,474
files checked. On the third run, this figure improved by one to 1,475.

In each case it detected all the files as being infected. The final run provided me with the somewhat confusing results of 1,927 files checked with 1,925 infected files found (out of a possible 1,536 files)! This bug aside, both the *DOS* and *Windows Toolkit* performed very well.

Central Point Anti-Virus and CPAVSOS Version 1.4

In The Wild   97.66%
Standard   96.98%
Enlarged   90.04%
Mutation Engine   Failed to complete

Two offerings from Central Point Software were entered: its commercial anti-virus product (*CPAV*) and a new, free, scanner-only version (*CPAVSOS*), which the company is distributing electronically. The principal difference between the two is that *CPAVSOS* has no cure capabilities. In terms of detection capabilities both versions fared the same, failing to detect the Father and Crazy Eddie viruses contained in the 'In The Wild' test set. Central Point's software suffers from a bug which meant that it failed to complete the Mutation Engine test, hanging the PC [*see VB January 1993, p.21. Ed.*].

F-Prot Version 2.06b

In The Wild   100%
Standard   100%
Enlarged   99.49%
Mutation Engine   100%

These excellent scores speak for themselves.

Package	In The Wild 128	Standard 364	Enlarged 783	Mutation Engine 1536	Overall Performance
Allsafe	104	344	685	0	78.82
AVScan	128	364	771	1536	99.92
Central Point AV & CPAV-SOS	125	353	705	Failed to complete	92.33
F-Prot	128	364	779	1536	99.97
HT-Scan	121	354	683	1446	94.72
Integrity Master	123	348	692	0	90.86
IBM AntiVirus	128	360	741	1536	99.62
McAfee Scan	128	360	751	1536	99.69
Norton Antivirus	122	359	732	1446	90.79
PC-Eye	126	361	732	0	93.34
Search & Destroy	125	356	735	1446	92.60
Sweep	128	364	755	1536	99.82
TBScan	126	358	715	1536	98.15
Toolkit (S&S)	128	362	776	1536	99.93
VI-Spy	128	363	763	115	94.85
Virex-PC	127	360	755	1535	94.09
Viruscure-Plus	103	296	505	0	75.74
VIS	127	364	782	137	94.37

Detection results: The overall performance of each product is in the form of a percentage, where each of the test-sets is weighted according to their importance. The appropriate weighting are: In the Wild 80, Standard 10, Enlarged 5, Mutation Engine 5. The scores for the Mutation Engine detection are calculated on an all or nothing basis.

Integrity Master Version 1.13d

In The Wild   96.09%
Standard   95.60%
Enlarged   88.38%
Mutation Engine   0%

The failure to detect any samples of the Mutation Engine, coupled with its poor performance in the 'In The Wild' test-set make this a disappointing result for this product.

IBM AntiVirus/Dos and IBM AntiVirus/2 Version 1.00

In The Wild   100%
Standard   98.90%
Enlarged   94.64%
Mutation Engine   100%

IBM AntiVirus is reviewed in *VB*, January 1993 [*pp. 18-20, Ed.*] and the reader is referred there for detailed information.

PC-Eye Version 2.1

In The Wild   98.44%
Standard   99.18%
Enlarged   93.49%
Mutation Engine   0%

PC-Eye performed tolerably well in the tests, even though it missed one Whale and one of the Tequila infections in the 'In The Wild' test set. Surprisingly, it is totally unable to detect any Mutation Engine-encrypted code; it is to be hoped that its author, PC Enhancements, develops and incorporates the necessary algorithms before viruses which use the Mutation Engine become commonplace.

McAfee Scan Version 99

In The Wild   100%
Standard   98.90%
Enlarged   95.91%
Mutation Engine   100%

McAfee Associates' *Scan* has consistently scored well in *VB* comparative reviews. This time is no different, although the results in the Standard test-set are a little disappointing.

Search & Destroy Version 25.08

In The Wild   97.66%
Standard   97.80%
Enlarged   93.87%
Mutation Engine   94.14%

Search and Destroy is a new product which Fifth Generation launched just before the end of last year. Like *Untouchable*, *Search and Destroy* has been licensed from BRM. It failed to detect Father and Penza from the 'In The Wild' test-set and while it reported the Dir II infected file as corrupted by a virus, the virus name itself was displayed as garbage characters.

TBScan Version 5.02

In The Wild   98.44%
Standard   98.35%
Enlarged   91.32%
Mutation Engine   100%

ESaSS, the Dutch company which writes *TBScan*, has clearly spent a great deal of time improving its product's user interface. It now sports a smart menu-driven front-end program which makes it much easier to use. It missed two viruses from the 'In The Wild' set - SBC and Spanz - but otherwise does reasonably well and is one of the faster products tested.

Viruscure-Plus Version 2.41

In The Wild   80.47%
Standard   81.32%
Enlarged   64.50%
Mutation Engine   0%

IMSI's *Viruscure-Plus* includes a customised version of McAfee Associates' *Pro-Scan* and this has the unenviable position of being the worst performer of all those tested. It missed too high a proportion of those viruses known to be at large - these include Father, Spanz, Vienna 2B, Warrier, Old Yankee 2, Penza, Spanish Telecom 1 and Spanish Telecom 2. It only found 81% of the infections in the 'Standard' test set, 64% of those in the 'Enlarged' test set and none of the Mutation Engine-encrypted samples. The version tested was unable to read any of the boot sector-infected disks - the only product to fail this test. These problems aside, *AVScan* detected the signature for the Slow virus in this scanner's executable file.

VI-Spy Version 10

In The Wild   100%
Standard   99.73%
Enlarged   97.45%
Mutation Engine   7.49%

Two things mar the performance of this product from RG Software. First, it was only able to detect only 115 of the 1,536 Mutation Engine-encrypted files and, secondly, *AVScan* detected the signature for Aircop within one of its executable files. In spite of this, *VI-Spy* continues to be a strong American contender.

Package	Hard Drive Scan 'Secure' Mode	Hard Drive Scan 'Secure' Mode	Floppy Drive Scan 'Turbo' Mode	Floppy Drive Scan 'Secure' Mode
Allsafe	0:54	2:16	0:08	0:13
AVSearch	0:29	1:10	0:03	0:07
Central Point Anti-Virus	1:30	2:35	0:06	0:11
Central Point Anti-Virus -SOS	Not Applicable	2:35	Not Applicable	0:11
F-Prot	0:16	1:12	0:03	0:06
HT-Scan	0:52	1:59	0:08	0:41
Integrity Master	0:50	1:45	0:03	0:08
IBM AntiVirus	1:38 0:30	3:11 1:20	0:14	0:51
McAfee Scan	1:18	2:56	0:05	0:12
Norton AntiVirus	0:56	2:04	0:07	0:10
PC-Eye	0:20	0:59	0:04	0:44
Search & Destroy	0:36	1:29	0:08	0:11
Sweep	0:21	1:52	0:03	0:05
TBScan	0:18	1:06	0:03	0:50
Toolkit (S&S)	0:25	0:55	0:03	0:04
VI-Spy	0:39	4:00	0:03	0:38
Virex-PC	1:10	3:31	0:03	0:49
Viruscure-Plus	0:53	Not Applicable	0:09	Not Applicable
VIS	1:26	4:44	0:18	0:31

Speed tests: While detection is more important than speed it is interesting to note the wide variations in scanning speed. A high scanning speed does not necessarily mean poor detection - the most accurate scanned in the test, F-Prot, was one of the fastest. The two times shown for the IBM product are respectively for building its integrity database and scanning, and integrity checking only.

VIS Anti-Virus Utilities Version 4.1

In The Wild	99.22%
Standard	100%
Enlarged	99.87%
Mutation Engine	8.92%

A disappointing result in the 'In The Wild' test-set and Mutation Engine test-set for this usually faultless scanner. Total Control has since informed *VB* that these problems are due to bugs in the software, which has just undergone a major upgrade, and that the version sent was part of an extended Beta test. The fact that the new version has been written in a high-level language and now features a *Windows*-like, DOS character-mode interface (a true *Windows* version is also supplied) has greatly impacted on its scanning speed: it is now the second slowest of all the scanners tested. *PC-Eye* reported that one of the *VIS* executable files was infected with the Not1491 virus.

Observations

Every product in this review should score 100% when tested against the 'In The Wild' test-set. It is also reasonable to expect a good score against the standard test-set, as all these viruses have been known for at least a year.

Mutation Engine detection is equally important, and is very much a case of all or nothing. If one sample is missed on an infected machine, the virus will simply continue its spread unabated. It is therefore unacceptable that some vendors, after many months of access to code, are still not achieving reliable MtE detection.

For many users, a scanner is the only line of defence against virus attack. If *your* scanner has performed badly, it is time to consider seriously just how well your PCs are protected.

The Test Sets

1. In The Wild

Where appropriate one genuine COM and one EXE file infection of: 1575, 2100, 4K, 777, AntiCAD, Captain Trips, Cascade 1701, Cascade 1704, Dark Avenger, Dark Avenger, Dir II, Eddie 2, Father, Flip (20 COM and 20 EXE), Hallochen, Jerusalem, Keypress, Maltese Amoeba, Mystic, Nomenklatura, Nothing, PcVrsDs, Penza, SBC, Slow, Spanish Telecom 1 (5 COM), Spanish Telecom 2 (4 COM), Spanz, Syslock, Tequila (5 EXE), Vacsina, Vienna 2A, Vienna 2B, Virdem, W13-A, W13-B, Warrier, Warrior, Whale (11 COM), Old Yankee 1 and Old Yankee 2.

The following genuine boot sector infections: Aircop, Brain, Disk Killer, Form, Italian Generic A, Joshi, Korea A, Michelangelo, New Zealand 2, NoInt, Spanish Telecom, Tequila.

2. Mutation Engine

This test-set consists of 1,536 genuine infections of the Groove virus which uses Mutation Engine encryption.

3. For details of the other test-sets used please refer to:

[1] Standard Test-set: *Virus Bulletin*, May 1992, p.23.

[2] Enlarged Test-set: This unofficial test-set comprises 783 unique infections.

Technical Details:

All speed tests were conducted on an *Apricot Qi-486/25*. The Hard drive speed tests were the time taken to scan a 30Mb partition containing 1,645 files (29,758,648 bytes) of which 421 (16,153,402) were executable. The floppy disk used was a 720 Kbytes disk containing 7 files (675,454) of which 3 files (25,805) were executable.

NLM Survey

Richard Ford
Virus Bulletin

Barrie Layfield
Information System Networks plc
VB December 1992

Virus Protection Under *NetWare*

This survey examines those scanners designed for use on *Novell* networks. All these products are NLMs, and offer centralised virus detection and reporting for systems running *Novell NetWare 3.1x.* NLM virus protection has many advantages over DOS-based scanning, and unless otherwise stated, all packages provide scheduled background scanning and real-time file scanning. For details of the hardware configuration used and the virus test set please see the *Technical Details* section at the end of the article.

Intel's *LANProtect*

LANProtect arrived on both 3.5 inch and 5.25 inch disks, of which only the 5.25 inch disk was permanently write-protected. The documentation supplied is a slim booklet, which gives an overview of the different programs which make up *LANProtect*.

The Supervisor is required to login from a workstation and execute the installation program from one of the disks supplied. The only criticism of this procedure is that at no time is the Supervisor warned to reboot the workstation from a clean system disk. While any network manager worth his salt is only too aware of the need to do this, a warning should be present in the manual.

Once installed, *LANProtect* is controlled from the system console. The screen offers a simple menu-driven interface which allows the software to be configured. The product is easy to use and the function of each menu is clear.

When a manual scan is in progress, the server displays the name of the current file being scanned, and any viruses found within it. When running a prescheduled scan this information is not displayed - instead, a report is generated. This report can be either viewed from within *LANProtect*, sent to a file, or sent to the printer queue.

LANProtect missed six of the viruses in the test set. This is a poor result which needs to be improved.

Workstations can also be scanned using *LANProtect*. This is done by executing the DOS program LPSCAN, which uses the same virus signatures as the NLM scanner. In addition to scanning for viruses, LPSCAN also has some disinfection capabilities. In tests, it successfully disinfected a number of programs. LPSCAN can be password protected so that it is only run by those authorised to use it. It should be noted, however, that because this program is a DOS executable, it is susceptible to stealth viruses which are already resident on workstations.

The last package in the suite is PCSCAN, a memory resident program which checks executed files for viral infection. It identified all but six of the viruses in the test set before execution and successfully prevented these infected programs from being run.

LANProtect is a carefully thought-out product, and is well written. The disk scanning part of the package is fast, and the pre-scheduled disk scan is sufficiently flexible to suit most users. In addition to this, the incoming and outgoing file scanning is a useful line of defence.

The largest drawback with *LANProtect* is its relatively poor detection rate. However, Novell has demonstrated great faith in the product by placing a worldwide internal licence for it - a recommendation in itself.

McAfee's *NetShield*

McAfee's *NetShield* is a shareware product. The review copy arrived on a 5.25 inch disk directly from McAfee Associates, but the software is also available via Bulletin Board Systems.

There were no installation instructions on the disk, so there was no choice but to leap in at the deep end and copy the NLM onto the file server. However, *NetShield* would not run until another file containing the virus signatures had been copied across.

The lack of documentation *could* be a major drawback with *NetShield*, especially during the installation procedure. However, once installed, the user interface is sufficiently good that this is not the case - running the software is easy due to the simplicity of the control system.

The configuration options provided are reasonably flexible, and are very similar to those offered by the other products. Periodic scanning is allowed, and this can be done either once a day, once a week or once a month. All these functions are controlled from the system console.

Scanning can be undertaken 'on the fly' on incoming and outgoing files. When a virus is detected, a message can be displayed on the workstation of the offending user, in addition to informing designated users. The infected file is then overwritten, deleted, moved to a specified directory or ignored, depending on the software configuration.

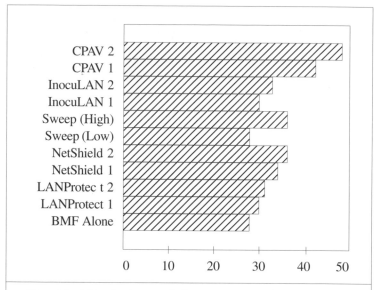

Network load. The time for a standard test program to run is measured during scanning of files. Where appropriate, the labels 1 and 2 refer to scanning with or without scanning of incoming files. For individual product details see text.

McAfee Associates' other anti-virus products have a good reputation for detecting viruses, and it is surprising that *NetShield* did not identify all the viruses in this test-set - it missed six, including a copy of the Syslock virus. This is a puzzling result, as all of these viruses were detected by the current version of McAfee's *Scan* product. McAfee Associates claims that it is aware of this problem and that it will be corrected in later releases.

Reports can be generated by *NetShield*, and are written to a log file. If the log file is viewed from within *NetShield* the contents of the file appear in a box which fills the lower portion of the server's screen. The log file contains all the relevant information which a network manager needs to know, giving details of which virus was found, when, and what action was taken. If the infected file was found when being accessed by a particular user, the user's name is also recorded. The options when viewing the log file are somewhat limited; a find function would have been useful, as would the ability to view the data from a specific date.

It is difficult to predict how network managers will receive a *shareware* product designed to protect the integrity of their LAN. Money is not such an overriding concern when protecting a network - the entire cost of the scanner will frequently be less than a day's downtime, and buyers may (incorrectly) assume that the more you pay, the better a package you get. However, the McAfee approach to network protection is direct, and has a clear and easy-to-use front end.

All in all, therefore, *NetShield* provides a no-nonsense approach to the job of virus detection under *NetWare*.

Sophos' *Sweep*

Of all the NLMs on offer at the moment *Sweep* from Sophos is the simplest. The installation procedure consists of copying one file from the installation disk into the system directory of the file server. *Sweep* is then executed by a simple LOAD command.

Sweep has been designed for operation from the system console, and is controlled by a series of easy-to-use menus which allow the various options to be set up.

All the other NLMs can optionally check all incoming and outgoing files for viruses. *Sweep* is not capable of doing this, but instead offers continuous background scanning of files in the server. This seems rather like closing the stable door after the horse has bolted, as it will only warn of virus infection *after* that infection has taken place. However, background scanning should detect virus infection quite quickly, so some users may feel that this is sufficient.

Sweep does have one advantage in that it is extremely easy to set up and use - while Sophos may not repeat Amstrad's offer of 'learn to use it in five minutes or your money back' it really was simple to operate. Scans can be optionally carried out in the background at scheduled times, or run immediately. In detection tests, *Sweep* scored very well, detecting all of the viruses in the test-set.

The *Sweep for NetWare* package comes complete with a site licence for the DOS version of *Sweep*, thus allowing all workstations to be swept. While the DOS version of *Sweep* can be run from the file server, Sophos still sensibly recommends a clean boot for complete protection of workstations.

Sophos says that it has omitted on-line file scanning from the current NLM because it can only be done by 'hacking' *NetWare,* and that this feature will be available for *NetWare* v4, which supports the necessary functions properly.

Sweep is entirely capable of protecting a network, and is easy to operate. The principal drawback ('hack' notwithstanding) is its lack of a 'real-time' file scanner.

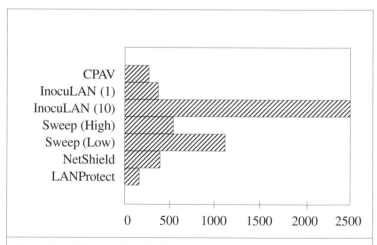

Comparison of the scan times. LANProtect was extremely fast, leaving all the other products behind. The scan times recorded are the time taken to scan all executable files on the file server. For individual product details see text.

Cheyenne's *InocuLAN*

InocuLAN by Cheyenne Software contained not only a manual for the Supervisor, but no fewer than *five* manuals explaining how the features offered to other network users function - an excellent idea. The Supervisor's manual is factual, though not very readable. However, it compensates for this with an easy-to-follow checklist for the installation process - another good idea.

Installation is easy: the user simply has to sit back and wait while the appropriate files are copied onto the workstation and the file server. *InocuLAN* is not fully configurable from the system console and so has a DOS-based control program which is executed from a workstation. This is somewhat unnecessary - all the options could just as easily be set from the console.

In addition to this, it detracts from the security of the system, as it requires the Supervisor to log on to control the software. DOS is inherently less secure than *NetWare*, and these NLMs should limit their reliance on DOS to a minimum. If a program *needs* to be reconfigured from a workstation, this can be done using the RCONSOLE utility.

The usual option of interception of incoming and outgoing files is offered, along with a scheduled file scan option. The scanner itself, however, did let the product down by missing six viruses from the test-set.

InocuLAN also comes with a number of TSR programs which are designed to help stop viruses from spreading on the workstations, as well as a generic detector. The generic detector, PREVENT, claims to detect virus-like behaviour 'such as unauthorised formatting of the hard disk'. Such claims are often treated with some scepticism, but PREVENT does appear to work: when run against some of the new viruses reported in *VB*, November 1992, it successfully detected all of the viruses when they were executed - an impressive result. It is not clear, however, how PREVENT works as in tests certain straightforward modifications to files went undetected - a puzzling result.

The remaining two TSRs check files for viruses at load time, and the user has the choice of either checking for those viruses deemed to be 'in the wild' or for all the viruses *InocuLAN* is capable of detecting. These programs seem to work as described in the manual, checking all files which are deemed to be executable when they are opened. Unfortunately, once loaded it was not clear how to unload these TSRs without rebooting the computer.

InocuLAN offers good protection for a *Novell* Network, and has a couple of nice touches to boot (such as five copies of the manual for the workstation software). The virus-specific detection ability of the software does need to be improved, but the generic detection offered appears to work well.

Central Point Anti-Virus for NetWare

Central Point's product arrived in two boxes, bearing the standard *Novell* badge with the words '*Novell* Network Aware' proudly printed in white on red. The package comes in two parts, a DOS part for the workstations and an NLM part (which requires *NetWare* v3.11) which provides the background scanning and file interception features which the products offer. Central Point's product is capable of detecting both MS-DOS viruses and Macintosh viruses.

All of the new *Central Point Anti-Virus* products have the ability to communicate with each other. By using this facility, the company offers a completely centralised anti-virus strategy which will automatically report all virus infections to one central point - no pun intended!

The Central Point product is designed to be controlled from a workstation. The configuration and control program which comes with the software is undeniably glossy and is easily used with or without a mouse. However, by making the software fully usable only from a workstation, one of the most important advantages of anti-virus NLMs is removed, since the Supervisor is required to log on to the system. If Central Point wants to offer system managers the option of a glossy interface it should be in addition to, and not instead of, a simple display on the system console.

When a virus is detected, the software updates the log file, and can inform designated users of the discovery. This can be done either by a Network Broadcast message, an MHS mail message or by paging the system manager using a modem connected to the server.

The virus detection ability of the software was good, missing only the Father virus from this test-set.

The package also offers generic virus detection, by monitoring the way programs access executable files. As this method is highly prone to false positives, the user is not informed of suspected virus behaviour. However, every time a possible virus is found, a note is made in the log file. The generic checker successfully identified the actions of several viruses, but also identified DEBUG as showing virus-like behaviour.

There were a couple of irritating bugs in the product. When operating in a DOS shell under *Windows 3.1,* every time a virus is discovered, the machine returns to the Central Point control program. This repeated return to *Windows* eventually managed to confuse the application running in the DOS shell to the extent that it crashed. Also, Network Broadcast Messages occur randomly - when a large number of viruses are discovered the user is not informed of all infections found. These bugs aside, the Central Point product does provide a good level of cover for the file server, and offers a complete package for virus protection.

Network Load

Possibly the most important aspect of the software is the question of network load. Virus protection is clearly unworkable if it loads the system so much that it is unusable. In order to determine some measure of the network overhead that the packages impose, a test program was run while scanning was in progress. The test program imposes overhead on the server by requesting a combination of random and sequential reads and writes. Clearly, the greater the overhead imposed by the anti-virus software itself, the longer this test program will take to execute.

A graph of the network overhead is shown. The network overheads are (products running in fastest modes without in/outgoing file scanning): *LANProtect* 3.4%, *InocuLAN* 3.4%, *NetShield* 17%, *Sweep* 24%, *CPAV* 48%.

Speed

Overall scanning speed is arguably not as important for an NLM as for a DOS based scanner, as the user is unlikely to sit waiting for the NLM scan to finish - one of the principal advantages of server-based protection is the automation of this onerous task. All products were tested over the same set of files, and asked to scan executable files only (86.2 Mbytes). The scan times are shown in Graph 2 (page 17). Products which appear twice in the graph have been run using different internal speed settings.

When comparing like with like (scanners running in 'Advanced' modes at full speed) the scan times in minutes and seconds were as follows: *LANProtect* 2:13, *CPAV* 3:38, *InocuLAN* 5:18, *NetShield* 5:29, and *Sweep* 9:58.

One point to note is that a scanner can be made faster by increasing its overheads on the file server. *NetWare* gives full control to any NLM running on the server, and the NLM is, in turn, expected to return control to the operating system to allow other products to run. Therefore, there is a trade-off between network overhead and scanning speed.

Conclusions

Choosing anti-virus software has never been easy, and with NLMs many different factors must be taken into account. The stability of the file server is of utmost importance and because NLMs operate at a low level within the system it is vital that they are well written. From this point of view Intel's *LANProtect* package seems to offer the best features as it is the only product tested which has been through the *Novell Laboratory's* testing procedure. It should be stressed, however, that this testing only ensures that the software is 'well behaved' and does not cause the system to become unstable.

The virus detection ability of the software is equally important. *Sweep* detected all the viruses in the test-set, with *Central Point Anti-Virus* coming a close second, missing only one infection. The biggest surprise of the review was the relatively poor detection performance of *NetShield*. McAfee Associates' *Scan* is capable of detecting all the viruses in the test-set, which implies that these false negatives are almost certainly due to teething problems with the new product.

Because of the large number of factors to be taken into account, it is difficult to choose a clear leader out of this range of products - the reader is left to decide for himself which product best suits his needs.

Supplier Details

Product: *LANProtect*

Version Evaluated: 1.5

Cost: Annual price per server £599

Manufacturer: Intel Corporation (UK), Pipers Way, Swindon, Wilts. SN3 1RJ, UK. Tel 0793 696000. Fax 0793 430763.

Product: *NetShield*

Version Evaluated: 1.02

Cost: Annual price per server £424

Manufacturer: McAfee Associates Inc., 3350 Scott Boulevard, Building 14, Santa Clara, CA 95054-3107, USA.

Tel (1) 408 988 3832. Fax (1) 408 970 9727.

Product: *Sweep*

Version Evaluated: 2.43

Cost: Annual price per server. 1-25 Users £495. 25+ Users £895.

Manufacturer: Sophos Ltd, 21 The Quadrant, Abingdon Science Park, Abingdon, OX14 3YS. Tel 0235 559933. Fax 0235 559935.

Product: *InocuLAN*

Version Evaluated: 1.1

Cost: $495 for up to 20 users. $995 for up to 250 users.

Manufacturer: Cheyenne Software Inc., 55 Bryant Avenue, Roslyn, NY 11576. USA. Tel (1) 516 484 5110. Fax (1) 516 484 5220.

Product: *Central Point Anti-Virus for NetWare*

Version Evaluated: 1.0

Cost: £699 per server, unlimited users.

Manufacturer: Central Point Software International Ltd, 3 Furzeground Way, Stockley Park, Uxbridge, Middlesex. UB11 1DA. Tel 081 848 1414. Fax 081 569 1017.

Technical Details

Hardware Used: 33 Mhz '386 PC with 300 Mbyte SCSI disk and *Adaptec* SCSI controller, and 8 Mbytes RAM, running *Novell NetWare* v3.11.

Viruses used for testing purposes:

777, 1575, 2100 (2), 4K (2), Anti-Cad (2), Cascade (2), Captain Trips (2), Tequila, Eddie, Eddie 2 (2), Dark Avenger (2), Darth Vader (3), Dir II, Father (2), Flip (2), Hallochen, Invader (2), Jerusalem (2), Keypress (2), Liberty (2), Macho (2), Maltese Amoeba, Mystic, Nomenklatura (2), Nothing, PcVrsDs (2), Penza, Slow (2), SBC (2), Spanish Telecom (2), Spanz, Syslock, V2P6, Vacsina, Vienna (4), Virdem, Warrier, Warrior, Whale, Yankee (2).

OS/2 Virus Protection

Mark Hamilton, VB August 1993

The new 32-bit operating systems from IBM and Microsoft will, both companies claim, revolutionise personal computing as we know it. Microsoft's *Windows NT* - the letters 'NT' standing for 'New Technology', 'Not There', 'No Takers' or 'No Thanks', depending on your point of view - has yet to be released. Even when it eventually is, Microsoft admits that it will support only a small subset of the millions of programs and applications that have been written for the PC over the last ten or so years.

OS/2, on the other hand, really became usable last year, when IBM launched version 2.0, and version 2.1 is now on general release. It supports over 90 percent of all applications out in userland and is starting to prove itself as an industrial strength operating system.

Although *OS/2* has not really caught on among the private users, several of the larger corporates have adopted it as their operating system of choice, and it is this carrot which has lured some of the big names in the anti-virus community onto the platform. To date, four different companies have announced the release of *OS/2* specific versions of their anti-virus software: IBM, Sophos, S&S International and McAfee Associates.

Featured Features

At the time of writing, there are no known *OS/2*-specific computer viruses. However, research shows that DOS file-infecting viruses are capable of infected files in DOS or *Windows* (*Win-OS/2*) sessions, although those which have low-level trigger effects will have their destructive attempts thwarted. In addition, boot sector viruses are to a certain extent platform-independent, and those users who use their *OS/2* machine as a file server (for example, sites using *LAN Manager*) also require a method of ensuring that the contents of the server are virus-free.

For the anti-virus company, *OS/2* provides certain benefits: the need to employ special anti-stealth tactics disappears, their product is operating in a protected environment and they have access to linear memory, rather than the segmented memory DOS imposes. For the users, the benefits are no less tangible: one should be able to run these products so that they check files in the background meaning that users can get on with real work and not have to 'play' at detecting viruses. *OS/2* provides the opportunity of relegating anti-virus software back to the utility category where pretty interfaces requiring human interaction are unnecessary: how many companies, I wonder, will rise to that challenge?

The following review examines the *OS/2* products from the four companies mentioned above, and forms *Virus Bulletin's* first ever comparative *OS/2* review.

IBM AntiVirus/2 - Version 1.02

IBM releases its product on a quarterly basis and this is the third such release. In designing this product, IBM went for the 'install and forget' philosophy - the user is not required to do anything, unless the product detects a virus.

My major criticism of this product is that, in the United Kingdom at least, it is not currently available as a shrink-wrapped product. With all other IBM hardware and software products, you simply send in a card to register for the IBM Helpline which is available 24 hours a day, 365 days a year - and an excellent service it is too. But not with *IBM Anti-Virus*: you have to subscribe to a special service and download the software from an IBM Bulletin Board. This is likely to restrict IBM's market share for *AntiVirus/2* which, like its DOS counterpart, could so easily be integrally bundled with the operating system.

The installation process is simple and efficient and it gives the user the option of invoking a DOS-based anti-virus TSR every time a DOS or *Win-OS/2* session is invoked. The software can also be configured to scan the files at periodic intervals: every boot, every day, once a week, once a month or only when specifically executed.

IBM AntiVirus/2 works in a different manner to the other products tested in that it includes both an integrity checker as well as a virus scanner. When it checks files, it looks to see if they have changed in

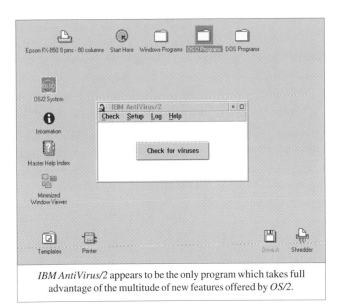

IBM AntiVirus/2 appears to be the only program which takes full advantage of the multitude of new features offered by *OS/2*.

any way and only scans those files which have been modified or are not included in the database for viruses. This makes it quite fast in operation since it does not need to wade through its virus signature database for every file - just those it finds suspicious. When it finds an infected file, it is capable of disinfecting it, as long as the file is infected with a virus which IBM deems common. Given that most virus infections are caused by a tiny minority of viruses, this restricted disinfection list is unlikely to cause any problems.

The on-line help system lists all the viruses detected by the current release as well as providing a brief description of the most common ones. Whilst this is not as comprehensive as Patricia Hoffman's VSUM database, it is nevertheless accurate and concise.

I do not have many criticisms with the IBM product. It is both fast and accurate, and I like the idea of combining an integrity checker with a scanner. One annoying quirk is that it insists on searching the whole disk before it begins virus checking to discover how many files it needs to check. Why?

The only other criticism I have of the product is its update frequency - all the others are updated every four to six weeks; *IBM Anti-virus /2* is updated on a quarterly basis. In a fast moving field, is that enough?

Dr Solomon's *Anti-Virus Toolkit for OS/2* - Version 6.53

The *OS/2* specific version of S&S's popular utility actually consists of the DOS version, an extra diskette and a very slim appendix for the DOS manual which contains details of the *OS/2* specific parts of the product.

Unfortunately, the documentation has not kept up with the software and the small card entitled 'Installing the *OS/2* Anti-Virus Toolkit' contains a completely fallacious set of installation instructions. There is even a typographical error on the card - it says 'OS\2'.

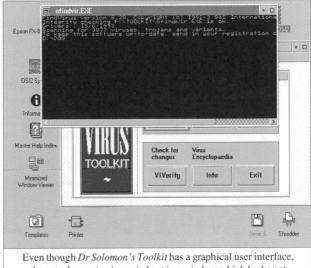

Even though *Dr Solomon's Toolkit* has a graphical user interface,
the actual scanning is carried out in a window which looks not
unlike the DOS version of FINDVIR

What the instructions should say - and what you in fact do - is run
the setup program provided on the disk to decompress and install the
OS/2 Toolkit (rather than copy the files from the floppy as the
instructions would have you believe).

The *OS/2 Toolkit* comprises just four programs: VISION, the *OS/2*
front-end menu program and equivalent to the DOS TOOLKIT
program; OVIVERIF, an integrity checker; OFINDVIR, the scanner;
and VDISPLAY, the on-line version of the virus encyclopedia. You
can, if you wish, also install the DOS version although the only
possible item you might want from it would be GUARD, the
monitor, to protect your DOS and *Win-OS/2* sessions.

The setup program creates a new folder on the Workplace Shell
Desktop - though I wish it had asked me first - which curiously
contains just the front-end program, VISION. This program - in
common with the DOS and *Windows* versions - has three big buttons

to scan drives A, B and C. If a machine has more drives than that, it is not possible to use VISION, and the user has to run OFINDVIR manually.

The programs themselves are rather disappointing as (with the exception of VISION) they do not take advantage of the *OS/2* graphical environment, running only in text mode.

The OS/2 Toolkit has none of the scheduling niceties found in the IBM product and surprisingly did not fare particularly well in the detection tests. It missed both Tremor and V2P6 in the 'In the Wild' test-set and was slower than the IBM product in two out of the three speed trials. When checking all files, it had problems with the Extended Attributes file and 'SWAPPER.DAT' (the swap file) - it really ought to know about the significance of these files, and be able to deal with their presence gracefully.

Product	Version evaluated	In The Wild Test-set (99)	Standard Test-set (364)	Mutation Engine Test-set (1536)
IBM Anti-Virus/2	1.02	100%	100%	99.9%
Sophos Sweep for OS/2	2.51	100%	100%	100%
Dr Solomon's Anti-virus Toolkit for OS/2	6.53	98%	98%	100%
McAfee Associates OS/2 Scan	106	97%	99%	100%

Didn't they do well! All the products scored well in the detection tests, although with products from these, manufacturers one would expect 100% scores in all tests. A question of poor quality control?

VDISPLAY, the on-line virus database (or encyclopedia as S&S calls it) is, like the other elements in this package, an *OS/2* text mode application. One factor I found particularly annoying is that it does not recognise the mouse. Users would normally access this through the *Toolkit* front end, which is mouse driven. However, the encyclopedia is displayed as an *OS/2* windowed application in text mode, so the user is relegated back to keyboard control. S&S might find that reconstructing the encyclopedia as an *OS/2* help file might alleviate this problem and make the whole package appear to be more of a real *OS/2* application.

I am somewhat disappointed with this offering from S&S - particularly when considering the high standard of many of its other products. The detection results are surprising, and the unimaginative use of the *OS/2* interface makes the overall result rather uninspiring.

Sweep for OS/2 - **Version 2.51**

The Sophos product is a command line program and appears to be a recompilation of its DOS product. Unlike its DOS counterpart, it has as yet no front-end menu to make life easier and the various different options within *Sweep* are controlled by a plethora of command line parameters.

The diskette contains just the *Sweep* executable and its signature file - there is no installation routine provided.

Like the S&S product, *Sweep* had problems opening the Extended Attributes file and it shared the *Toolkit's* problem concerning the *OS/2* swap file. It also reported a spurious 'DOS error code'.

The documentation is a little misleading in places, and looks like a rewrite of the DOS *Sweep* manual. For example, it states 'SWEEP may be incorporated into the AUTOEXEC.BAT file...'. Following these instructions produces an error message whenever a DOS or *Win-OS/2* session begins. This is because the AUTOEXEC file is run under the DOS emulator, which does not understand *OS/2* executables. The manual should read 'SWEEP may be incorporated into the STARTUP.CMD file...'.

Sweep's operation is controlled by both command line parameters and a configuration file that stipulates which areas should be included in the scan. This latter file, SWEEP.ARE, was designed by systems programmers for the *cognoscenti* and not dumb users. It can be somewhat intimidating to set up, until you realise that '80' refers to the first hard drive and '81' to the second (physical) hard drive.

Like its DOS counterpart, the *OS/2 Sweep* does not disinfect infected files but it can optionally delete them. When *Sweep* discovers a virus, it turns the screen background colour to a vivid red and flashes 'Sweep Alarm!' on the screen.

Sweep proved to be the slowest of the four products tested as it took over three minutes to scan 649 executable files. Nevertheless, *Sweep* discovered all the viruses... speed isn't everything, but would be nice!

McAfee Associates' *OS/2 Scan* - Version 9.17 V106

McAfee Associates' *OS/2 Scan* is just like the company's other shareware scanners in that it presents a 'no frills' approach to the task. Like Sophos' and S&S's products, McAfee's *OS/2Scan* looks like a simple recompilation of the DOS version's source code. Indeed, in McAfee's case, the developers have even left the SCAN name in an error message ('Type SCAN /help').

OS/2 Scan comes with no fancy installation routine - but really does not require one. Installation is simply a matter of copying the single executable OS2SCAN onto the hard drive. The product also comes with a documentation file, OSCNnnn.DOC, which explains how OS2SCAN is designed to be used.

OS/2SCAN has no pretty GUI and is controlled by command line parameters. The switches used are a subset of those understood by

SCAN, so regular McAfee users will have no problems converting existing batch files and modes of operation to the *OS/2* platform

Although quite fast, McAfee's *OS/2SCAN* is not one of the most accurate scanners: it missed infections of Loren, Powerpump and Whale in the 'In The Wild' test-set - indeed it missed more viruses than the other three products making it the least reliable of those reviewed.

Like its DOS counterparts, McAfee's *OS/2* scanner is shareware which might make it an unacceptable choice for more traditionally minded business who prefer to purchase their software through conventional sources.

Speed Tests

Due to the multitasking nature of *OS/2*, the speed tests are rather less important than they would be for a DOS machine. However, for reference, they are given below:

Product	Diskette	HD (Turbo)	HD (All)
IBM Anti-Virus/2	0:45	0:53	2:15
Sophos Sweep for OS/2	1:56	3:41	8:41
Dr Solomon's Anti-virus Toolkit for OS/2	0:52	0:56	1:59
McAfee Associates OS/2 Scan	0:35	1:13	4:20

Conclusion

It is early days for *OS/2* scanners and the anti-virus companies are only just starting to dip their development toes in the water. If I were actively looking to purchase an *OS/2* hosted anti-virus product, I would be disappointed by the lack of choice and, except in one case, the lack of attention paid by the anti-virus developers to *OS/2's* potential. Only one product, *IBM AntiVirus/2,* offers scheduling and, from a dumb user's point of view, seems better integrated into the environment and makes full use of its facilities.

Needless to say, IBM's product is the only one I didn't erase from my hard drive following the testing phase of this review - the other products don't really hit the mark. It is interesting to note that some of the other products seem to perform less well than their DOS counterparts. With reviews of *OS/2* products being a relatively new feature within *Virus Bulletin* it will be interesting to see if those caught on the hop improve their scores next time.

Vendor Details

Product: *OS/2 Scan*

Vendor: McAfee Associates, 2710 Walsh Ave., Suite 200, Santa Clara, CA 95051-0963, USA.

Price: $375, including *OS/2 Clean* and *Vshield*.

Product: *IBM AntiVirus/2*

Vendor: IBM AntiVirus Services, 1 East Kirkwood Boulevard, Roanoke, TX 76299-0015, USA

Price: $29.95, but prices vary according to country.

Product: *Sophos Sweep for OS/2*

Vendor: Sophos Ltd, 21 The Quadrant, Abingdon Science Park, Abingdon, Oxon. OX14 3YS

Price: £295 for Single User, £495 for the File Server, with monthly upgrades.

Product: *Dr Solomon's Anti-virus Toolkit for OS/2*

Vendor: S&S International Ltd, Berkley Court, Mill Street, Berkhamsted, Herts HP4 2HB, UK.

Price: £149 +VAT with quarterly upgrades.

Technical Details

Test Platform:

I used a *SIR 486DX50* with 8MB memory, 170MB IDE hard drive and a *Panasonic* Phase-Change Optical drive provided a further half Gigabyte of disk storage. The machine was running under *OS/2* version 2.1 DAP (Developer Assistance Programme) release.

The IDE drive was used for the speed tests and there were 2,732 files, split across 126 directories, occupying 123,081,356 bytes of which there were 649 executable files occupying 46,236,452 bytes. For the diskette test, I used the OS/2 Disk 1 which contains 52 files occupying 1,435,106 bytes.

Test-Sets Used:

Only the Common, or 'In The Wild', test-set has been updated, and now contains the following 99 viruses:

File Infectors: 1575, 2100 (C+E), 4k (C+E), 777, AntiCAD (C+E), Captain Trips (C+E), Cascade 1701, Cascade 1704, Dark Avenger (C+E), Datalock (C+E), Dir-II, Dos Hunter, Eddie, Eddie 2 (C+E), Father (C+E), Flip (C+E), Hallochen, Helloween (C+E), Invader (C+E), Jerusalem 1 (C+E), Keypress (C+E), Liberty (C+E), Liberty- E, Loren (C+E), Maltese Amoeba, Mystic, Necropolis, Necros (C+E), Nomenklatura (C+E), Nothing, PcVrsDs (C+E), Penza, Pitch, Powerpump, SBC, Slow (C+E), Spanish Telecom 1, Spanish Telecom 2, Spanz, Syslock, Tequila, Todor, Tremor, V2P6, Vacsina, Vienna 2a, Vienna 2b, Virdem, Virus, W13a, W13b, Warrier, Warrior, Whale, Winvir14, Yankee 1 and Yankee 2.

Boot Sector Infectors: Aircop, Beijing, Brain, Disk Killer, Form, Italian Generic A, Joshi, Korea A, Michelangelo, New Zealand 2, NoInt, Spanish Telecom and Tequila.

For details of the other *Virus Bulletin* Test-sets, please consult *Virus Bulletin,* May 1992, page 23.

```
1D9F:04F2 B409        MOV     AH,09
1D9F:04F4 CD21        INT     21
1D9F:04F6 B81C35      MOV     AX,351C
1D9F:04F9 CD21        INT     21
1D9F:04FB 891EAA03    MOV     [03AA],BX
1D9F:04FF 8C06AC03    MOV     [03AC],ES
1D9F:0503 B81C25      MOV     AX,251C
1D9F:0506 BA4503      MOV     DX,0345
1D9F:0509 CD21        INT     21
1D9F:050B B80935      MOV     AX,3509
1D9F:050E CD21        INT     21
-u
1D9F:0510 891E0A04    MOV     [040A],BX
1D9F:0514 8C060C04    MOV     [040C],ES
1D9F:0518 B80925      MOV     AX,2509
1D9F:051B BAAE03      MOV     DX,03AE
1D9F:051E CD21        INT     21
1D9F:0520 BA0E04      MOV     DX,040E
1D9F:0523 83C20F      ADD     DX,+0F
1D9F:0526 B104        MOV     CL,04
1D9F:0528 D3EA        SHR     DX,CL
1D9F:052A B80031      MOV     AX,3100
1D9F:052D CD21        INT     21
1D9F:052F 880D        MOV     [DI],CL
```

Virus dissections

Sweet is the lore which Nature brings
Our meddling intellect
Misshapes the beauteous forms of things:
We murder to dissect.

W. Wordsworth

4K - A New Level of Sophistication

VB May 1990

4K is a memory resident, COM and EXE infecting virus from Israel. The size of most PC viruses is 1000 - 2000 bytes, which makes 4K one of the largest for as its name implies, its length is 4096 bytes. This virus is also known by two other names, 'IDF' and 'Frodo'. 'IDF' refers to the Israeli Defence Forces, where the virus was originally found late in 1989. 'Frodo' refers to the on-screen message displayed by the virus, as described later. Two versions of the virus exist, the significant differences between them surround the effects after triggering. The 4K virus may occasionally cause damage to files. It manipulates the number of available clusters, which can result in files becoming cross-linked.

Most of the virus code is devoted to making the virus 'invisible' when it is active. Other recent viruses attempt this, for example 666 [*see VB, May 1990, p.13. Ed.*]. The difference is that 4K uses a more comprehensive method, intercepting a greater number of DOS functions than any other virus.

From a technical viewpoint, 4K is very advanced - it uses more undocumented features of the MS-DOS operating system than any other known virus, but it requires DOS 3.x because some of the undocumented features function differently under DOS 2.x and 4.x.

It is clear that the author of the virus has a very good knowledge of the internal workings of the MS-DOS operating system.

Installation

When an infected program is run, the virus will attempt to disable tracing, by manipulating INT 01h (single step), the flag register and the 8259 chip.

It then alters the Memory Control Blocks (MCBs) and creates a 'gap', 6K in size just below the end of memory. The virus code is written there, overwriting the part of COMMAND.COM stored there. COMMAND.COM will therefore be reloaded and infected when the infected program terminates. The virus will intercept INT 21h, but not in the usual way - instead it will overwrite the first 5 bytes of the current INT 21h routine with a FAR JMP to itself. Most of the virus is devoted to processing various INT 21h functions. They are:

- Disk I/O Using File Control Blocks
- Function 0Eh (Open file)

The virus first calls the original DOS function, and if the file is successfully opened the FCB is examined for the infection marker (year of creation > 2043). If an infection is found, the 'file size' field is decremented by 4096.

Function 11h (Find first matching file), Function 12h (Find next matching file)

The original DOS function is first called and if a file is found the 'year' field of the timestamp is examined. As in the 'Open' function, if the highest bit is set, the file is assumed to be infected and the 'length of file' field in the FCB is decremented by 4096.

Function 14h (Sequential read), Function 21h (Random record read), Function 27h (Random block read)

If a program is attempting to read from the beginning of an infected file, the virus returns the original contents of the first bytes, before they were overwritten by the virus.

Function 23h (File size)

The virus makes a copy of the FCB, opens the file and closes it again. The FCB will then contain various information, including the creation year and the true size of the file. If the file appears to be infected, the virus will once again subtract 4096 from the true length and return that value.

Disk I/O using handles/ASCIIZ

Function 3Ch (Create file)

If the file being created has the 'Read only', 'System' and 'Hidden' attribute bits set, control will simply be given to the original DOS function. This is probably done in order to avoid infecting IBMDOS.COM and IBMBIO.COM. [*Under certain versions of DOS, both these files have the extension SYS. Ed.*] In other cases the virus will call DOS to create the file, close it and transfer control to the 'Open file' function.

Function 3Dh (Open file)

First the extension of the file is checked, in a highly unusual manner. The ASCII codes for the three characters in the file extension are added together. If the sum is 223 or 226 the file may be subject to infection. Entering a command such as COPY X.WEF Y.BMP will result in the infection of X.WEF and Y.BMP. If the sum does not match, the virus will return to the original program.

4K maintains an internal table of open file handles and the process IDs of the 'owner' of the file. The term 'process ID' refers to the segment address of the Program Segment Prefix (PSP). If this table has any room left, the process ID and the file handle will be stored there, for future use by the 'Close' function.

Function 3Eh (Close file)

When a file is closed, the process ID of the current process is first obtained and the table mentioned above is searched for a record containing it and the file handle. If it is found, the file is assumed to be a COM or EXE file and will be infected before it is closed.

Function 3Fh (Read)

If a program attempts to read from an infected file, the virus will 'disinfect' the file as it is read, which may cause problems for checksumming programs because the file may appear unmodified.

Function 40h (Write)

When an infected file is being written to, the virus will disinfect it, only to re-infect it as it is closed.

Function 40h (Lseek)

When a program seeks to the end of an infected file, the reported value of the file pointer (position within the file) is decremented by 4096.

Function 4Bh (Load/Execute)

Instead of loading and executing a program, the virus will only load it, using an undocumented sub-function of INT 21h (4B01h). The loaded file will then be checked for disinfection and any trace of infection will be removed before it is executed. However, if the file is not infected, the infection routine will be called.

Function 4Eh (Find first), Function 4Fh (Find next)

Just like their FCB counterparts, these functions only check whether the file is infected, in which case 4096 will be subtracted from the reported file length.

Function 5700h (Get date/time of file)

If this function is used to obtain the creation year of an infected file, the virus will subtract 100 from the value.

Function 5701h (Set date/time of file)

4K will not permit any program to set the date of a file later than December 31, 2043.

Miscellaneous Functions

Function 30h (Get DOS version)

This is perhaps the most interesting part of the virus. It will first check the current date. Before September 22nd nothing happens, but after that date a mysterious routine is executed. One version of the virus will cause indefinite results, probably causing the machine to 'hang'. This version contains some garbage bytes as well as the POP CS instruction, which is illegal on '286, '386 and '486 machines. The other version of the virus attempts to overwrite the boot sector with the 'Frodo' code described later.

Function 37h (Get/set switchchar, device availability)

The reasons for hooking into this function remain unclear.

Infection

4K may infect programs when they are executed or when an executable file is closed. The second possibility implies that copying a non-infected program (on a machine where the virus is active) will result in the infection of the target file as well as the original.

The virus starts by checking whether or not the target file has the extension EXE. It reads the first two bytes and checks to see whether they are 5A4Dh or 4D5Ah (which represent the ASCII characters MZ). Virtually all files in the executable format start with 4D5Ah. But it is little known that MS-DOS will assume that a file starting with 5A4Dh is also one in the executable format.

The virus code is written to the end of a file. In the case of a COM file, the first three bytes are overwritten with a JMP into the virus code. EXE files are modified in a different way, by changing the information in the header, including the initial CS and IP values.

As might be expected, 4K removes the 'read only' attribute before infecting files and restores it afterwards.

The directory entries of infected files are modified using a method similar to that adopted by the Vienna virus. Vienna modifies the 'seconds' field of the timestamp, setting it to an impossible value (62), but 4K adds a century to the year. A file created in 1990 will appear to have been created in 2090. When the user issues the DIR command, no change in the date is visible because MS-DOS only displays the last two digits of the year. This method will not work after the year 2007, however, because the last date which MS-DOS can represent is December 31st 2107. This date modification prevents reinfection and allows the virus to identify uninfected target files.

There is thus an easy way to check whether 4K is active in memory - just set the date to January 1st 2044, create a small file and issue a DIR command. If the file is reported as having a length of 4 Gigabytes and having been created in the year 100, the virus is active. The reason that DOS reports a length of 4 Gigabytes is that the virus subtracts 4096 from the file size which it assumes is infected. This produces a negative number, which DOS treats as an unsigned binary equivalent.

'Frodo' Code

4K contains a routine which attempts to modify the boot sector to display the on-screen message

```
FRODO LIVES
```

when an infected machine is booted. This text, in large letters, is surrounded by a moving pattern. This routine does not, in fact, work. The keyboard interrupt is re-directed, probably to disable the Ctrl-Alt-Del combination, forcing the user to turn the PC off and to boot from a non-infected diskette. [*Frodo is one of the 'hobbit' characters in J. R. R. Tolkien's fairy-tale 'The Lord of the Rings'. Ed.*]

Final Notes

4K conceals itself quite efficiently but it can be detected in a number of ways. The loss of 6K of memory provides an immediate indication to the observant user that the machine is infected. Changing the date as described above will also reveal its presence.

A hexadecimal search pattern for this virus is:

```
E808 0BE8 D00A E89A 0AE8 F60A E8B4 0A53
```

Apart from these characteristics the virus will probably remain unnoticed until September 22nd 1990, although it may be detected on some computers earlier, as it seems unable to co-exist with some items of network software.

Users of checksumming software, and indeed all anti-virus programs, should take note that such software can only be effective if run from a clean system disk.

If the 4K virus is active in memory it could fool checksumming programs into 'thinking' that system attributes are unmodified.

High-level security checks using anti-virus software must be run from a write-protected 'clean' system floppy disk. Anti-virus programs invoked from AUTOEXEC.BAT can be undermined by second generation viruses. However, running secure checksumming programs from the hard-disk will still provide a high degree of protection on a day-to-day basis.

1575 - Attack of the Mutant Green Caterpillars

VB October 1991

Following the small number of common viruses which contribute to the greater part of reported 'real world' infections comes a long trail of lesser protagonists in the virus battle. Though hugely overshadowed by such names as New Zealand 2, Cascade and Jerusalem, reports of all manner of viruses are increasing and specimens which numerically represent only a few percent of total reported infections are still taking hold and causing problems.

One contender that is moving up the ranks of those jostling for a place behind the 'leaders' and currently being reported out in the field is the Green Caterpillar virus (aka 1575). This is now overhauling the likes of Italian and Plastique, and on a par with Joshi, Dark Avenger and Nomenklatura.

A COMMAND.COM Infector

Some viruses specifically avoid infecting COMMAND.COM despite the fact that this file is one of the first to be executed, which logically should increase the potential for any virus to propagate.

It has been suggested that the virus writers' general aversion to the COMMAND.COM file is because its infection is altogether too obvious to the user resulting in the early detection of the virus.

However, the widespread Cascade virus infects COMMAND.COM with no apparent risk of such premature discovery, so the perceived risk of infecting this file may be over-estimated by the virus writers.

The Caterpillar virus specifically looks for C:\COMMAND.COM on every invocation (the string is encrypted within the code) and actually targets this file for infection - this may explain why the virus has become relatively widespread in a short space of time.

Operation

Caterpillar infects both COM and EXE files. It goes memory-resident by manipulating DOS arena pointers (though it does not lower the BIOS available memory information) and traps the DOS FCB find-file functions - thus infecting files when the DIR command is used to examine disk contents. This additional disk activity ought to alert users, at least when using diskettes, but makes this virus highly infective if it is not noticed.

Only files in the inspected directory are infected, and a bug in the interrupt routine causes the virus to miss all files that have the full eight characters in their base name. [*On the machine used to compose this article such files comprise about 8 percent of the number of executables on the hard disk. Ed.*] The DOS critical error handler is trapped, so users will not see failed attempts to write to a protected diskette. Infected EXE files have a tendency not to run correctly due to corruption by the virus.

Trigger

The trigger routine of this virus occurs when a file which has been infected for over two months is run, COMMAND.COM is already infected (or does not exist in the root directory) and there is another copy of the virus already resident in memory.

In the idiosyncratic manner which we have come to expect from virus authors, the user is subsequently greeted with an animated green caterpillar crawling down the screen, munching through characters and turning the text yellow in its wake.

If uninterrupted, this display lasts some three minutes. Any input which causes the screen to scroll up results in the caterpillar jumping back and continuing from its new position. It cannot be scrolled off the top of the screen and only stops when it finishes its journey.

Technically, the programming is a curious melting pot: neat, legible code interspersed with long-winded meandering, trivial errors and some arcane structuring (or lack thereof). Instead of a simple JMP linking the virus code to the start of a COM program, 12 bytes of instructions are used to set up the code segment for the virus.

The next piece of code manipulates the program stack in highly dubious ways and jumps all over the shop but eventually achieves absolutely nothing. Its only function seems to be to foil an automatic debugger - this particular section cannot easily be traced as it uses a part of the Interrupt Table as its stack. Another possibility is that it is related to a launch or dropper program which is not carried with the virus.

Even before becoming resident in memory, the virus checks for the existence of an uninfected C:\COMMAND.COM and infects it. A data string of 'C:\COMMAND.COM' might arouse suspicion so this string is 'encrypted' (to use the term very loosely) by the addition of 32 (decimal) to each character. Infected files are marked by having the last two bytes as 0Ch 0A.

If the virus finds that another copy of itself is already installed in high memory (by searching for the 0Ch and 0Ah bytes file signature), it checks its own date of infection to ascertain whether it is more than two months old. If it is, the BIOS timer tick (interrupt 1Ch) is trapped and the already-installed copy services these interrupts to produce the animated caterpillar. Note that if

C:\COMMAND.COM has just been infected the caterpillar display
will not initiate.

On going resident, interrupt 21h (the DOS function executor) is
trapped to intercept functions 1Ah (set DTA address), 11h (FCB
find-first) and 12h (FCB find-next). From that point on, all results
from a file find are examined after letting DOS go ahead with the
operation. Returned filenames are parsed and examined for COM
and EXE extensions, except, as noted above, this parse routine fails
for 8-character base names. The surrounding code confirms that this
is not a deliberate 'sparse infection' ploy. The first suitable
executable is opened in read/write mode and updated with the virus
code, with the current month being planted in the new virus.

Naturally, the virus prefers to let DOS initially process the find
functions. As the virus has already trapped these itself, it needs to
bypass its own interception to let DOS do the job; the usual way is by
a FAR CALL to the old address, but this author chose the tack of
providing a 'pass-thru' code. Interrupt 21h is still used within the
handler - a potential recursive death - but the only two calls it needs
to make do not use the processor's AL register and it places a hex 57
in AL to avoid tying itself in knots. Its own intercept routine catches
this signature and passes the request to DOS.

Detection and Removal

The Caterpillar virus has an infective length in COM and EXE files
of between 1575 and 1591 bytes, and may be detected by the
following hexadecimal pattern:

```
0E1F A12B 018E D087 ECBE 3C01
BF00 00B9 1000 FCF2 A4E9 DEFE
```

Caterpillar is not encrypted and makes no attempt to hide itself in
memory or on disk, not even hiding the increase in file size. Infected
program files should be deleted and replaced with clean write-
protected copies of the master software.

Batman - Robbin' Users of Security

Eugene Kaspersky, VB March 1993

Whenever a new virus lands on my desk it falls into one of four broad categories, which do not really align themselves with the usual system for classifying viruses. In my personal system the first group, which is also the most numerous, contains all the standard variations on the theme of COM and EXE infectors or boot sector viruses. These viruses are now sufficiently common that they usually receive no attention save their inclusion in the *VB* list of known PC viruses. Most do not utilise stealth techniques, and they are usually bug-ridden scraps of code - really nothing more than computer graffiti.

Another group of viruses are those which are polymorphic, or which use increasingly complex methods of stealth in order to hide their presence on infected files or disks. Examples of viruses which fit into this group are MtE-based viruses, Girafe, and the Uruguay series to name but a few. These viruses are frequently more difficult to detect reliably, and can be a cause of much head scratching among those developing anti-virus software.

The third group contains attempts to write the shortest possible virus. Due to this self-imposed length restriction, these viruses contain no trigger routines. Although none of these viruses has a significant chance of spreading, the virus authors seem to be continually trying to outdo one another. The whole thing looks rather like a competition between the virus writers, though I have no idea what the prize is!

The most interesting group of viruses are those which use new algorithms for infection or disguise. All virus researchers will remember, for example, the first stealth file virus (4K or FRODO), the new method of the file infection used by DIR-II, or the way the Starship virus infects the boot sector of a disk. Although the vast majority of virus writers are unusually inept at assembly language, every now and then they have the unfortunate habit of coming up with the occasional cunning idea.

The latest new development I have seen is a memory-resident virus which is capable of infecting batch files. While there are a couple of supposed batch files infectors known, this virus infects in a somewhat unusual way. The virus has no trigger routine, and while it is relatively easy to remove, has a high nuisance value. It is to be hoped that Batman does not herald a new age of infectors which target slightly more unusual objects.

Simple Tricks

It is easier to show part of the text of an infected batch file than to explain the technique used by the virus. The text inserted into the batch file is very simple:

```
@ECHO OFF
REM <<< binary code: jmp installation,
int_21 handler part 1 >>>
copy %0 b.com>nul
b.com
del b.com
rem <<< binary code: TSR installation,
int_21 handler part 2 >>>
```

(*Note*: the brackets <<< >>> mean that the non-text bytes of the virus would normally be located here.)

The unusual thing about this virus is that the code can be executed as one of two different file types: either as a batch file or as a COM file.

When this file is executed as a batch file it can be seen that the virus will create a copy of the batch file with the extension COM by using the command

```
copy %0 b.com
```

The %0 parameter substitutes the name of the batch file as it typed at the command prompt. The newly created COM file is then executed.

Inside The COM File

When the batch file is renamed to b.com the start of this file still begins with the text string

```
@ECHO OFF
REM
```

However, because this file now has a COM extension, this text is interpreted as the i8086 instructions

```
INC AX
INC BP
INC BX
DEC AX
DEC DI
AND [BX+46],CL
INC SI
OR AX,520A
INC BP
DEC BP
AND ??,??
```

These 'junk' instructions do not influence COM program execution (just as the remarked binary code does not effect the execution of the batch file). Once they are executed, the virus code stored in the batch file after the REM statement is executed. It is this binary code which allows the virus to become memory-resident.

The virus uses standard DOS function calls to go resident, and makes no attempt to hide its presence. It hooks INT 21h by using the DOS functions GET INTERRUPT VECTOR and SET INTERRUPT VECTOR and then goes resident exiting used an INT 27h (TERMINATE AND STAY RESIDENT) call. The virus does not have an 'Are you there?' call, and so will multiply infect memory every time an infected batch file is run.

The virus' INT 21h handler only intercepts the WRITE FILE function (INT 21h, AH=40h). The virus checks the beginning of the write buffer for the string '@ECHO'. This string is commonly found at the start of many batch files. If it is present the virus writes itself into the file before saving the contents of the buffer. Therefore any batch files which start with this text string will be infected upon creation, copying or modifying.

When this part of the virus returns control to the batch file, the newly created COM file is deleted from the disk, thus leaving no evidence of the foul play which has gone on.

Poor Coding

This virus is not well debugged - it looks more like the trial of a new idea than a serious attempt at writing a virus. There are several errors in the infection algorithm.

Every now and then the batch file will cause DOS to display the error messages

```
Bad command or file name
```

or

```
File not found
```

during execution. This is caused by the presence of redirection signs
('>' or '<') or pipe ('|') in the virus code commented out by the
REM instruction.

The virus stores the original INT 21h handler address in its own
code, and that address in ASCII form can contain any characters
including '>', '<' and '|'. When the batch file is run, DOS rather
surprisingly interprets these signs and will report an error.

The second error manifests itself on execution infected batch file by
typing in the batch file name without its extension. The %0 batch
parameter will be equal to file name only and DOS cannot execute
the command

```
copy %0 b.com
```

because that file is absent. In this case DOS displays the message:

```
File not found
Bad command or file name
File not found
```

However, this error is trivially avoided.

Due to the lack of an 'Are you there?' call or any form of self-
recognition on files, the virus also multiply infects files. In the
extreme case, when several copies of the virus are resident, each
resident copy of the virus will infect the batch file before it is written
to disk.

What Next?

This virus is not a significant threat in itself, as it is unlikely to
spread. However, it does illustrate that new methods of infection are
being thought of all the time. Any object which can form executable

code is a possible target for infection. This includes object files or even files which infect C source code or libraries. Therefore it is important that those relying on integrity checkers as their main line of defence are aware of which objects they need to protect.

Some manufacturers exclude certain files (for example, CONFIG.SYS) arguing that this drastically reduces the number of alarms given by the product. If so, then great care should be taken when deciding whether a system is truly virus free. What next - a multi-partite BOOT-SYS-BAT-DLL infector? - the possibilities are endless. Well, we have no choice but to wait and see. Meet Batman - the memory-resident BAT file infector.

Batman

Aliases: None known.

Type: Memory-resident, Parasitic file infector.

Infection: Batch files which start with the text @ECHO OFF.

Self-Recognition:

Files   None

System   None

Hex Pattern:

```
4045 4348 4f20 4f46 460d 0a52
fc40 756f 9c50 5351 5256 571e
```

or the text string:

```
copy %0 b.com>nul
b.com
del b.com
```

Removal: Under clean system conditions delete the first six lines of infected batch files using any text editor.

The Cascade Virus: Falling Down

Richard Ford (updated analysis from VB September 1989)

One of the most famous viruses to date, and one without which any anthology of computer viruses would be woefully incomplete, is the Cascade virus. There are several different reasons for the celebrity status of Cascade, but the two most important are as follows. Firstly, the virus is highly prevalent in the wild [*See VB, August 1993, p.15. Ed.*]. Secondly (and probably most importantly) the trigger routine is the much loved falling characters effect, where text appears to fall to the bottom of the computer screen.

Overview

Cascade is a memory-resident parasitic file infector. It is only capable of infecting COM files (including COMMAND.COM) and adds 1701 or 1704 bytes to the length of infected files. Cascade was the first virus which used encryption in an attempt to make it more difficult to detect and analyse, though the encryption used is so simple that it does not present any real problem to scanner manufacturers.

There are now several different variants of the Cascade virus known, but this report will concentrate on the two most closely linked (and the most often encountered) variants, Cascade 1701 and Cascade 1704.

Operation

When a file infected with the Cascade virus is executed, processing is passed immediately to the virus code by means of a JMP instruction inserted at the start of the file. This JMP points to a decryption routine which is 35 bytes in length. The encryption algorithm is extremely simple, and consists of XORing bytes of the virus code with a variable key.

One unusual feature of the virus is that the decryption routine tests a byte within the virus code, which is used as an encryption marker - if the marker is zero, it assumes that the body of the virus is unencrypted. The most likely reason for this is that the author of the virus would not have written the virus in an encrypted form, but as unencrypted code. This marker would therefore allow the author to create an unencrypted 'seed' version of the virus, from which the encrypted variant could be produced.

The entire decryption routine is reproduced at the end of this report. The reader should not be concerned that by publishing this short snippet of code, *VB* is encouraging the would-be virus author: the routine is so simple, not to mention well known, that using it in a virus today would be a liability, rather than an asset!

Once decryption has completed, the first action taken is to determine whether the virus is already memory-resident. This is done by calling INT 21h with AX set to 4BFFh. If the virus is memory-resident, the value 55AAh is returned in the DI register, the virus rewrites the start of the host program in memory and returns control to it.

If the system is not already infected, the virus searches for the string 'COPR.IBM' at offset 8 of the BIOS. This string is a copyright message, and is found in the BIOS of XTs and PS/2s in this location. However, for IBM ATs, the message is found at offset 7. If the message is not found, the virus returns control to the host program. The routine which tests for this string is flawed and will not function correctly. The later Cascade variant, Cascade 1704, appears to be an attempt to correct this (and several other) bugs, but the routine will still not function correctly.

The virus then alters the contents of MCBs and the PSP in order to become memory-resident, before hooking the DOS Services Interrupt, INT 21h. In addition to this routine, Cascade checks the date and, if it meets certain requirements, hooks one of two different services. Firstly, the date is checked to see if it is set to October, 1988. If it is, the timer interrupt INT 1Ch is hooked. If the year is set to 1980, the virus hooks both INT 1Ch, and also the DOS idle interrupt, INT 28h. This completes the installation process, and control is then passed back to the host program.

Interrupt Handlers

The INT 21h handler inserted by Cascade is very simple, and serves a dual purpose. It is designed to function as an 'Are you there?' call handler and also as the vehicle to infect files when it receives a Load and Execute request. When such a call is made, the virus code gains control and loads the first three bytes of the program into memory. If the first two bytes are 'MZ' the file is assumed to be an EXE file, and the Load and Execute request is passed on to DOS.

If the program does not start with this identifier and the file is short enough so that if it were infected, its length would be less than 64K, the virus checks to see whether it is already infected. This is done by examining the first three bytes of the target file. If this corresponds to the JMP address instruction which the virus would insert, the file is assumed to be infected and the installation routine is aborted. Note that the offset to which the jump points varies between the two variants. This means that the 1701 variant does not recognise files infected with the 1704 variant and vice versa.

Trigger

The trigger routine of the virus is called when the clock date is set to between October and December, 1988. In this case, a timer is loaded with a random value, which corresponds to a time of not more than five minutes. When this reaches zero, the cascade display routine is activated, and the count is reset to a random interval of not more than one minute.

The cascade display causes text characters on the screen to appear to 'fall' to the bottom of the display, accompanied by a clicking from the PC's speaker. One character is dropped down the screen within its column until it encounters an obstruction, whereupon processing is moved to another column.

Falling characters do not overwrite other characters, but stack up at the bottom of the screen. Graphics characters (such as those used to create boxes) do not fall, nor will other characters fall past them. In addition to this, if two adjacent lines have different display attributes, they do not fall.

The first time the cascade routine is activated, it is confined to one column. For each subsequent display, the number of columns is multiplied by a random number between one and three until eventually the whole screen is involved.

Cascade

Type: Memory-resident, Parasitic

Files: COM files (including COMMAND.COM)

Self-recognition:

Memory   'Are you there?' call. INT 21h with AX=4BFFh returns
               55AAh in DI

File   Presence of JMP offset instruction at start of the file.

Hex Pattern

```
FA8B  EC08  0000  5B81  EB31  012E
F687  2A01  0174  0F8D  B74D  01BC
```

Intercepts: INT 21h 4Bh for Infection and 'Are you there?' call.

INT 1Ch and INT 28h for trigger

Trigger: Causes text to 'fall' to the bottom of the screen, accompanied by a clicking noise from the PC speaker.

Removal: Under clean system conditions, identify and replace infected files.

Cascade Decryption Routine

```
DB0100    DB   1                             ; Encryption indicator

ENTRY:    CLI                                ; Virus entry point
          MOV  BP,SP                         ; Save stack pointer
          CALL BP0010                        ; Get address of BP0010
BP0010:   POP  BX                            ; into BX
          SUB  BX,OFFSET BP0010+2AH          ; Relocation register
          TEST DB0100[BX+2AH],1              ; Is virus encrypted?
          JZ   BP0030                        ; Jump to the body if not
          LEA  SI,BP0030[BX+2AH]             ; Address of encrypted area
          MOV  SP,OFFSET ENDADR-BP0030       ; Length of encrypted area
BP0020:   XOR  [SI],SI                       ; Decrypt virus body
          XOR  [SI],SP                       ; with double XOR
          INC  SI                            ; Next decryption address
          DEC  SP                            ; Counter
          JNZ  BP0020                        ; Until body decrypted
BP0030:   <encrypted body of the virus follows>
```

The CMOS1 (Exebug) Virus

Tim Twaits, VB January 1993 (updated)

It is rare that a virus introduces a completely new idea - most are simply adaptations of existing viruses with small modifications or additions. The author of the CMOS1 virus, however, seems to have managed to find a new approach. To the best of my knowledge it is the first virus which modifies the non-volatile system configuration data in the CMOS RAM in anything other than a destructive way: hence the name CMOS1.

In The Wild Origins

It was unusual to receive this virus from a user whose PC had been infected rather than from one of the many virus researchers and collectors. As such, it provides an insight into how a new virus is first detected and countered. The first suspicion of something amiss arose because of an error condition detected by the *Windows 3.1* 32-bit disk driver. It would have been easy to ignore the message, since *Windows* still ran successfully without using the 32-bit driver. Luckily somebody decided to investigate.

The first step taken was to attempt to scan the machine for known viruses. However, after performing a clean boot from a system diskette prior to running the virus scan, the hard drive could not be accessed. Armed with this knowledge of the symptoms, the investigator identified another infected machine. Both machines were immediately isolated and all associated diskettes quarantined.

At this point I received a copy of the virus. As soon as a recognition pattern had been extracted, a complete scan of all machines and disks was undertaken. In this case the virus had been contained and no new infections were discovered. The source of the infection was later traced to a golf game which had recently arrived from Taiwan. This game had also been sent to an office in South Africa, so the virus may well have spread further afield.

Operation

CMOS1 is primarily a Master Boot Sector virus. When the computer is booted from an infected disk the virus gains control. It creates a 'hole' in memory by decrementing a data value in the ROM BIOS data area which contains the useable memory size. This has the direct effect of reducing the available DOS memory by 1K. The virus then installs its own Interrupt 13h handler, which intercepts all calls to the BIOS disk services, before allowing the boot sequence to continue normally.

CMOS Modifications

The CMOS battery backed RAM in an IBM compatible PC contains the non-volatile system configuration information. The CMOS1 virus modifies this information to indicate that there is no floppy drive installed, forcing the system to boot from the fixed disk and load the virus, regardless of whether or not a floppy disk is present in the A drive. Once the virus has become memory-resident, the normal boot sequence is started from the expected drive leaving the user totally unaware that the virus is active in memory.

Fortunately the CMOS modification does not have the desired effect on the majority of systems where the changes are either ignored or detected as corruption of the information in CMOS. This technique is, however, effective on some PCs such as those containing the AMI BIOS. The CMOS1 virus will often not function as expected due to a number of errors in its code. An effective virus based on this technique is possible and all virus scanners need to be able to detect this type of virus in memory.

Infection

The virus always infects drive 80h (normally drive C) immediately after booting from an infected diskette. Further diskettes are infected when their contents are read. Thus simply inserting a diskette and typing DIR A: will cause the diskette to become infected.

When infecting a disk, the virus needs to keep a copy of the original boot sector so that the boot sequence can be completed successfully after the virus code is executed. On a hard disk the original MBS is stored in sector 17, cylinder 0, head 0. On a diskette an extra track (number 40 or 80, depending on the disk size) is formatted at the end of the normal data area. Creating this extra track has the advantage that the storage capacity of the diskette is not affected. However, not all systems can access this extra track successfully, and this will cause some machines to hang when booting from an infected diskette.

Stealth

The virus intercepts all requests to read the Master Boot Sector and returns the contents of the original sector to the caller. This effectively hides the virus from scanning software unless a clean boot is achieved. It also provides the mechanism by which the virus invokes the original boot code at initialisation. The virus issues an INT 19h call to restart the system once the intercept handler is installed. The system then starts normally since the bootstrap code will now load the original boot sector.

All requests to write to the Master Boot Sector are also intercepted, allowing the write operation to complete, but then immediately reinfecting the disk. The result is that one can run utilities which modify the boot sector, such as FDISK, without displacing the virus.

The virus contains another feature, which could perhaps be described as stealth. As well as overwriting the code in the Master Boot Sector, the virus also overwrites the partition table with invalid data. Thus when booting from a clean system diskette the hard drive cannot be accessed directly. Although one cannot scan the drive to detect the virus, the absence of logical drive C betrays its presence.

Increased Contagion and Trigger

In an attempt to make itself more contagious the virus will infect some EXE files written to drive A. The infection routine is primitive, as the file is simply overwritten by the virus. The program infects drive 80h immediately upon execution. This type of infection occurs whenever data starting with 4Dh (the EXE header identifier) is written to sector 3 on any cylinder of the diskette. This not only produces infected EXE files but will also corrupt any files which contain a sector starting with 4Dh.

While the creation of infected program files will undoubtedly help the virus to spread, it also significantly reduces the chance that the virus will survive in the wild. Since the infected programs are overwritten with the virus code they no longer retain their original function, providing an immediate signal that something has gone awry. While I do not think that it is beyond the (limited) technical ability of the virus author to devise a more sophisticated strategy, the code size has been restricted to less than 512 bytes, and there is simply no room for a routine which would make this virus truly multi-partite.

A proportion of EXE files written to fixed drives will be similarly modified, although in this case the modified program has a more disastrous effect. It will overwrite the first track of the first fixed drive, effectively making all data inaccessible. The data on any diskettes is also overwritten. These files are only produced when writing the EXE header to sector 3 on any cylinder in the range 512-767. The disk must contain a significant amount of data before this occurs.

Removal

After performing a clean boot, one can detect the presence of the virus both in the boot sector and in any files by using a simple search pattern. It is important to check data files as well as executables, since they may have been corrupted. If the machine is one which can be prevented from booting from the A drive, it is possible to erase the CMOS contents by removing its battery.

The virus can be removed from the Master Boot Sector on hard disks by copying the original contents which were stored by the virus (sector 17, cylinder 0, head 0) back to the boot sector (sector 1, cylinder 0, head 0) using a disk editor such as *The Norton Utilities*. Alternatively, the Master Boot Sector can be rewritten by using the FDISK /MBR command or by performing a low-level format. Be warned that because the virus corrupts the partition data stored within the Master Boot Sector, using the FDISK /MBR command will not recover the data stored on the drive; it will simply overwrite the virus code.

CMOS 1

Aliases: Exebug

Type: Resident semi multi-partite.

Infection: Master Boot Sector and EXE files.

Recognition: Hard drive not accessible after clean boot. *Windows 3.1* 32-bit disk driver will not load. Location 28h in Master Boot Sector is 7Ch.

Hex Pattern

```
B0FF E621 BA80 00B9 0100 B811
039C 9A?? ???? ??FE C680 E607
```

Intercepts: Interrupt 13h for stealth (boot sector only) and infection.

Trigger: Creates trojanised EXE files when writing to certain areas of a disk. The programs destroy disks.

Removal: See text.

Commander Bomber

Jim Bates, VB December 1992

A favourite pastime of virus researchers has always been to try to second-guess the virus writers by predicting just what future developments might entail. Such discussions are seldom published because this might feed ideas to the virus writing community.

Many researchers have always believed that a successful virus would always contain some self-recognition capability on disk to prevent multiply infecting the same file. However, the latest virus to arrive on my desk for disassembly has destroyed part of this cherished assumption in a way that was speculated upon over two years ago, and does it with the most complex code yet seen in a virus.

There is no immediate cause for concern, since this virus has not been reported at large, does not use code encryption and is easily recognisable with even a simple file examination utility. However, the first sample brought to the West (apparently from Bulgaria) reportedly caused certain vendors to decide to suppress all information (even amongst known genuine researchers) 'because it was so dangerous'. It is debatable whether such a decision was genuinely in the public interest - the virus represents more of a threat to product manufacturers' methods than it does to users.

The virus has been called Commander Bomber, after an internal text message which reads 'COMMANDER BOMBER WAS HERE'. It is reported as the work of the so-called 'Dark Avenger', and although there are some similarities of style, my own feeling is that this code is beyond his limited capabilities.

Commander Bomber is a resident virus that infects memory image files between 5120 and 61183 bytes in length which are invoked by a LOAD-and-EXECUTE system call. Infected files grow by exactly 4096 bytes, although the actual virus code is only 2496 bytes long. The reason for the discrepancy is that the virus needs space for data used in reconstitution and repair of host files.

Code-In-The-Hole

Where other parasitic viruses prepend, overwrite or append their code to the host file, this virus inserts its code at a randomly chosen position between 32 bytes from the beginning and 4064 bytes from the end of the host file. At this random position, 4096 bytes of host code are removed and added to the end of the file. The virus code, together with its attendant data areas, is then inserted into this 'hole'. This on its own would create only minor problems if the virus code was then executed by a simple jump from the beginning of the file, but this is where the devious and malicious mind of the writer has expended most of its considerable effort.

The virus contains several routines which generate random code. This 'junk code' does nothing except bring processing (eventually) to the virus code proper. The effect is to produce a file which does not start with a jump or call, but has code which seems 'normal' inserted at random spots throughout the file. The integrity of the code is maintained and the range of op-codes generated is almost complete - even memory modifying instructions are included.

To any cursory inspection, the 'junk code' appears quite normal and contains conditional and unconditional jumps and calls exactly like proper code. There is no attempt to maintain the value of any registers with the single exception that the condition of the stack is monitored. The random generation routines include occasional checks for processor type so that processor-specific op-codes are not generated incorrectly. While the code is sophisticated, there are several bugs which may cause system malfunction when an infected file is executed.

Installation

When the virus code is executed, it first checks the DOS version and exits directly to the host code if the version is earlier than 3.*xx*. The code then searches the environment to locate the path and name of the program being executed. Once this has been obtained, a familiar 'Are you there?' call routine is executed which calls INT 21h with a value of 424Fh in the AX register. If the virus is resident, the call returns a value of 4D42h in AX (these values represent the ASCII letters BO and MB), and processing is passed to the host code.

If the virus is not resident, a secondary rebuilding routine is processed which repairs various sections of the virus pre-processing code before re-writing the infected program back to the disk. Due regard is taken of the existing Time and Date stamp of the file, but any Read Only setting in the file attributes will be removed.

The virus code (2596 bytes) is then relocated to the normal COM offset in memory and the intercept routine is hooked into the system at INT 21h using the normal system services. The next phase of installation calls the infected file and executes it as a child process before finally exiting via the system TSR (Terminate and Stay Resident) function.

Commander Bomber uses a clever trick to avoid multiply infecting files. Whenever a file infected with Commander Bomber is run, the virus saves the memory image of the file to disk before disinfecting the file in memory and passing control to the host program. Therefore, if a file is doubly infected with the virus (as is briefly the case when running an infected file with the virus resident), the host is rebuilt as it was when it was first infected - i.e. a program which is infected *once*. When control is passed over to this host program, the second infection of Commander Bomber saves the memory image of the file (i.e. with only one infection) to disk. Therefore even though the virus cannot recognise itself in files it will not multiply infect them. [*Simple! Ed.*]

Operation

The complexity of this virus code precludes a detailed description of its operation but the general operation of the intercept code works as follows:

In order to load and execute a program, the name of the program must be passed to system function 4B00h of INT 21h. The virus intercepts this function call and stores it, while locating and opening the target file. The first word of the file is examined to see whether it is either the 'MZ' or 'ZM' header which signifies a segmented EXE file. Files containing this header are *not* infected and execute normally. This process does not test the filename extension.

However, the virus does check to avoid infecting files with a name of COMMAND (with or without an extension). The length of the file is also checked, and only files between 5120 and 61183 bytes long are infected. The virus does not check that the target file is already infected: *all* files of an acceptable length are infected as a matter of course. Thus the virus does not need to recognise its own existence within an infected file (see above) and this particular Achilles' heel has been protected.

Once the file has been infected and re-written to disk, the original function request is allowed to continue.

The Implications

Plain pattern recognition scanners which scan only the beginning and end of files (to increase scanning speed) will need to be modified to allow them to complete an exhaustive scan of files.

The other so-called 'smart' scanners which use processing flow analysis to locate the virus code, may find that their analytical capabilities will need considerable enhancement to cope with the range of 'junk code' which this virus generates. The absence of a self-recognition signature within the code is particularly alarming. The hallowed precept that a virus must always recognise itself on file if it is to avoid multiply infecting its host, has been shown to be false. This discovery, if further developed, will contribute significantly to the difficulties faced by scanner developers who have traditionally relied on this self-recognition file signature as a part of the detection process.

Fortunately, good generic integrity checking software will have no problem in noticing that a file has changed.

Commander Bomber

Aliases: Bomber

Type: Parasitic, inserting virus.

Infection: COM and memory image files invoked by the LOAD and EXECUTE function, between 5120 and 61183 bytes in length. COMMAND.COM is exempted.

Recognition:

File   The text message 'COMMANDER BOMBER WAS HERE' is plainly visible within an infected file and the file will be 4096 bytes longer than it should be.

System   An 'Are you there?' call which returns 4D42h in AX if

INT 21h is called with a value of 424Fh in AX.

Hex Pattern

```
E852  FFD1  E096  2EFF  9400  04EB
BE2E  0460  066F  0685  06A3  06E0
```

Intercepts: INT 21h for infection and detection of 'Are you there?' call.

Trigger: There is no trigger routine, but infected files may fail because of bugs in the code generation routines.

Removal: Specific and generic file disinfection is not possible. Under clean system conditions, identify and replace infected files.

Cruncher - The First Beneficial Virus?

Eugene Kaspersky, VB June 1993

The first time I ever heard about the dispute over whether there could ever be such a thing as a useful virus was many years ago, when I was analysing the first virus I had ever seen. One of the articles which I read at the time was about the definition of a computer virus and the philosophical aspects of viruses. The article went on to discuss what the future might hold, and whether or not one could ever have a useful virus.

At the time, I was not ready to take a firm standing point on this issue - in fact, I am still not ready to decide. For example, a well-written boot sector virus which looked for lost clusters could arguably be useful. Once you begin to consider the beneficial things a virus could do, the list is rather long. There is a multitude of small 'housekeeping' tasks which a virus could perform, all of which could be inserted into the virus' algorithm.

I hope that this does not appear to be propaganda for the legitimacy of virus writing. Computer viruses bring immense problems with them, and seriously compromise the security of machines. However, life brings a lot of surprises, and to become fixed with one particular viewpoint is always a bad idea - one of these surprises was that the Earth is not flat, but round as a ball. In the 15th Century, who would have thought it!

However, regardless of all of the above, the question remains - can we have a useful virus? If we can, then the Cruncher virus could well be it.

The Virus which Saves You Disk Space

This virus takes its name from an internal text string 'Cruncher V1.0ß' which is inserted into the end of the virus body. This word has a special meaning in the world of file compression - 'crunching' is the name of one of the file-packing methods used by most popular data compressors.

On the face of it, Cruncher looks like an ordinary memory-resident parasitic COM-file infector. It hooks Int 21h when it is executed and then alters the Memory Control Block list, leaving itself neatly installed in high memory.

When Cruncher is memory-resident, it infects on the DOS Load and Execute function. During the infection process, the virus intercepts Int 24h (the DOS Critical Error Handler) to ensure that spurious error messages are not displayed. The virus does not alter the time and date stamp of infected files, nor their attributes.

So far, Cruncher appears to be almost an ANSI-standard file infector virus, but unfortunately things are not nearly as simple as this first analysis would show. The additional code in the virus makes up a complete data compression routine. The Cruncher virus compresses the body of the host file when it infects it - so a hard disk thoroughly infected by this virus will have more space on it than before the infection - with no resulting loss of data!

The Origin

The virus contains the text string '[MK / Trident]'. This message is present in several of the more complex hacker products, including the four versions of the TPE - the Trident Polymorphic Engine, which is rather like the MtE.

This means that virus writers can append that object module to their viruses to make them polymorphic and difficult to detect. About six TPE-based viruses are known at this time, including the Girafe virus and the last version of the Coffeeshop and Civil War viruses.

The 'MK' label is present in several other viruses which are comparatively advanced - these are the MtE-based version of the Coffeeshop virus and WinVir-1.4, which is capable of infecting *Windows* executables.

Resident Operation

When the virus is memory-resident, it intercepts the main DOS interrupt Int 21h and checks function 4B00h (Load and Execute) and function 33E0h which is used by the virus as an 'Are you there?' call.

When a Load and Execute (AX=4B00h) function is trapped, the virus checks the file's name and extension. Version one of the virus only infects COM files, although it excludes any files which have the first letters CO. Version two of the Cruncher virus infects both COM and EXE files, but excludes files which begin with the letters SC, CL, VS, NE, HT, TB, VI, FI, GI, RA, FE, MT, BR, or IM.

The virus opens the file and examines five bytes of its header to ensure that the file is not already infected. If the target file length is less than 256 bytes, or above 61440 bytes, the virus will not infect it.

Slimming Down

If the file is deemed suitable for infection, the virus reads the whole file contents into one of two temporary segments (128k) of system memory. The virus then infects the file *in memory*, by appending the virus code and adding a jump instruction at the start of the host file.

Up to this point, the virus has acted like any other file infector. However, the virus now starts to pack the infected memory image of the file using the same algorithm as the DIET utility. This compression is used over the entire file, i.e. the host and the virus body.

The infection routine ends here, and the compressed file is copied back to disk. The virus closes the file, restores the file attributes and time/data stamp and releases the temporarily allocated segment of system memory which was used during infection. The result of this is that the virus code is now stored within the file compression - and therefore not immediately visible. The compressed file is completely DIET-compatible to the extent that it is possible to use the DIET utility to decompress the executable!

Unpacking and Installation

When an infected file is executed, the file begins to unpack itself, using the DIET algorithm. When the unpacking routine is complete, the virus installation code is executed. This checks the system memory to see whether the virus is already resident by using an 'Are you there?' call. If it is not, the interrupt handlers are hooked into place and the virus becomes memory-resident.

Detection Problems

Reliable detection of the Cruncher virus is a very difficult task because the actual virus code is hidden within the compressed file. In this case it is not acceptable to search for the decompression routine (effectively, the decryption routine) because that code has a perfectly legitimate role in other programs. It is also not possible to use a Hex pattern search (even with wildcards) as the contents of the compressed file will depend on the contents of the host file.

When a file is compressed using DIET, an algorithm developed by Lempel and Ziv is used. The compression is based on creating a dictionary of 'words' which make up the majority of the file. Compression of this type is known as 'adapted word compression', which can be thought of as creating 'abbreviations' for longer expressions - just as one abbreviates Terminate Stay Resident to TSR.

For example, by using this method the string '111122231111' will be compressed to '11 [repeat 2 bytes from offset 0] 2223 [repeat 4 bytes from offset 0]'.

The contents of a file are therefore packed as the sequence of new words and pointers to words which have already occurred in that file.

This means that the byte sequences contained in the compressed file will depend not only on the contents of the virus code but also on the contents of the host file. Therefore the contents of the compressed infected file will differ vastly for different host files.

This presents rather serious problems when considering how to detect the Cruncher virus. I can see no way of detecting every single infection of the virus unless the entire file is unDIETed [*Fattened? Ed.*], and then scanned. However, this process is both time and resource consuming - if the target disk contained a number of legitimate DIETed files, the scan time for the disk could be unacceptably high.

It is probably possible to search for the strings '[MK / Trident]' and 'Cruncher V1.0ß'. Although these are nominally compressed, the brief experiments which I have conducted show that infected files are detected in 75% of cases - which is enough to raise the alarm, but not nearly enough for reliable detection.

Cruncher

Aliases:	Cruncher-2092, Cruncher-4000
Type:	Memory-Resident, Appending Parasitic, Polymorphic
Infection:	COM files only (Cruncher-2092) COM and EXE files (Cruncher-4000)

Self-Recognition:

Files	Checks contents of first five bytes
Memory	'Are you there?' call using INT 21h with AX=33E0h.

Hex Pattern

No simple search pattern is possible. Many infected files contain 'corrupted' incidences of the following strings

Cruncher-2092:
```
[ MK / Trident ] Cruncher V1.0ß
```

Cruncher-4000:
```
*** CRUNCHER V2.0*** Automatic file
compression utility
```

Trigger:	None
Removal:	File disinfection is possible but difficult. Under clean system conditions, identify and replace infected files.

DIR II - The Much Hyped 'Linking' Virus

Jim Bates, VB November 1991

Once again certain sections of the anti-virus industry have been crying wolf. Global virus alerts and panic bulletins have been posted on countless BBS forums - the end of computing, we have been assured, is imminent. While this activity undoubtedly does no harm to their sales figures, once again it is the user who is left confused and frightened by unconfirmed reports of uncontrolled infections in Eastern Europe by a new virus. One report describes it as '*A new, fast moving, and very destructive virus ... uses a completely new technique ... cannot be easily identified or removed*'. Small wonder that normal research work has been punctuated by frequent telephone calls from concerned users enquiring about the imminence of the annihilation of their programs and data.

Facts not Fiction

The facts, simply, are these: the virus uses a new infection technique; it spreads rapidly within a machine environment by virtue of its infecting whole directories; and (incidental to its method of operation) it displays a certain stealth capability. However, it is not 'very destructive'; it is extremely *easy* to identify and it can be disabled and removed with no risk to existing files. Its potential for corrupting existing data is limited to a single cluster (probably unallocated) on each infected disk. All of this information, together with a simple and effective disinfection technique, was gleaned from disassembling and analysing a sample of the code and took under 24 hours of research effort.

The virus comes from Bulgaria. It is known as DIR-II and the fact that most researchers agree on this name is an indication of how rapidly a sample was distributed amongst researchers around the world. The fact that the sample was accompanied by unconfirmed tales of the virus 'running rampant' in Eastern Europe is probably the reason for the panic, as to date only a single report of it being 'at large' (which subsequently turned out to be false) has been received from my own contacts.

General Analysis

Since this virus does not attach itself to executable file contents, the term 'linking' virus has been coined to differentiate its infection method. The code is 1024 bytes long and is written in assembler. It does not subvert any of the interrupt vectors although it does collect one of the antique access points designated for compatibility with CP/M. Access to the system is gained by attaching the code to the existing device drivers which handle part of the DOS file services.

The infection technique links a single cluster containing the virus code to each file that is infected, while preserving the original location of the start of the file in an encrypted form within the directory entry. This means that the actual contents of each infected file are not altered in any way and can be accurately and completely recovered.

The virus makes no attempt to encrypt its code and it is therefore easily identified by even the simplest scanning program when used 'clean' to scan suspected floppy disks. However, it should be noted that if any other parasitic virus occurs on such a disk, the scanning program will not find it until the DIR-II infection has been removed.

The virus infects all EXE and COM files (including COMMAND.COM). This virus will **not** propagate across a network unless an infected file is copied to the file server.

Installation

The virus code begins by setting up its own local stack and then incrementing a single word data value. This word is not referenced elsewhere in the code and may be a simple infection counter. The interrupt table is then examined and an address is collected from a position reserved solely to maintain compatibility with CP/M type programs. This address points to an entry point within the operating system and after a small modification (to skip certain initialisation code) it is stored via the local stack in the virus' data area for later use as the main link between the virus code and DOS.

A normal interrupt request is then issued to determine the version of DOS and the virus then attempts to initialise a data value. The attempt fails because of a bug in the code but this does not affect the overall operation of the virus.

After modifying the amount of memory used by the virus, the code examines the chain of device drivers and modifies all those found to be resident within the DOS segment so that they become linked to the virus code. Calculations are then performed on specific memory allocations to determine whether the virus code is being processed before COMMAND.COM is loaded. This information is vital to the successful installation of the virus in low memory.

Once the virus is installed as an extension of the operating system, the addresses of the strategy and interrupt routines of the device driver are collected into the virus' data area for use later. The next part of the installation routine is reminiscent of other Bulgarian viruses and begins by collecting the Disk BIOS address from within the device driver. This is stored within the virus' data area, but an additional routine searches for any ROM modules and examines them for their own Disk BIOS address. If found, this address is used in preference to the one from the device driver.

The final part of the installation routine collects the name of the host program and executes as a child process via the normal LOAD and EXECUTE function of DOS. After execution, any returned error code is collected and the code exits normally to DOS. Provision is made for the execution of COMMAND.COM since it is possible for the virus code to be processed before this file is loaded.

Operation

Once installed, the virus code remains resident and is invoked whenever DOS issues commands to the device drivers associated with the Disk BIOS. Thus all disk accesses requiring collection of the directory structures become routed through the virus. The connection to the device drivers functions in a similar way to the redirection of interrupt services in other viruses - various commands are intercepted and others are allowed to continue unchanged. In this case only the Read, Write, Write/Verify and Build BIOS Parameter Block (Build BPB) commands are intercepted.

The Read and Write commands are intercepted **before** processing by the device driver, while the Build BPB command is intercepted **afterwards**.

Build BIOS Parameter Block

The interception of the Build BPB command is implemented to prevent possible corruption of the disk structure either by DOS or CHKDSK and similar utility programs. The BIOS Parameter Block is of vital significance to DOS when calculations are undertaken to ascertain the location and volume of available space on the disk. Remember too that the BPB is constantly being rebuilt as different disk types and sizes are accessed.

After the device driver has completed the command, the virus code regains control and copies the newly built BPB into its own buffer. The contents of the request header are modified to point to the virus copy of the BPB and the block itself has an appropriate number of sectors (corresponding to the virus' requirements) subtracted from its Total Sectors field. Thus, on an infected machine, CHKDSK does not indicate any errors or orphan clusters. Note, however, that if an infected machine is booted from a clean system disk, CHKDSK will indicate an indeterminate number of cross-linked and orphan clusters.

Output and Output/Verify Commands

These commands, which are issued to the device driver when directory sectors must be rewritten, are intercepted by a single routine in the virus before the device driver receives them.

This routine begins by checking to see whether the media has changed in the target drive (new floppy, etc.). If the media has changed, the original output request is issued to the device driver request and when processing returns, the virus continues with the disk infection routine. If the media has not changed, processing jumps to the sector infection routine.

Input Commands

Intercepting the Input commands to the device driver involves first checking to see whether the media has changed. If it has not, then the sector infection routine is called - if it has then the disk infection routine is invoked.

Infection Routines

The two infection routines are where this virus differs from other types and it is important to understand the mechanisms involved before describing the routines themselves.

On a single infected disk (hard or floppy) the virus code usually resides in only one place - the final one or two clusters on a disk. Differentiation between disk types is according to how many sectors are allocated to each cluster on that particular media. The routine that locates and places the virus code in this area is referred to here as the disk infection routine. Once a disk has been infected in this way, the other infection routine is used to link the virus cluster to target files. This is done by directly accessing the directory sectors on the disk and modifying the directory entry for each suitable file.

Only COM and EXE files are affected and modification consists of replacing the First Cluster Pointer (FCP) of each file entry with a pointer to the single virus cluster (thus effectively cross-linking the files). The original FCP is then encrypted and stored in a different section of the directory entry which is apparently unused (marked as 'reserved' by reference books). This routine is referred to here as the sector infection routine and it should be noted that regardless of size, the whole of a target directory is infected in a single pass. It is this process which makes the virus spread so rapidly within a single PC [*the intra-machine environment. Ed.*].

It is interesting to note that the virus only examines the *file extension area* of the directory entry and does not check to see whether the target file has been deleted - although this has no effect on the normal virus operation, it does make this the first virus I have seen which actually 'infects' deleted files!

Disk Infection

This routine completes a simple series of calculations to determine the number of the last available cluster on the target disk. The relevant FAT entry is then inspected and if a bad cluster is indicated the position is decremented and the routine tries again.

Once a usable cluster is located, the FAT entry is marked with an End of File (<EOF>) indicator and the virus code is copied to that cluster. The <EOF> marker used is FFFEh instead of the more normal FFFFh, this is perfectly acceptable to DOS and enables the virus to detect whether the disk is already infected. This is the only section of the virus code that might cause damage to an existing file since no notice is taken of whether the cluster is already allocated to a file. If the cluster was allocated, the file to which it belonged will be irreparably damaged. Deleting the file will temporarily free the virus cluster but the disk infection routine will immediately re-allocate it and the only side-effect will be that any subsequent portion of the file's cluster chain will become orphaned.

During the disk infection routine, the master encryption key (based upon part of the virus cluster number) is generated and stored within the virus code.

Sector Infection

This routine first calculates the size of the target directory and then calls an infection toggle routine. The toggle process examines each directory entry in turn to see whether the FCP points to the virus cluster. If it does not, the existing FCP is collected, encrypted and placed in the reserved area of the directory entry. The true FCP field is then altered to point to the virus cluster. If the entry is already infected, the reverse happens and the virus disinfects the entry by repairing and replacing the original FCP.

The process of switching First Cluster Pointers is incidentally responsible for giving this virus a spurious stealth capability since while the virus is resident, DOS operations will only occur on disinfected files and cannot access the virus cluster.

This toggling of infection/disinfection provides a useful Achilles' heel through which the virus can be de-activated and made to clean up infected disks and machines. Classical scholars will recall that the original Achilles only had one vulnerable heel - this virus has two, and a glass jaw as well! These flaws in the virus are described in detail later.

Observations

As noted above, scanning floppy disks on a clean machine will instantly reveal the presence of the virus. In fact, if the target disk is infected with the virus (rather than containing just a single program containing the virus code), the result of a scan will indicate all COM and EXE files in a particular directory as infected, thus reducing the possibility of false positive identifications from a single file which just happens to contain a sequence similar to the recognition string.

However, the infection technique does pose some new problems for users when dealing with infected machines and disks. To explain these problems it may be easier to describe various sequences of actions and their results:

Since without the virus being resident and active in memory all infected files appear to point only to the virus code, copying (on a clean machine) an infected file from an infected diskette will result in the destination file being exactly 1024 bytes in length. This is regardless of the length reported by any directory listing of the source diskette. If this copied file is then executed, nothing will appear to happen (the DOS prompt will just re-appear). However, the virus will load into memory and activate and the files on the infected floppy will now appear 'normal' to the system and may be freely copied and executed.

Infection of the fixed disk in this way will almost invariably lead to the infection of COMMAND.COM (or whatever the command interpreter is named) and thereby ensure the survival of the virus at the next reboot. If instead of copying the original file from the floppy, it is simply run from the diskette, the same result will occur - the virus will be resident and active and infect the fixed disk (and probably COMMAND.COM).

Detection

The virus employs no encryption and is easily detected on disk. As with all cases of suspect virus infection the PC should be booted from a clean, write-protected system diskette before scanning commences. Note that the virus will be found in all COM and EXE files in each directory scanned - if the presence of the virus is detected in only a single file, a false positive should be suspected.

The following hexadecimal pattern reliably detects the DIR II virus:

```
BC00 06FF 06EB 0431 C98E D9C5
06C1 0005 2100 1E50 B430 E824
```

Disinfection

Once a machine becomes infected, COM and EXE files cannot be backed up by copying them to an appropriate floppy disk because doing so will infect the target diskette. Booting the machine from a clean floppy is also no use because without the virus active in memory, all infected files will only contain the 1024 bytes of virus code.

This apparent dilemma is described in one panic message as a 'Catch 22 situation'.

In fact the solution is simple and obvious. Far from being the dangerous and frightening beast that these 'experts' suggest, this virus is one of that rare breed which can be removed **completely** by any reasonably literate user without the use of **any** specialist tools (i.e. anti-virus software) whatsoever. The removal procedure (which is astonishingly straightforward) goes like this:

Boot the machine normally from its hard disk so that the virus is resident and active, and then rename all COM and EXE files to different extensions (perhaps .CO and .EX), thus:

```
C:>REN *.COM *.CO
C:>REN *.EXE *.EX
```

The result of this renaming process is that the virus fails to identify the .CO and .EX extensions as suitable target files as its own method of infection requires the presence of full COM and EXE extensions. Note that this renaming process must be undertaken in *all* directories.

The machine should then be rebooted from a clean system diskette to remove the virus from memory and the renamed files can be renamed back to their original COM and EXE extensions - the machine is then clean. It really is that simple!

By following this procedure the execution route of the virus is **completely** severed and the link by which the virus points to COM and EXE files is broken. The final virus cluster which is unallocated (i.e. an orphan cluster) can be recovered using CHKDSK in the normal way.

There are two *caveats* to the above procedure. First, if your machine uses something other than COMMAND.COM as a command interpreter this file must be replaced under clean conditions with a known clean copy. The name and location of the command interpreter is usually displayed as the COMSPEC variable which may be displayed by typing SET at the DOS prompt.

Second, in order to determine whether your COMMAND.COM file is infected, you should boot your machine from a clean write-protected system diskette and then copy the suspect file onto a separate floppy disk. If the file is infected, the resulting copy will only be one cluster (usually 2048 bytes) long.

It should also be remembered that as the virus infects a disk, it overwrites the last usable cluster on the disk whether it has been allocated to another file or not. Thus it is possible for one file to be corrupted by this process. Since the average user has no way of knowing exactly where particular files reside, he should use a scanner capable of exhaustively searching all bytes of all files to check whether this has happened.

The Patch

Another interesting facet of this 'now you see it, now you don't' virus, is that we can appeal to its 'conscience' by changing just 7 bytes. If these changes are introduced into the virus cluster on the disk, a subsequent reboot makes the patched code automatically disinfect any infected files until there are no more and thereby 'self-destructs' by becoming completely disconnected from system operation. Using this patch also has the effect of making the machine immune to further infections of this virus from external sources as long as the orphaned cluster at the end of the disk is not removed.

It would be irresponsible to publish exact details of the patch here since eager pimplies would be queuing up to produce version two [*DIR II-II? Ed.*]. An information sheet giving details of the patches is available from *Virus Bulletin* to *bona fide* users.

The use of either the patching method or the renaming process may also show which file was responsible for introducing the virus if it was originally copied from an infected floppy. What happens is this: all infected files maintain their integrity even under infection. Disinfecting these files restores their original condition and since the originally copied file consisted only of the virus code, it will be restored along with the rest. Thus if a scanner is run after disinfection and finds a one-cluster file which contains the virus code at its beginning, this is almost certainly the one that caused the problem in the first place. Exhaustive scanning is desirable to locate the single file that may have been actually damaged by the virus code.

The Big Myth

The myth that the Bulgarian viruses are somehow 'cleverer' than other common specimens needs to be exploded once and for all - the DIR-II virus is not clever; it is ingenious but stupid, complex and totally impractical.

The Bulgarian (and other Eastern bloc) authorities should get their acts together and introduce legislation to make this childish pastime illegal. Any computer technology from these countries carries a high degree of risk. If the authorities let them play like this with software, who is to say that some of them have not introduced malicious or mischievous code into some machine ROM chips, or even safety-critical hardware.

Less Than Twenty Four Hours of Research

The DIR-II code has obviously been painstakingly pared down to fit into 1024 bytes and further tampering or optimization of this virus appears to be unlikely. I suspect that many weeks of some individual's programming and testing went into this latest production, but however long it took him to produce, his effort was negated in less than 24 hours of research.

His brainchild is now nothing more than a curiosity.

The Form Virus

Fridrik Skulason, VB November 1991

This boot sector virus from Switzerland makes noises, like the Music Bug virus, and infects the DOS Boot Sectors of diskettes and hard disks, but there the similarity ends.

When the Form virus is executed, it reserves 2 kilobytes at the top of RAM and reads the second half of itself from disk. The virus does not retry the read operation if it gets a read error, but simply hangs the machine. This means that booting from an infected floppy may often result in the machine hanging, because a time-out error is somewhat likely at this point. The virus will then read the original boot sector and attempt to infect the hard disk.

Hard Disk Infection

The Form virus reads the Partition Table and locates the active DOS partition. It will then read the DOS Boot Sector of that partition and check whether it is already infected or whether the sector size is something other than 512 bytes. If it is a 512 byte sector, the original DOS Boot sector is written to the last sector of the partition and the second half of the virus is stored in the preceding sector. Finally the virus overwrites the first sector of the partition (i.e. the location of the original DOS Boot sector) with the first half of itself. As the sectors used by the virus are not allocated by the virus they have a chance of being overwritten, but this will only happen if the partition fills up completely.

Activation Day?

After having infected the hard disk the virus hooks INT 13h, but if the current date is the 18th of any month, the virus also hooks INT 09h - the keyboard interrupt. The new INT 09h handler produces a click whenever a key is pressed - a harmless, but annoying effect.

The INT 13h Handler

The Form virus only intercepts requests to read from track 0 on drives A and B - in all other cases control is simply passed directly to the original INT 13h handler. This will generally result in the infection of diskettes the first time that they are accessed.

Diskettes are infected in standard fashion. The virus attempts to infect all densities of diskettes as long as the sector size is a standard 512 bytes. As in the case of hard disk infections the virus starts by verifying that the sector size is 512 bytes and that the boot sector is not already infected. It then proceeds to locate an unused cluster, marking it as 'bad' in the FAT and moving the original boot sector there, as well as the second half of the virus code.

This is all quite ordinary boot sector virus activity - indeed there is very little remarkable about the Form virus, except maybe the following text message which it contains:

```
The FORM-Virus sends greetings to everyone
who's reading this text. FORM doesn't
destroy data! Don't panic! Fuckings go to
Corinne.
```

Form Removal

The simplest way to disinfect diskettes is to boot from a clean write-protected system diskette, transfer data or executables using the DOS COPY command and then format the diskette. It is essential that this process is done in a clean DOS environment. Do not use DISKCOPY as this is an image copier and will copy the infected diskette *exactly* and in its entirety - including the virus in logical sector 0 of the diskette.

The Form virus can be removed from the active hard disk partition using a method similar to that used to remove Music Bug - simply by locating the original boot sector and writing it back to its original location.

The FAT might need slight fixing to recover the lost clusters, but that is not strictly necessary and should only be done with virus removal tools which recognise the Form virus.

Finally...

For any boot sector virus to spread and do damage it must first be executed. A machine will only become infected if you boot from an infected diskette. **Remind all PC users never to leave diskettes in drives for longer than necessary**.

ROM start-up code always tries to boot from the diskette drive in preference to the hard drive and if an infected diskette is present, the virus will be read into memory.

Joshi - Spreading Like A Forest Fire

Richard Jacobs, VB December 1990

One of the most common viruses in recent months has been the New Zealand (2) virus. This was, until recently, the only virus to infect the Master Boot Sector of a disk.

Joshi is the second virus of this type to be seen. Removal of a Joshi infection from hard disks is complicated by the fact that this virus, like New Zealand, is unaffected by a DOS FORMAT. It is therefore necessary either to perform a low level format of the disk, followed by repartitioning, and then a DOS FORMAT of all DOS partitions on the disk, or to replace the original Master Boot Sector.

The first of these options is painstaking and involves replacing all files on the hard disk from backups. Fortunately in the cases of both Joshi and New Zealand, the 'non-destructive' option is a straightforward procedure involving the restoration of the original Master Boot Sector using utilities such as *Norton* [*see VB, September 1990, p.9. Ed.*].

Joshi was first reported in August of this year. The virus originated in the Indian sub-continent and is now widespread in Europe and has recently appeared in the wild in the UK. Unlike many new viruses, Joshi does not employ self-modifying encryption, so every copy is identical. However, the virus does use 'stealth' which makes it undetectable if it is active in memory.

The virus consists of a boot sector and then uses a further 8 sectors elsewhere on the disk. One of these sectors contains a copy of the original Master Boot Sector, the next two sectors are not used, and the remaining five contain the virus code.

As with the majority of viruses, Joshi is not deliberately destructive. However, due to an oversight by its author, Joshi is likely to corrupt some data on infected 720 K diskettes.

Intentional Side-Effects

The only deliberate side effect of Joshi occurs on January 5th of any year. If one boots from an infected disk, the following message will be displayed on a cyan background:

```
Type "Happy Birthday Joshi" !
```

This message remains on screen until the required text is typed in, unless the PC is switched off and booted from a clean disk. Once the text has been entered, the boot process continues normally and no further evidence of the virus is seen.

Survival and Deception Features

There are several features of this virus which are of particular interest. First of all this virus will survive a warm boot (Ctrl-Alt-Del). Secondly, on floppy disks the virus formats a new track at the end of the disk, which it then uses to store itself and the original boot sector of the disk. Also, on floppy disks some or all of the error messages contained within the original boot sector are copied to the virus boot sector, so if an infected disk is inspected on a clean PC, using a utility such as *The Norton Utilities*, it will look like a clean this reason dedicated virus detection software is essential for reliable diagnosis.

As with New Zealand, the Joshi virus can only infect a PC if the machine is booted from an infected disk. Non-system disks can spread infection to a PC; the usual

```
'Non-system disk. Please insert a system
disk and retry'
```

will be displayed as the virus goes into memory. This re-emphasises the danger of negligently leaving diskettes in the floppy drive when the machine is shut down. Once the machine is powered up again, it will automatically boot from the floppy drive, providing the opportunity for a boot sector virus to infect the hard disk.

Note: Boot sector viruses will infect any DOS-formatted diskette, regardless of whether it is used to transfer pure data or executable images.

Operation

When the PC is booted from an infected disk, the virus checks as to whether or not it is already in memory. If it is, control is passed straight to the virus, otherwise the amount of available memory is reduced by 6 KBytes. The virus boot sector plus the 8 sectors assigned to the rest of the virus, including the original disk boot sector, are loaded into this 6 KBytes reserved block of memory and control is transferred to the virus in memory.

Next the virus checks the interrupt vectors for INT 8h, INT 9h and INT 13h. If these vectors do not already point to the virus' own sub-routines, they are altered to do so and the previous settings are stored for later use. The virus then sets markers to indicate that it does not know whether the first two floppy drives and the first two fixed drives are infected. It then copies the original disk boot sector stored in the virus' 6 KByte reserved memory block to the address to which it would have been loaded by the computer's start up process. The virus jumps to that address, thus returning control to the normal boot up procedure.

The memory-resident part of the virus is subsequently accessed through INT 8h (Timer Interrupt), INT 9h (Keyboard Interrupt), INT 13h (ROM BIOS disk services) and INT 21h (DOS services).

At this stage INT 21h has not been set. This is because the Master Boot Sector executes before DOS is loaded into memory and any setting of this vector would be overwritten by DOS. This problem is solved by using INT 8h to set the vector for INT 21h. INT 8h is generated 18.2 times per second to keep the time-of-day clock current. The INT 8h handler monitors the INT 21h vector and does nothing until the vector changes. It then changes the vector to point to its own routine and saves the previous value.

The other function of the INT 8h handler is to monitor the state of the floppy drive motors. If it detects that a motor has stopped, a marker is set so that next time that drive is used the disk is checked for infection. This means that all uninfected floppy disks used in an infected PC will be infected.

The INT 9h handler monitors what is typed at the keyboard. If the 'Happy Birthday Joshi!' message is displayed, this routine supplies the codes of the keys typed to the INT 21h handler rather than to the normal operation of INT 9h. The second function of this routine is to intercept a warm boot request (Ctrl-Alt-Del) and prepare the PC so that the virus remains intact in memory during the boot process.

The INT 13h (ROM BIOS disk services) handler checks for disk infection and infects all clean disks. Every time INT 13h is called, it checks whether or not a disk is infected. If it is, the disk function is checked and if it is not a request to *read*, *write* or *verify*, the Master Boot Sector control is returned to the INT 13h handler.

Otherwise the first sector on the disk is loaded and 344 bytes of its contents are checked against the copy of the virus boot sector originally loaded during the bootstrapping process. If they match, then the disk is already infected and control is returned to the normal INT 13h handler unless the INT 13h is a call to *read, write* or *verify* the Master Boot Sector. If it is, the call is redirected to the original Master Boot Sector rather than the virus boot sector.

Any attempt to read the Master Boot Sector of a disk will show the clean original Master Boot Sector rather than the virus boot sector. This will cause any virus scanning program to diagnose a PC as uninfected if the virus is memory-resident at the time of checking. This re-emphasises the need to boot the PC from a clean write-protected system diskette prior to using virus scanning software. Scanning software should not be installed or run from a hard disk in order to scan the hard disk.

Infection Routine

Infection is the same on floppy disks and hard disks, except for the location at which the virus is stored on disk.

For hard disks the virus is placed on the first track of the disk, which is unused in almost all cases. For floppy disks an extra track is formatted after the last track and this track is used to store 8 sectors of data. On floppy disks the number of sectors per track is checked and if it is less than 15, the disk is assumed to have 40 tracks, otherwise the disk is taken to have 80 tracks. This assumption is incorrect in the case of 3.5 inch 720 K disks, which have 9 sectors/ track and 80 tracks, which causes corruption of track 40.

The virus alters the copy of its own boot sector in memory to contain the correct BIOS Parameter Block (BPB) (for hard disks this will be meaningless data). It then copies itself from the reserved 6 Kbyte memory area, which now includes the original Master Boot Sector, into 8 sectors chosen for the type of disk and writes the virus boot sector to the Master Boot Sector location. The marker is set to indicate that the disk has been infected and control is returned to the start of the virus INT 13h handler.

The INT 21h handler checks the date, and if it is the 5th of January of any year, it starts the message routine, which retains control until the correct key sequence is entered.

Disinfection

The PC must be switched off and booted from a clean write-protected system floppy disk before commencing disinfection. A warm boot (Ctrl-Alt-Del) is **not** sufficient to remove Joshi from memory.

For floppy disks, all files can be copied safely to another disk and the disks then reformatted using DOS FORMAT. To copy the files use the DOS COPY command or a file-by-file backup program. **Do not use DISKCOPY or any image copier as this will copy the virus onto the destination diskette.**

For hard disks there are two methods:

1. Backup any data needed and then do a low level format*, followed by FDISK and a DOS format (FORMAT C:/S/V), and then restore all files. [*See VB, July 1990, pp.3-5. Ed.*]

2. Use the routine described in *VB*, September 1990, p.9 except that stage 10 of the process should be changed to 'Select: "Side 0","Cylinder 0", "Sector 9","Number sectors 1"' for Joshi. It is advisable to take a full backup before undertaking this procedure, as a mistake could make the disk inaccessible.

* The low level formatting procedure will be described in the manual supplied with the PC. Some system disks are also supplied with a low level formatting utility.

The Mutation Engine - The Final Nail?

Fridrik Skulason, VB April 1992

Last year a note was posted on Fidonet's virus conference, where 'Dark Avenger' announced his soon-to-be-released Mutation Engine (see *VB*, April 1991, p.19). He has now done so - releasing the engine with documentation, sample code and he even offers technical support via a virus exchange BBS in Bulgaria. [*Dark Avenger's tech support is presumably better than that offered by certain anti-virus vendors - see VB, April 1992 pp. 17-24. Ed.*]

The Mutation Engine is a logical extension of the process which began with the 1260 virus [*VB, March 1990, p.12, April 1990, p.10. Ed.*]. In that exercise the author (Mark Washburn) proved the possibility of variable decryption whereby no code remained static as the virus 'copied' from file to file. At the time 1260 was cited as the 'first nail in the coffin of virus-specific detection'. For certain simple scanning products, the Mutation Engine may well prove to be the final nail.

The current version of the engine (MtE 0.91) contains the following files:

```
MTE.OBJ        The main engine
MTE.DOC        Documentation
DEMOVIR.ASM    The source to the
               'Dedicated' virus
```

DEMOVIR.OBJ	Same, in object form
RND.ASM	Source code to the random number generator
RND.OBJ	Same, in object form
MAKE.BAT	Used to create an executable virus
NOPS.BIN	Data file
READ.ME	Some comments from the author

The whole package might best be described as a virus writer's 'Toolkit', the intention being that a virus writer can utilise the Mutation Engine via a single subroutine call, thus rendering his code extremely difficult to analyse and detect. The generic term for viruses which demonstrate the encryption processes used in the Mutation Engine is 'polymorphic'.

The documentation is quite interesting to read. The following excerpts are reproduced exactly from file MTE.DOC:

```
1. Licence
You are free to include this Engine in
viruses. Using it in another ways is
prohibited. You are free to give it to
people that will only use it in this way.
MuTaion engine is free.

2. How it works
Please read the whole document before
trying to do something with the Engine. If
you have never written a virus in
Assembler, DON'T start with the Engine.
First do this, then return back to the
Engine.

MuTation Engine is an object module that
could be linked to any virus. It has been
written in Assembler and assembled under
Turbo Assembler 2.5. We recommend that you
```

use this assembler to compile the viruses
that will carry the Engine. Linking it to
an object file produced by other
assemblers, or high-level languages
compilers is theoretically possible, but we
never tried and do not recommend it. We
decided NOT to give up the Engine's source
code at this time.

The Engine will encrypt your code each time
with a different encryption key. It will
also generate a routine to decrypt it,
which will also differ each time. Both the
decryption routine and the encrypted code
will have variable lengths. Thus your virus
will be hardly detectable. The Engine's
code is about 2KB; we believe this is not
too big.

To say the decryption routine 'differs each time' is an understatement
- the code produced by the engine is far more complex than the code
which Whale [*VB, November 1990, pp. 17-20*] and V2P2 [*VB, April
1991 pp. 18-20*] generate. It is totally impractical to attempt detection
with a set of signature strings (i.e. straightforward hexadecimal
patterns) - the code is simply far too variable.

Structurally the decryption routine can be divided into the following
five steps:

Step 1: Generate a pointer to the start of the encrypted code. This
may be done with a simple instruction such as 'MOV BP,1F4B', but
probably a more complex method will be used, such as:

```
MOV  AX,8DEE
MOV  DX,184B
MUL  DX
MOV  DI,AX
```

Step 2: Generate a decryption key. Again, this may be done with a single instruction, but also with a long, complicated sequence.

Step 3: Decrypt a word. This is only rarely done with a single instruction such as XOR [DI+0CEA],BX, but usually in a convoluted way, such as:

```
MOV  AX,[BP+0D22B]
SUB  AX,SI
MOV  DX,7D67
MUL  DX
MOV  DX,7E3B
MOV  CX,AX
MOV  AX,2386
SUB  AX,CX
XCHG AX,CX
XCHG AX,[BP+0D22B]
```

Step 4: Increment the pointer register. This is quite often done with just two INC instructions, but as one would expect, much more complicated ways may be used as well.

Step 5: Branch back to step 2

Significance and Implications

At the moment three viruses are known which use Dark Avenger's Mutation Engine. They are Dedicated, Fear (a variant of Dedicated) and Pogue (which belongs to the Gotcha! family). The latter virus contains a text string 'TNX2DAV' - Thanks to Dark Avenger.

The appearance of these viruses is not particularly significant. What *is* significant is the availability of the engine *itself* and the fact that virus writers are *already* using it in order to conceal their code. It is inevitable that a series of MtE-encrypted viruses will appear in the near future.

As long as Dark Avenger does not release the actual source code, any anti-virus program which detects the current MtE viruses should also be able to detect any new ones. However - the current version is only 0.91 - which indicates that version 1.00 is under development. There are numerous ways in which the engine could be 'improved' - for obvious reasons they are not listed here.

As would be expected, anti-virus products written before the release of the Mutation Engine were generally ineffective in detecting it. Integrity-checking programs such as those which use cryptographic checksumming were of course able to catch it, *after* it had infected files, but all existing scanners will have to be updated. A handful of static analysis tools were able to determine the presence of highly suspicious self-modifying code in files containing the engine.

Detecting the current version of MtE is not easy - at least not without running the risk of causing regular false positives which will prove unacceptable to the end-user.

A Torture Test

Perhaps the appearance of the Mutation Engine should be considered a torture test for the R&D departments of all the anti-virus companies - if they are not able to detect it in a couple of months they would be well advised to redirect their efforts to other pursuits.

Anti-virus programmers (and teams) are already stretched - the Mutation Engine may well be the straw that breaks quite a few camels' backs. This is the technical editor's personal opinion, but those who disagree are reminded that, even now, some 18 months since its development, only about half of the virus scanners on the market detect V2P6 with 100% consistency and the encryption used in Mr. Washburn's V2Pn series is orders of magnitude simpler than that used in Dark Avenger's Mutation Engine.

New Zealand - Causing Chaos Worldwide

Fridrik Skulason, VB May 1990

This virus originated in New Zealand. The author, a student in Wellington, claims he never intended the virus to run wild. His story is that he destroyed all copies of the virus except one which he kept under lock and key at his home. This copy was stolen and used to infect computers at a local computer store. This happened in early 1988, but the virus has now spread all over the world, although it is still rather rare in Europe - at least in comparison to several Asian countries where it is understood to be rampant.

New Zealand (aka Stoned/Marijuana) is a boot sector virus capable of infecting hard disks as well as diskettes. One in eight times a computer is booted from an infected disk the virus will display the on-screen message:

```
Your PC is now Stoned!
```

The virus seems to have been designed to be non-destructive, but it is capable of causing considerable damage due to the author's lack of technical knowledge.

Operation

When a computer is booted from an infected diskette, the virus
becomes memory-resident. It will first create a hidden 2K block at
the top of memory by decreasing the value stored at the location
0040:0013. The virus then copies itself into this block. All other boot
sector viruses currently known to be in circulation use a similar
method to obtain a memory block for their use, but the size varies.
When DOS is loaded it will use the value stored at the location
0040:0013 to determine the amount of usable memory, but the
memory block reserved by the virus will remain hidden.

The virus then hooks into INT 13h, the disk I/O interrupt. If the
computer was booted from a diskette, there is a one in eight chance
that the screen message above will appear. The method used by the
virus to determine whether the message should be displayed is to
check if the bottom three bits of the byte at 0040:006C contain 000.
This byte is incremented 18.2 times every second and is often used to
provide a simple random number generator. If booting from the hard
disk, the message will not appear.

If the computer was booted from an infected diskette, the virus will
attempt to infect the hard disk. The Partition Boot Record (PBR, also
called Master Boot Record or Disk Bootstrap Sector) is read into
memory and examined. If no hard disk is present, the read operation
will fail and the virus will skip this operation. If the first four bytes
of the PBR do not match the corresponding bytes of the virus, the
hard disk will be infected.

The PBR is stored on track 0, head 0, sector 1 of the hard disk. In
many cases the rest of track 0, head 0 is unused, a 'feature' which
the virus exploits by moving the original PBR to track 0, head 0,
sector 7. The virus code is then written to track 0, head 0, sector 1,
ready to be executed the next time the hard disk is booted. It should
be noted that the New Zealand virus is the only PBR-infecting virus
currently known. [*At the time of writing there are about two hundred
known PBR-infecting viruses. Ed.*]

Finally the virus will load and execute the code found on the original boot sector.

Infection

Infection of hard disks at boot-up has already been described, but diskettes are infected in a different way. When a program performs an INT 13h call, the virus intercepts it. The function number in AH register is checked to see if it is either 2 (disk read) or 3 (disk write). If not, the virus will pass control to the original BIOS routine. Otherwise it will check whether the calling program is attempting to use drive A. If so, the virus will check whether the motor timeout counter at 0040:0040 contains zero - probably to avoid suspicious delays whenever the disk is accessed.

If these conditions are met, the boot sector is read from the diskette and checked for an existing infection. If no infection is found, the original boot sector is moved to track 0, head 1, sector 3. On a 360K diskette this is the last sector of the root directory, so no problems will arise unless the root directory is almost full, containing more than 96 entries. The virus completes the infection by copying itself to sector 1.

Problems Encountered

The New Zealand virus seems to have been designed to be 'benign'. However, the author did not consider the existence of diskettes containing more than 360k of memory. On a 1.2 megabyte diskette, track 0, head 1, sector 3 is not at the end of the root directory, but rather the third directory sector. Since each directory sector contains 16 entries the New Zealand virus may prove highly destructive if the root directory contains more than 32 entries. A similar problem arises in the case of 3.5 inch diskettes.

Another potential problem is that track 0, head 0, sector 7 is not always unused on all hard disks. In certain cases it contains a part of the File Allocation Table and, in such instances infection of the hard disk will cause considerable damage. Such damage would be reparable, however, because DOS stores two copies of the FAT on the hard disk.

Recognition

The easiest way to spot an infected diskette is the absence of the usual DOS messages in the boot sector and the presence of the text strings:

```
Your PC is now Stoned!
```

and

```
LEGALISE MARIJUANA!
```

Text strings can searched for by using the Search Disk for Data option provided by *The Norton Utilities*.

The virus signature stored in the first four bytes of the PBR sector is EA 05 00 C0.

Alternatively use the Search facility of *The Norton Utilities* (or a virus-scanning program) to search for the following hexadecimal patterns:

```
0400 B801 020E 07BB 0002 B901 0033 D29C
0400 B801 020E 07BB 0002 33C9 8BD1 419C
```

Variants

Several variants of this virus have been reported, but only one variant can be confirmed (but see below). The only difference is a relocation of the original PBR to track 0, head 0, sector 2.

One variant is said to display the second message 'LEGALISE MARIJUANA!' (included in the text strings above). Another variant is said to display no message at all making it harder to detect. The existence of both reported variants has not been confirmed.

Editor's note: *Virus Bulletin received a further variant of the New Zealand virus. The virus was reported to have resided on a free disk distributed with a computer magazine. It contains the text message 'Your PC is now Sanded!'. This is a very simple mutation of the existing New Zealand virus which could have been completed within a matter of minutes using a utility such as Norton. The addition of this text string to a search option may be warranted. The hexadecimal patterns above will detect this variant.*

Peach Virus Targets Central Point

VB May 1992

As a rule, computer viruses are badly written and often convey the impression that they are the author's first attempts to write assembly language programs. Indeed, the programming of some viruses is so execrable that most analysts have occasionally felt the irrational desire to tear the diskettes containing some of the worst examples to pieces.

The Peach virus is a refreshing exception - the code is clear and easy to understand. It is a shame that somebody who obviously has a fair understanding of assembly language should choose to waste his time writing viruses.

Structure and Operation

Structurally and functionally, this virus is unremarkable - 887 bytes in length, it is a memory-resident COM (including COMMAND.COM) and EXE file infector, which infects programs on execution. The only unusual feature of the virus is the method it uses to subvert the *Central Point Anti-Virus* product (*CPAV*).

When run, the Peach virus first checks whether it is already resident. Unlike most viruses it does not define a special interrupt function for this purpose, but instead it stores the text string 'Roy' at memory location 0040h:00FCh.

This text is also located at the beginning of a longer message inside the virus - which may be the author's genuine address, or that of someone he wishes to harass or inconvenience (it may also, of course, be completely bogus).

```
Roy Cuatro
No 2 Peach Garden
Meyer Rd. Spore 1543
```

File Infection

If the virus is already resident, it determines whether the current program is structurally a COM or EXE file by looking at the second byte of the internal buffer which stores the beginning of the original program. If that byte is 'Z', the file is assumed to be an EXE file (virtually all EXE files start with 'MZ'). The virus then restores SS:SP and jumps to the original entry point.

If the file is structurally a COM file, the virus restores the first 19 bytes to their original values and jumps to address 100h in the current code segment - transferring control to the original program.

If the virus is not already memory-resident it allocates memory by manipulating the Memory Control Blocks and reducing the size of the last block. The virus then copies itself to the newly created hole and intercepts INT 21h, before returning control to the original program in the way previously described.

The INT 21h Routine

The INT 21h interception routine is straightforward - the virus only intercepts the Load/Execute function (4Bh), which is called whenever the user runs a program. Peach then hooks into interrupts 23h and

24h. The reason for intercepting INT 24h (critical error handler) is obvious - otherwise the familiar 'Abort, Retry, Ignore?' message would appear whenever the virus tried to infect a program on a write-protected diskette. The interception of INT 23h is quite unusual and is probably intended to prevent the user from aborting the infection routine by pressing Ctrl-C.

The virus increments an internal counter and checks whether it is equal to 1. If so, the string 'Roy' is stored at location 0040h:00FCh, to indicate that the virus is resident. Why this is not done at the same time as the virus goes memory-resident is not clear. If the counter has reached 27 the virus jumps into ROM at address FFFFh:0000h, which reboots the computer. This means that with the virus active, every 27th program run will cause a reboot, regardless of whether any other programs actually become infected. The virus also subverts *CPAV* at this time, as described later.

In order to determine whether to infect a program, the virus reads its first 24 bytes. If it appears to be an EXE file (again determined by checking whether the second byte is 'Z'), the virus checks the initial IP value. If it is equal to the one used by the virus, the program is assumed to be infected and is allowed to run normally. The virus next checks the initial SP value and does not infect the program if the value is equal to 7200h or 7600h. The virus presumably does this to avoid infecting an as yet unidentified program which uses self-checking code (the most obvious candidate would be McAfee's *SCAN* but this program has different initial SP values, as do the EXE files in *Central Point Anti-Virus*).

At this point the virus checks whether its INT 21h routine has been modified starting with a PUSH AX instruction. The reason for doing this is not clear. The most probable explanation is that this checks for the presence of an INT 21h-monitoring program. If the PUSH AX instruction is not found, the virus proceeds with the infection by modifying the header to reflect the necessary changes and appending its code.

COM files are processed in a slightly different way. Files shorter than 512 bytes or longer than 64511 bytes are never infected. Otherwise the virus compares the beginning of the program to a 19-byte stub of code located at the beginning of infected files. The purpose of this code is to transfer control to the virus located at the end of the file. This is a more complex procedure than the more usual modification of a JMP instruction. If the blocks do not match, the program will be infected.

Attacking *CPAV*

As mentioned before, the unusual feature of the Peach virus is its ability to attack the *Central Point Anti-Virus* package. This is done by exploiting a fundamental design flaw in this anti-virus program. When *CPAV* is run for the first time it creates a file (called CHKLIST.CPS) containing a checksum and other information for every executable file. On subsequent executions the scanner calculates the checksum for the file, and only if it does not match the stored checksum will the file actually be scanned for known viruses.

The *CPAV* authors took some precautions against one line of attack; by not publishing the details of the checksumming algorithm used they denied the attacker proprietary information which might enable him to infect a file, and then update the relevant checksum. Such subversion appears possible: all copies of *CPAV* seem to use the same, apparently trivial method to calculate the checksum. However, the Peach virus exploits a far more fundamental weakness within CPAV which its designers overlooked.

The Peach virus simply deletes file CHKLIST.CPS (the checksum file). It seems incredible, but this method actually *works* - the *CPAV* program recreates this file the next time it is run, calculating a new checksum for infected file(s) and fails to indicate a change to the integrity of the files. Central Point Software will presumably close this loophole in the next version; in the meantime, users of the package should be grateful that this virus has not yet been reported 'in the wild'.

Peach

Aliases:	none known
Type:	Appending Parasitic on COM files (including COMMAND.COM) between 512 bytes and 64511 bytes in length and EXE files. Code becomes resident in newly created MCB.
Infection:	887 bytes
Intercepts:	INT 23h
	INT 24h (Critical Error Handler)
	INT 21h for infection route via 4Bh only
Trigger:	Every 27th program executed causes a reboot. The virus subverts checksumming method employed in Central Point Anti-Virus versions 1.00 through 1.20
	System recognition via 'Are you there?' call which places text 'Roy' at memory location 0040:00FCh

File recognition:

```
33C9  33D2  E851  FFB4  40B9  1800
8BD7  807D  015A  7406  B913  00BA
```

Spanish Telecom

Jim Bates, VB January 1991

Another virus attempting to make a political (?) point has recently come to hand from Spain. [*The virus was identified at two separate academic sites - Oxford University and City University, London, UK, in December 1990. Ed.*] The virus has been called 'Spanish Telecom' for reasons which will become apparent as this analysis progresses.

Multi-Partite Structure

This virus is a true multi-partite virus in that it functions both as a **parasitic virus** infecting COM files, and as a **boot sector** virus which infects the Master Boot Sector of the first fixed disk drive as well as the boot sector of **any** type of floppy disk. The code contains a particularly vicious trigger routine which will overwrite all data on both the first and second fixed disk drives. The trigger routine is invoked from the boot code section of the virus after the 400th infected boot cycle. The parasitic code is encrypted and contains plain text at the end of the code which reads:

```
Virus Anti - C.T.N.E. (c)1990 Grupo
Holokausto.
Kampanya Anti-Telefonica. Menos tarifas y
```

```
mas servicios.Programmed in Barcelona
(Spain). 23-8-90. -666-
```

The final '666' may be a reference to the 666 (Number of the Beast) virus since certain techniques first noticed there have been used here! The phrase translates roughly as 'Lower tariffs, more service.' Another message which is separately encrypted is displayed during the overwriting activity of the trigger routine:

```
Campana Anti-TELEFONICA (Barcelona)
```

Analysis of this code is best undertaken by considering the parasitic and boot sections separately.

Parasitic Analysis

This is undoubtedly the most untidy code which I have examined. There are many repetitions and several bugs which will reveal the presence of the virus long before the trigger routine is invoked.

The virus code is attached at the end of COM files between 128 and 60999 bytes in length (inclusive). COMMAND.COM is specifically excluded from infection as is any file beginning with the letters 'IBM' (the IBM system files). The initial four bytes of the host file are saved within the virus code and overwritten with an appropriate jump instruction to pass processing to the virus code.

The infective length of the parasitic code is 3,700 bytes (this includes the boot code). The virus code begins with an 85 byte section which contains 'armoured' code to detect debugging software and several random instructions which are presumably intended to prevent the extraction of a reliable search string. There are two different versions of this 85 byte 'header' routine, only one of which is actually positioned for use during the file infection process. There are, therefore, **two** distinct search strings for the parasitic code although each confirms the existence of the same virus.

Both 'header' code routines perform the same functions: check for debug presence, locate the position of the virus code within the host segment and decrypt the remaining code.

Processing then checks to see whether the virus is memory-resident . This is done by collecting the byte at offset 1BCh of low memory and XORing it with 13h, the result is then checked against the next byte at offset 1BDh. If they are the same then the virus is resident and processing returns to the host program. The values of these two bytes are changed regularly by the virus during its intercept operations but by simply XORing them together, regardless of their values, the result will be 13h if the virus is resident in memory.

If the virus is not resident, the current INT 21h vector is collected and stored in memory via direct access to page zero of memory where the interrupt vectors are stored. The virus code is then installed in high memory and 3984 bytes are removed from system memory to accommodate it.

The next set of instructions collects a pseudo-random number from the system clock and uses it to index into a table of word addresses. The selected word is then inserted as the offset portion of the INT 21h vector in low memory, the segment portion being set to the virus' own segment in high memory. This random process of selection ensures that the actual offset stored in the interrupt table will vary from infection to infection. Each address, though different, points to a jump instruction which takes processing to a single INT 21h handler within the virus code. There are 14 entries in the address table although only 7 of them are used and this, together with other sections of the code, suggests that other techniques may have been tried (or are being prepared). Once the interrupt handler has been installed, a special call is made to it which completes the installation process. This call consists of putting 4B21h into AX and issuing an INT 21h request.

The special call is routed by the virus' handler to an installation routine which uses the single step INT 01h capability in the same way as the Flip virus [*see VB, September 1990, pp.18-20. Ed.*] to 'strip' out any extraneous handlers from the targeted interrupt chain. Interrupts treated in this way are 13h, 21h and 40h and the stripped vectors are temporarily installed during file infection and repaired when the process has completed. Thus any TSR monitoring software which uses installed handlers will need to contain reliable self-testing routines to guard against this type of subversion.

Interrupt Handling

The virus interrupt handler intercepts six different function requests within the DOS services interrupt: function 4B21h has already been mentioned and there is another special call using a value of 4B20h which does nothing. This gives rise to speculation that further developments may be planned. The SEEK function (42h) is intercepted when accompanied by subfunction 02 (from End of File). This checks to see whether the file has been infected and if so, modifies the pointer to subtract the length of the virus code before returning the End of File position. The two alternative sets of Find First and Find Next functions (11h - 12h and 4Eh - 4Fh) are similarly intercepted to return a modified file size on infected files. The main intercept however, is that applied to the Load and Execute function (4B00h). This is used to select and infect files with a COM extension (subject to the name and size exceptions mentioned earlier). Once a suitable file has been identified, the INT 13h and INT 40h vectors are temporarily replaced with their stripped equivalents and a simple handler for the critical error interrupt (24h) is installed.

The usual process of file infection is then invoked whereby the target file date, time and attributes are collected and stored, and the file is opened for Read/Write access (attributes are modified if necessary). The correct initial jump is calculated and the first four bytes of the target file copied and stored before being overwritten by a jump to the virus code. Certain sections of the virus code are then modified by the addition of random data values generated from a system clock reading.

The next stage involves using one of these data values as the new encryption key into one of the two 85 bytes decryption headers (chosen at random). The header is written (unencrypted) to the end of the host file. All the virus code is then encrypted and written to the end of the host file one byte at a time - each byte is collected, encrypted and written on an individual basis. This removes the need for a special buffer or a decrypt/recrypt cycle.

The final stage is to close the file and reset the date, time and attributes to their original settings. As a marker to indicate that the file is infected, the date setting is modified in a similar way to the 4K (or Frodo) virus by adding 100 to the year field. Modified interrupt vectors are reset to their previous values before processing returns to the calling routine.

During the installation of the handlers, a check is made to see whether the Master Boot Sector of the first hard drive is infected with the virus' boot code. If the disk is not infected then the boot section of the virus code is installed in sector 1, head 0, track 0. The second sector of virus code is stored in sector 6 of the same track and the original boot sector is stored in sector 7. This will cause problems of access on some machines which use these sectors for other purposes.

Boot Sector Analysis

The boot section of this virus functions completely independently of the parasitic portion and both sections will almost certainly be in memory simultaneously. This may explain the almost obsessive concern with revectoring interrupts during the parasitic file infection. However, while the parasitic code contains all the virus routines, the boot section is limited to two sectors of self-contained code. **Thus a machine infected with only the boot code will not infect files, only other disks**.

The only items worthy of note in the boot code are the trigger routine, the floppy infection routine and the interrupt redirection.

The interrupt redirection intercepts requests to INT 13h for both floppy and hard drives. A Read or Write request to either the first or second floppy drive will result in the disk being checked for infection and infected if possible. The routine is unusual in that it will only complete the check and infection if the motors of both the first two floppy drives are **not** running.

INT 13h requests to the first hard drive are intercepted and tested to see whether they are Read or Write. A Write request to the Master Boot Sector of the first hard drive is changed into a Verify call so that the sector will not be overwritten if the virus is resident. Read requests are tested to see which sector (on head 0, track 0) is wanted and re-routed accordingly. Requests for sector 1 are given sector 7 (where the original boot sector is stored) and requests for either sector 6 or 7 are given sector 5. In a similar way to the Brain virus, Spanish Telecom, when resident, will attempt to prevent inspection of the true boot sector by ordinary utilities.

Floppy Infection

If an uninfected floppy is accessed, the virus will attempt to infect it and the storage sectors used for the second sector of code will vary according to a table maintained within the virus code. Remember that both the first and second (A and B) drives are affected.

Floppy disk infection indicating the head and sector location of the virus code on diskettes is shown below:

Floppy Type	Virus Location	
	Head	Sector
160K - 5.25"	0	6
180K - 5.25"	0	8
320K - 5.25"	1	1
360K - 5.25"	1	2
720K - 5.25" or 3.5"	1	4
1.2M - 5.25"	1	0Dh
1.44M -3.5"	1	0Eh

It will be seen that infected disks may become unreadable as virus code overwrites sections of the FAT or root directory. To complete this information you should note that the virus code occupies sectors 1 and 6 of a hard disk, with a copy of the original boot sector being stored in sector 7 (all on head 0, track 0). [*This is the first virus known to VB which will infect all diskettes regardless of density - the table above is a graphic reminder of the need to write-protect floppies, even those dedicated to pure data transfer. Ed.*]

Trigger Routine

When a PC is booted from an infected hard disk, a counter within the boot code is incremented and tested to see whether it has passed 400 (190h). If it has not, the code is written back to the boot sector and processing continues normally. However, when the counter does reach this number, processing immediately passes to the trigger routine. This is one of the nastiest, most destructive triggers I have seen; it overwrites all sectors of both the first and (if there is one present) the second hard drive with random information from boot-time low memory. The overwriting routine will be completed a number of times (for each drive) depending upon the number of heads on the drive. On each pass, the encrypted message reproduced earlier in this analysis will be displayed.

Detection

It has been necessary to extract a different recognition string for each version of the parasitic code and these are as follows:

```
Header 1 - 8B1D B200 83FB 0074 18BF 5500 B2

Header 2 - 83ED 09BE 2001 03F5 FCB6
```

It should be noted that the presence of **either** of these strings at the appropriate offset (into the virus code) is an indication of infection.

Infective length of the parasite is 3700 bytes (appended on LOAD and EXECUTE).

Recognition of the boot virus code is simpler but note should be taken of the interrupt redirection discussed above. The code is not encrypted and the recognition string is as follows:

```
8A0E EC00 BE70 0003 F18A 4C02 8A74 03C3
```

The Starship Virus

Jim Bates, VB November 1992

When taking virus code apart, it is my practice to produce, by the end of it, a full printed disassembly which is commented on every line. This is not because I am any sort of perfectionist but simply because if I need to refer to the work later, I invariably find myself unable to remember much more about the virus than its name. As well as the normal disclaimer and limitation messages for the benefit of other researchers to whom these listings are passed, the disassemblies are usually liberally sprinkled with salty observations on the personality, physical attributes and parentage of the virus writer. Of course I have a much freer rein when making these remarks than that allowed within the sober pages of *Virus Bulletin* (maybe one day a virus writer will try to sue me for libel!). However, even my copious store of coarse, cutting and disparaging phrases was stretched when dissecting the latest virus - Starship.

The Starship virus is undoubtedly the most convoluted collection of garbage it has yet been my misfortune to examine. The best that can be said of it is that it is significantly less boring than the usual offerings.

My information is that this is yet another product of the misbegotten group of virus writers in Bulgaria and it certainly contains many of the tricks and devices which are common in their operations. Despite the convolutions however, this virus is quite easy to detect and remove in its boot sector form.

An Overview

The name Starship exists within the encrypted portion of the code and is obviously intended by the writer to be the name of his creation. From a research point of view, this virus has some interesting variations on several themes: code encryption, both static and dynamic, interrupt stripping, code randomisation, mobile routines, armouring, stealth, multi-partite - about the only classifications missing are companion and linking!

A simple search pattern is not possible for the parasitic form of the virus, but the initial sector of the boot infection is not encrypted and can easily be recognised. On a clean machine, once the virus has been detected it is also quite easy to remove, and even disks partitioned in a non-standard way can be disinfected, if care is taken.

This specimen is somewhat different from other multi-partite viruses in that the same code functions as a boot sector virus (infecting the MBS) on fixed disks, and as a parasitic COM and EXE infector on floppy disks in drive A or B. It should be noted however, that since the parasitic portion infects any COM file greater than 1917 bytes in size, on an infected machine a floppy disk formatted with the install system option set (/S) will certainly have COMMAND.COM infected and possibly the system files too (if they have a COM extension).

This report describes both boot and parasitic installation and infection processes, as well as the more unusual techniques, although the nature of the internal operation rather precludes the usual blow-by-blow description without an abundant collection of diagrams.

Boot Infection and General Operation

As mentioned above, this virus only affects fixed disks and a further limitation is that only disks with an active partition whose type number is below 5 are infected. For reference the relevant type numbers are as follows:

- Type 1 is a DOS 12 bit FAT partition

- Type 2 is a XENIX file system partition

- Type 3 is the obsolete XENIX /usr file system

- Type 4 is the DOS 16 bit FAT partition

This excludes the common Huge DOS partition type and therefore will thankfully limit the platforms on which this virus can exist.

The virus infects the Master Boot Sector of the disk (at track 0, head 0, sector 1) by changing only three bytes. These constitute the progression or Partition start address in the active entry of the Partition Table itself and result in the master boot code loading the first sector of the virus rather than the Partition Boot Sector. The actual virus code will be located in the last six sectors of the active partition and is in two parts.

The practical upshot of this method of infection is far-reaching. No actual code is changed within the Master Boot Sector; only the size of the active partition is altered. This does mean that some minor work will need to be done to certain scanners to ensure accurate detection of the virus.

The first section of the virus to be loaded is not encrypted and contains code which will load and decrypt the remaining five sectors of viral code and place them into the initial memory locations together with the relevant system insertions. This virus does not 'hook' the interrupts in the usual way via the interrupt table, but inserts new addresses into the DOS function dispatch routine. Thus straight examination of the interrupt table will not reveal tell-tale addresses, although another area of low memory does show positive indications of the virus presence.

The bulk of the code is also mobile, being dynamically encrypted and relocated during machine operation - with special attention being given to this during the operation of TSR programs. Presumably this is done in an attempt to remain difficult to locate. However, as with all of the memory resident viruses that I have examined, these attempts to remain hidden are eventually futile since there must always be some point where the virus code keeps contact with the system services and that remains one of their most vulnerable areas.

In this instance, there is a highly specific memory area at 0000:04B0h which reveals instantly whether the virus is resident. On most machines, this area is reserved for Optical Disk Driver software and will normally contain zeros. The virus checks this area during installation and only becomes resident if it contains zeros. In this case, the virus inserts either an INT 0B0h instruction (0CDh, 0B0h) or two NOPs (90h, 90h). The third byte is a FAR CALL instruction (9Ah).

Self Protected Code

Normally, resident viruses use the DOS services to protect their memory locations in the same way as TSR programs, or else they manipulate the memory control blocks so that the virus code appears to be a legitimate part of the system. The Starship virus occupies around 2.5 KBytes of memory and the fact that it makes its own arrangements for protection means that simple memory tests such as that done by the CHKDSK program do not detect any reduction of system RAM.

During the initialisation phase of the infection, the virus uses the single step interrupt to monitor the disk BIOS routine and strip it back to a ROM entry point. This technique (sometimes called tunnelling) is a favourite trick of the Bulgarian virus writers, although it was first demonstrated as one of the hardware features of the *Intel* 8086 series of processors.

Boot Stealth

Once installed and initialised, the virus monitors system activity in a number of different ways. To avoid the possibility of system malfunction due to the mismatch of parameters within the Partition Table, the virus examines disk access calls and intercepts requests for the Master Boot Sector. These are held while the MBS is read into the caller's buffer and then the three address bytes are replaced with their correct values. The request is then returned with the corrected MBS.

Once again this is a vulnerable point of the virus, since use of a simple Partition Table Editor (such as the Disk Editor in *The Norton Utilities*) after booting from a clean floppy disk will immediately show that the partition appears to be only 6 sectors long! For example, if the partition table normally shows the active partition starting at track 0, head 1, sector 1 and finishing at track 449, head 6, sector 17 - this will show a partition size of 53,533 sectors. If this machine was infected with the Starship virus, *Norton* would show the starting address as track 449, head 6, sector 12 and all the other details would be the same - plainly a conflict of values.

System Monitoring

Apart from the detection of programs becoming TSR, other system activity monitored by the code concerns the creation of files. Here, the monitoring routine intercepts system requests to CREATE a file (function 3Ch) by first testing if the file is to be created on either of the floppy drives A or B. It if is, the extension is checked to see whether it is either COM or EXE and if so the name is copied into a buffer maintained by the virus. Only one buffer exists, so a check is made to ensure that it is empty before being used (thus only one file at a time can be marked for infection). The allocated handle is also stored for similar reference along with the creation date and time and the file attributes.

The DOS CLOSE function is also monitored and when the file being created (and referenced by the virus) is closed, the interception routine checks that the file is greater than 1917 bytes and is not already infected. If it meets these requirements, it is infected, then closed and the virus buffer is cleared for the next target.

At first sight this might seem to be an attempt to subvert development machines where program files are continually being created. However, it should be noted that internally, whenever a file is copied, a CREATE file request is issued for the destination filename. Thus on an infected machine, just copying suitable files from the fixed disk to a floppy disk will cause the destination file to become infected. It is important to appreciate that the infection process does not happen when files are copied in the reverse direction (i.e.: to the fixed disk). Only if a file is being created on a floppy disk, regardless of where it comes from, will it be infected.

Parasitic Encryption

When a file is to be infected, the virus encrypts the whole of its code before writing it to the file. It does this by first making a copy of itself at offset 50h of an available segment (usually in high video memory) and then building a variable and randomised decryption routine into the preceding space (this does not mean however, that the decryption routine is always 50h bytes long). The encrypted virus code preceded by the decryption routine is appended to the target file and appropriate changes are made to the initial bytes (in the case of COM files) or the program header (for EXE files). So when an infected file is run, the virus decryption routine is executed first.

Quite simply, when this virus is invoked from an infected file, it will immediately attempt to infect the Master Boot Sector and active partition of the first fixed disk. If it succeeds, the virus becomes resident and functions exactly as if it had been loaded from an infected boot system.

File Recognition

Because both the encryption key and the method change with each infection, simple string recognition will not uniquely identify this virus. However, within the virus code there are two distinct recognition techniques used to prevent re-infection of files. I have not been able to check the uniqueness of these methods, so there is a possibility that they might cause false positives if used without any other qualifying conditions. False positives, of course, cause no problems within the virus code, they simply mean that the identified file will not be infected even though it was clean. However, the identification methods are interesting and might prove useful, so I will describe them here:

EXE file infection recognition is achieved by first checking that the header contains the required 'MZ' identifier. The contents of the header are then checked to ensure that the SP field contains a value of 800h - the IP field is 13h or lower - and the result of subtracting the CS field from the SS field is 100h. If these three criteria are met, then the file is deemed already to be infected.

COM file infection uses a completely different routine which checks to see whether the first byte of the program is 0E9h. This signifies a jump instruction and if this byte is found, the virus collects the succeeding word offset and calculates where in the file the destination of the jump is. If this jump is not found, the file is treated as an EXE file.

Once the jump offset has been calculated, the virus reads seventeen bytes from that position in the file and then applies an algorithm which determines whether within those seventeen bytes there exists a word which represents a call to interrupts 01h, 02h, 03h, 11h, 12h or 13h. Any of these will result in the infection routine aborting since one of them will exist in the entry code to an infected COM file.

Armouring

The writer has expended tremendous energy in an attempt to armour this virus - that is, attempting to make disassembly as difficult as possible by introducing spurious bytes and code instructions intended to trip up automatic disassemblers. The fact that this report has been written is ample evidence that he failed miserably. While I am dissecting virus code I use a number of different monitors, disassemblers and debuggers (both hardware and software) - some commercially available and others that I have developed for my own highly specific purposes. I am delighted to report that even with the heavy armouring in Starship, no modifications were needed to any of my tools in order for them to break down the code accurately into its constituent parts. This is no testament to my ability but rather a measure of the virus writer's programming ability. Any armouring is a challenge; it could slow down the disassembly process considerably - but not in this case!

Trigger

The trigger routine appears similar to a published routine which displays a simulated moving starfield. Typically however, the writer appears not to have understood the algorithm and the routine contains several bugs which result in random garbage being displayed on the screen at random intervals. When this happens, the user should wait until keyboard control returns and then exit the current application as soon as possible (saving any work as necessary). Only video memory is affected and any other corruption can be avoided with care.

Damage

Apart from the deliberately disruptive trigger routine, this virus does not apparently set out to cause deliberate corruption. However, since I contend that there is no such thing as a 'benign' virus, it is relevant to note that when the fixed disk boot infection takes place, the virus makes no attempt to determine whether the disk sectors it uses are already occupied by legitimate files. Thus this virus will cause damage on machines where any of the final six sectors of the partition are currently in use. Conversely, once the virus has occupied these sectors, they are not marked as being in use and they will therefore in due course probably be allocated for use by DOS and be overwritten by legitimate data. This will certainly cause affected machines to crash during the boot sequence.

Starship

Aliases: None known.

Type: Memory-resident, multi-partite.

Infection: COM and EXE files longer than 1917 bytes, and Master Boot Sectors.

Recognition:

Files   See analysis.

System   90h 90h 9Ah or 0CDh 0B0h 9Ah in 0000:04B0h to 0000:04B2h indicates that the virus is resident.

Hex Pattern

for the boot sector pointed to by the address within the active entry of the Partition Table:

```
B937  00BE  D606  BFC0  02F3  A4BF
B004  B908  00F3  A41E  C506  4C00
```

Intercepts:

INT 13h DISK READ. Cleans MBS and returns.

INT 20h EXIT PROGRAM. Used to indicate to the virus that relocation is necessary as memory allocation will change when an application terminates.

INT 27h TSR. Used to indicate to the virus that some memory manipulation will be necessary.

INT 21h functions:

31h TSR. Re-routed to virus INT 27h handler.

3Ch CREATE FILE. Collects filename if target is floppy disk and extension is COM or EXE.

3Eh CLOSE FILE. Infects if file to be closed was noted by 3Ch intercept.

4Ch EXIT PROGRAM. Re-routed into the virus INT 20h handler.

Trigger: Displays multicoloured garbage to the screen at random intervals.

Removal: Specific and generic disinfection of the MBS is possible. Under clean conditions, identify and replace infected files.

Tequila - A Cocktail of Viral Tricks

Richard Jacobs, VB June 1991

The Tequila virus was originally sent to *VB* under the guise 'Yugoslavian Virus', however the virus contains an encrypted text message declaring its Swiss origin. This message starts with the greeting:

```
'Welcome to T.TEQUILA's latest production'
```

This message suggests that the writer of this virus has also written other, less sophisticated viruses. The text goes on to give a Swiss post office box number, through which the author, supposedly, can be contacted. [*The alleged authors of this virus were arrested by Swiss police on May 20th 1991 - see VB, June 1991, p.24. Ed.*]

Self-Modifying Encryption

Tequila is a sophisticated, self-modifying, encrypted virus using techniques similar to those of Mark Washburn in his V2P6 virus [*see VB, April 1991, pp.18-20. Ed.*]. It was expected that Washburn's tactics would be adopted quickly by virus writers in their efforts to conceal their programs - this virus provides further and somewhat alarming evidence that this is the case. It should be noted that the encryption method used in this virus has not been copied from any of

Washburn's viruses - the author has developed a proprietary method. The virus is also the latest in the current trend of multi-partite viruses, infecting both EXE files and the Master Boot Sector of fixed disks. No hexadecimal search pattern can be extracted to identify infected programs but a search pattern can be located in infected boot sectors.

Trigger Routine

The virus contains a non-destructive memory-resident routine which conceals increases in the size of infected files and which triggers the virus' only visible side-effect. Under certain conditions, depending on the date and number of files infected, the virus displays a crude on-screen Mandelbrot (fractal) set. The virus then prompts the user to execute an INT 21h function, which displays a text message giving the name T. Tequila and the Swiss P.O.Box number. The message continues with the text:

```
'Loving thoughts to L.I.N.D.A. BEER and
TEQUILA forever !'
```

Operation

When an infected file is run the virus decrypts itself in memory, reads the Master Boot Sector of the first fixed disk and checks it for previous infection. If the disk has not already been infected, this sector and the virus are written out to the last six sectors of the DOS partition. The size of the partition is reduced by 6 sectors so that the virus will not be overwritten. The virus boot code is copied over the copy of the Master Boot Sector in memory, preserving any error messages and the Partition Table. This new infected sector is written out to the normal Master Boot Sector, which closely resembles a normal boot sector in all but execution. This is one of several features to reduce the likelihood of detection. Finally, the virus returns control to the original program.

The majority of the virus only executes when a PC is booted from an infected disk. Should this happen, the virus reserves the top 3 KBytes of base memory, loads itself into this area and transfers control to this copy of itself. Next the virus reads the original Master Boot Sector. The interrupt vectors for INT 1Ch and INT 21h are then read and INT 1Ch is redirected to point to a routine within the virus, before control is transferred to the original Master Boot Sector and the boot procedure is allowed to continue.

INT 1Ch is the clock tick interrupt and is generated 18.2 times a second. This routine checks whether or not the INT 21h vector has changed (i.e. whether or not DOS has been loaded). If it has not, normal processing resumes. Once INT 21h has been altered, INT 1Ch is returned to normal and INT 13h (BIOS disk services) and INT 21h (DOS functions) are redirected to routines within the virus.

The INT 13h intercept passes calls straight through to the normal routine unless an attempt is made to read from, or write to, the Master Boot Sector of the first fixed disk. In this case the call is diverted to the original Master Boot Sector, thus concealing the presence of the virus.

The INT 21h routine has four different functions. The first of these is a simple check to find out whether the virus is already memory-resident. The second intercepts any FindFirst, or FindNext, file calls. Both ASCII and FCB calls are intercepted. Calls to ascertain the length of files are subverted. If a file has its seconds field set to 62, then the length of the virus is subtracted from the file length. Again, this is another stealth feature to render the virus invisible to the operator.

The third routine handles the screen display, when triggered.

The final INT 21h function intercepted by the virus is function 4Bh. This is the DOS Load & Execute call and is the normal way of loading programs to be executed. First, the virus checks the name of the file. If the name contains 'SC' or 'V', then the file will not be infected. This is probably a crude attempt to avoid infecting **Virus**

SCanning software. Otherwise INT 24h (Critical Error handler) is disabled and the file attributes are read and saved, before being cleared. Next the file is opened and the date and time it was last written to are saved. The first 28 bytes of the file are then read. The file will only be infected if it is an EXE file.

62 Seconds Stamp

Although Tequila uses the ubiquitous 62 seconds stamp to identify infected files in the FindFirst/Next file routines, it does not rely on this for determining whether or not to infect files. Instead the checksum stored in the file header is read. This checksum is calculated by the linker when the program is first created, but is not used by any current versions of DOS. When the virus infects a file, it overwrites the checksum with a word taken at random from the virus decryption routine.

In order to check for a previous infection, the virus scans its own decryption routine for this checksum. If it finds the checksum with the decryption routine, it assumes the file is already infected. The virus then sets the seconds field of the file time stamp to 62, closes the file and restores INT 24h and the file attributes. If there is no match with the checksum, the virus assumes the file has not already been infected.

Variable Decryption

The encryption method used in this virus is somewhat more advanced than that used in the 1260 [*see VB, March 1990, p.12*] and V2P2 viruses but less flexible than that of V2P6 [*see VB, April 1991, pp.18-20. Ed.*].

Once an uninfected file has been identified, the virus adjusts the values stored in the EXE file header to provide a stack for the virus, to set up the virus entry point and to allow for the increased length of the infected file.

The virus then generates a new copy of itself and attaches it to the end of the original file. This process involves generating a new decryption routine. First, the old decryption routine is overwritten with a random word obtained from the system time. This random number is then used to build up the decryption routine. The routine is generated as several modules which can be put together in any combination. This provides a much more flexible set of routines than seen in the Whale virus [*see p.268*].

Each module can also contain randomly placed instructions that have no effect on the functionality of the virus, but further increase the differences between each copy of it. Although Tequila always uses the same registers for the decryption routine, it does not always use each register for the same purpose - for example, SI and BX can be interchanged.

Likewise, the virus does not always use the same instructions in the decryption routine. For instance the actual encryption can be performed either by an XOR or by adding a key to the value of each byte in the virus.

One unusual feature of this virus is that the decryption routine itself is used as the *key* for decryption. Once the new decryption routine has been created, the virus is encrypted in memory, written to the end of the file and then decrypted in memory again. The file time stamp is then set to 62 seconds and one word of the decryption routine is written to the checksum in the file header, for identifying infected files. The new file header is then written out to the file. Finally, the file date and time are restored along with INT 24h and the file attributes. Control is then returned to DOS, which will load and execute the program normally.

Detection and Removal

Removal of this virus from infected files is by the normal procedure of deleting the files and replacing them with write-protected backup copies of the master software.

Disinfection of the Master Boot Sector sector is less straightforward unless you keep a backup of the Master Boot Sector on floppy disk. If such a backup is available removal of this (and all other currently known boot sector viruses) is simple! Otherwise some work with a disk editor is required to locate and replace the original Master Boot Sector. In both cases reboot the PC from a clean, write-protected system floppy disk before starting. **Unless all of the infected program files are replaced, the boot sector will be reinfected immediately an infected program is run**.

Detection of the virus in the Master Boot Sector can be determined using a straightforward hexadecimal pattern, shown below:

```
B82A 0250 B805 028B 0E30 7C41 8B16 327C
```

However, no pattern can be used to detect the virus in program files. The use of professional virus scanning software capable of algorithmic detection is essential if the above pattern is located in the Master Boot Sector.

Conclusions

The Tequila virus displays a veritable cocktail of programming techniques designed to increase its chances of spreading undetected. The use of various stealth techniques, self-modifying encryption and multi-partite characteristics infecting both programs and boot sectors places it in the 'hybrid' category.

Ironically, despite all the author's efforts to conceal this program, it is comparatively easy to develop reliable detection routines for inclusion in scanning software.

Tremor - A Shaky Start For DOS 6?

Jim Bates, VB March 1993

It is unfortunately true that no matter how well written an anti-virus program is, it can be targeted by appropriate code. Part of the skill in writing anti-virus software is to appreciate this problem and install comprehensive precautions that make targeting as difficult as possible. The author of the Tremor virus, which is at large in Germany, has obviously disassembled several anti-virus packages and built an awareness of their methods into the virus. Some are avoided and others are subverted as the virus tries to wriggle its way through the defences. Disassembly and analysis of this virus reveals routines which target specific packages, but there are other routines which I was unable to identify. All of the testing and analysis of this virus was done on machines using DOS 5.0 and below.

There is a strong possibility that most of this virus is directed at DOS 6, which I understand contains some built-in anti-virus precautions. If this *is* the case, it simply confirms that any sort of global attempt to include virus protection within a system will provide an easily accessible target that virus writers will be unable to ignore. Even with the highest internal security checks, such protection is bound to be extremely vulnerable.

General Information

Tremor is an encrypting, resident, parasitic virus which appends 4000 bytes of code to COM and EXE files. It marks infected files by adding 100 to the year value in the Date/Time field of the file directory entry. This marker has been used by other viruses (notably the 4K, or Frodo, virus) and many packages will detect it quite easily. However, when the virus is resident, a stealth routine removes the marker if any attempt at monitoring is detected. This virus is capable of using the upper memory blocks or extended memory when it becomes resident.

Tremor infects files by simply appending its code to the end of the file and altering the file header to ensure that the virus code is executed first. It is therefore possible to recover the original file image by removing the virus code and repairing the file header. Once infected by this virus it is essential that a machine be booted from a clean system disk because the virus will invariably infect COMMAND.COM or any other file named in CONFIG.SYS as the command interpreter.

Virus Installation

When initially executed, the virus first decrypts itself and enters an installation routine. This collects the current system date and compares it against a date inserted when the file was infected. If the current date is less than three months after the file was first infected, the code is modified to prevent the shake effect trigger from being processed. The virus then checks the DOS version and aborts if it is 3.29 or below.

Next, a check is made which depends upon previous infection conditions. If when the file was originally infected an INT 01h routine was installed and a function 30h request (get DOS version) was detected which had the current date in the CX:DX registers, the code which processes the installation check is modified so that the virus will not function. This INT 01h check is presumably a test for the existence of an anti-virus monitor. The design is such that if the check fails, installation continues - otherwise installation is aborted and processing eventually returns to the host program. In this way, the check also functions as an 'Are you there?' call.

Installation continues by testing for the presence of extra memory. This virus first attempts to install into extended memory and if that fails it tries the upper memory blocks. If this too is unsuccessful, the virus installs itself into the top of conventional memory.

Once the code has been copied into the chosen memory block, the INT 21h and INT 15h vectors are collected and stored within the virus code. Then an INT 01h routine is invoked which uses the techniques known as tunnelling to determine the true system entry point of the INT 21h service routine. The virus then checks if an additional TSR has been hooked into this interrupt and if so, this entry point is also stored and the MCB marker is checked for the unusual value of 44h. This too is probably a check for the presence of anti-virus software!

Processing continues by creating a temporary disk transfer area and searching for the first file in the root directory with the archive bit set. The date stamp of this file is checked and compared to a previous date collected in similar fashion when the file was first infected. If these dates do not match then the shake effect trigger routine is disabled. Thus a newly infected file introduced to a machine will not cause the trigger to activate.

The system environment is then examined for the file specified in the 'COMSPEC=' variable. This file is infected by using a special call to the newly resident virus code. This means that the command interpreter file (usually COMMAND.COM) will become infected during the first execution of the virus code. This special attention to the command interpreter ensures that on subsequent reboots, the virus code becomes resident before most anti-virus software. After this infection, the installation routine concludes by repairing the host file image in memory and erasing all traces of the initial virus code from memory (leaving just the resident code active).

Resident Operation

Most DOS function requests are intercepted, but under a varying range of conditions. A large proportion of the resident code is involved with avoiding detection by different checking programs. For example, special code is included to ensure that the DOS CHKDSK program does not show anything amiss. These tests are too convoluted to list here and include several self-modifying options which are applied under highly specific circumstances.

However, one check worthy of special mention concerns *Central Point Anti-Virus*. Some anti-virus detection software needs to disable its own activities under certain circumstances and such potential security loopholes are usually well protected within the code. During the DOS interception routine, the Tremor virus issues a special INT 13h call which appears to turn off the Central Point vector checking routines and thus allows unimpeded changes to be made to the system vectors.

Infection of files seems to take place during most of the intercepted functions but conditions vary according to the prevailing system condition.

Within the resident code there is a check to see if the target file name begins with CH, ME, MI, F2, F-, SY, SI and PM. If so, temporary changes are made to the allocation of system memory to avoid detection. Similarly, if the second and third letters of the file name are 'RJ' then part of the interception routines are disabled.

Triggers

This virus has two trigger routines. The first is called very rarely (on a random basis) and produces a slight vertical movement in the screen display before causing the machine to hang. The second routine is hooked into the INT 15h intercept routine and as this interrupt service is used by many different packages (*MultiDos*,

DesqView, etc) it is impossible to forecast when this will execute. The routine displays the message

```
-=> T.R.E.M.O.R was done by NEUROBASHER
/ May-June '92, Germany <=-
-MOMENT-OF-TERROR-IS-THE-BEGINNING-OF-LIFE-
```

on a cleared screen, waits a few seconds and then continues normal operation.

Conclusions

The internal security of some anti-virus packages is obviously called into serious question by this virus. It is not my place to reverse-engineer commercial anti-virus software but during investigation into this virus I had occasion to check the primary operation of several packages against the various routines that were obviously attempting subversion. The Central Point checks were certainly the most obvious and seemed to take no special security precautions against being targeted.

I am seriously concerned that such a widely used package as *Central Point Anti-Virus* is so open in its internal construction that targeting becomes extremely simple. Writing anti-virus code that does not incorporate in-depth security checking is a little like designing a brand new lock and then placing it inside a transparent casing - with a little inspection, anyone can pick it!

Because of the complexity of this virus, my commented listing is available to anti-virus vendors, who may recognise a potential threat to their own package.

Tremor

Aliases:	None known.
Type:	Resident, Parasitic file infector.
Infection:	COM files less than 60,001 bytes and EXE files below 1,048,576 bytes.

Self-Recognition:

File	Year field in file Date/Time stamp is greater than 100.
System	INT 01h handler present.

Hex Pattern

No simple recognition pattern is possible.

Intercepts:	INT 21h (most functions) for stealth and infection, INT 24h for internal error handling, INT 15h for trigger 2, INT 03h for armouring, INT 01h for tunnelling.
Trigger:	Vibrating screen effect or message display routine.
Removal:	Specific and generic disinfection is possible. Under clean system conditions, identify and replace infected files.

The Volga Virus Family

Eugene Kaspersky and Vadim Bogdanov, VB May 1993

The vast majority of all virus trigger routines simply involve either displaying a silly message, overwriting the hard drive or both. Indeed, while virus authors seem to spend a great deal of time thinking of new ways to infect a system, little thought ever seems to be given to the trigger routine, which is the virus' *raison d'etre*. Unfortunately the Volga virus family is an exception to this rule.

The family consists of several variants which are all related to the New Zealand II virus. They were discovered in the Volgograd State University in Russia and are internally dated from July 1991 to the end of April 1992. All of the members of the Volga family occupy one disk sector and take up one or two Kilobytes of memory when resident.

Operation

There is nothing particularly novel about the way the Volga viruses replicate. When a machine is booted from an infected hard or floppy drive, the virus installs itself into high addresses of system memory, then checks the hard disk Master Boot Record to see whether it is infected.

If the hard disk is not infected, the virus uses a standard boot sector virus infection routine. The original contents of the MBS are encrypted and stored in an unused sector of the hard drive, and the virus code is inserted in its place. The encryption algorithms vary between different members of Volga virus family. Once the virus is resident, it hooks INT 13h and infects any suitable floppy disks placed in the disk drives. None of this is particularly noteworthy, however the Volga family of viruses is interesting because of an unusual (and extremely annoying) trigger routine.

Destructive Trigger

All the viruses in the Volga family have the unfortunate side-effect that once a PC is infected, it is very difficult to recover the information stored on the drive. Even after the virus has been removed from the machine, a further clean-up procedure is required to restore normal functionality.

The virus author uses the fact that the fixed disk controller stores an error correction code (usually four or six bytes in length) at the end of every sector. The disk controller uses this information for error checking and error correction of the data stored within that sector.

If the extra information stored at the end of a sector is not what the disk controller expects, then an error code is returned, and the read request fails. However, IBM was prepared for this eventuality and implemented a call which allows software to read the entire contents of a sector, including this extra information.

When one of the Volga viruses is resident, it intercepts calls to INT 13h and substitutes the two calls

```
INT 13h, AH=02h    read disk sector(s)
INT 13h, AH=03h    write disk sector(s)
```

with

```
INT 13h, AH=0Ah    read long hard disk sector(s)
INT 13h, AH=0Bh    write long hard disk sector(s)
```

These substituted calls use exactly the same registers and return the same values, so no additional programming needs to be done to ensure that the read long calls function correctly. However, this is a process fraught with potential pitfalls. The IBM BIOS Interface Technical Reference Manual states that services 0Ah and 0Bh are 'reserved for diagnostics' and that these calls should be used with care.

The Trigger in Action

Therefore, when an INT 13h write request is issued, the virus intercepts the call and changes it into a 'write long sector' call. As discussed above, this means that the sector is no longer readable by standard calls to the BIOS.

However, when the virus is memory-resident, all read requests (INT 13h, AH=02h) are altered to 'read long sector' requests (INT 13h, AH=0Ah). This 'read long sector' call will read not only sectors which have been altered by the virus but also sectors which have been written by DOS in the standard format. As long as the virus is memory-resident, the computer will appear to operate normally.

The catch is that if the hard disk is accessed without the virus being memory-resident (either after clean booting or after the machine has been disinfected), the standard DOS functions will not be capable of reading the rewritten long sectors. This occurs because the standard INT 13h call cannot read these altered sectors correctly.

Cleaning Up

Even though it is relatively easy to disinfect machines infected with these viruses, recovering the data stored on affected hard drives is a tricky task, best carried out by a program written specially for that purpose. This program has to read all sectors on the hard drive and if it encounters an error, has to attempt to use the 'read long sector' function call. If this call is successful, the sector should be rewritten using the standard write sector call.

As the only way to test if a sector is affected is to read data from it, this procedure can take a lot of time to complete - from several minutes to an hour, depending on hard disk size and speed. This makes the Volga family of viruses one of the most difficult from which to recover.

Although the trigger routine should not cause data loss, the time taken to recover data from the hard drive classes it as one of the most irritating viruses in the wild. One can only hope that the last virus in the Volga series marks its author's last attempt at virus writing.

Volga

Aliases:	VolGU
Type:	Resident, Master Boot Sector.

Self-Recognition:

Disk	Text string at the beginning of MBS. Varies for different variants.
System	Varies for different variants.

Hex Pattern

Positioned at offset 0 of sector 0

```
Volga-A:  BE00  7C33  FFFA  8ED7  8BE6  FB9A  3000  C007
Volga-B:  BE00  7C33  FFFA  8ED7  8BE6  FBEA  3A00  C007
Volga-C:  BE00  7C33  FFFA  8ED7  8BE6  FBEA  3000  C007
Volga-D:  BE00  7C33  FFFA  8ED7  8BE6  FBEA  3000  C007
Volga-E:  BE00  7C33  FFFA  8ED7  8BE6  FBEA  2901  C007
Volga-F:  BE00  7C33  FFFA  8ED7  8BE6  FBEA  3301  C007
```

Intercepts:	INT 13h for infection and damage.
Trigger:	Rewrites sectors on the hard disk drive using the INT

13h 'write long sector' request, making sectors unavailable when the virus is not memory-resident.

Removal: Specific and generic removal is possible under clean system conditions.

V-Sign

Jim Bates, September 1992

The increasing prevalence of the V-Sign virus warrants a supplementary report to the analysis of this virus which appeared in *Virus Bulletin*, July 1992, page 6.

Unusual Features

The virus is known as V-Sign due to its display when the trigger routine executes. V-Sign is a boot sector virus which infects floppy disks and the Master Boot Sector of hard disks. It hooks itself into the system at boot-time in the usual way via INT 13h and it attempts to detect and remove the New Zealand (Stoned) virus. In this respect, it may have some claim to being an anti-virus virus but the implementation is so convoluted and so poorly executed that it actually increases the chance of system malfunction.

The infection method differs from most boot sector viruses in that no attempt is made to store a clean copy of the original boot sector. The integrity of the bootstrap process is maintained by swapping chunks of code around.

Another new development in a boot sector virus is the use of code randomisation to make pattern recognition difficult.

Installation

During infection, the virus collects 38 bytes of code from the Master Boot Sector of the target disk, stores them within itself and replaces them with code that redirects the boot process to load the remainder of the virus from elsewhere on the disk. The virus itself is actually only 786 bytes long but this hook which is inserted into the original Master Boot Sector could be said to extend its total length to 824 bytes.

Once the virus is in memory, it checks whether it is already installed. This might seem superfluous but with the increase in alternative and selective boot software, it is quite possible for a machine to initiate a warm boot sequence where existing system hooks have not been reset. The method of self-recognition is to collect the segment portion of the INT 13h vector and check that segment of memory for a recognition word of 9876h at offset 0D6h.

An 'Anti-Virus Virus'

If this is not found, a check is then attempted to detect the existence of the New Zealand virus. The intention is to compare a 10 byte fragment of code found in the New Zealand virus with a specific memory location. The code fragment is obviously there simply for pattern matching since it is never executed. However, this check fails due to an error in the program and V-Sign will not detect New Zealand at this stage. Because this check fails, the code to unhook the New Zealand virus is never executed and processing passes immediately to the installation routine.

Installation is achieved by the familiar method of locating the top of conventional memory and moving the code up into it. Then the memory pointers are modified so that subsequent programs will not use that space and finally any relevant interrupt handling routines are hooked into the system interrupt table. The virus then repairs the displaced boot code in memory and finally passes control to it so that the normal boot routine may continue.

Operation

V-Sign only intercepts the BIOS INT 13h system function. During these system requests, the interception routine examines the status of the floppy drive motors. If neither the A or B drives is running, the routine aborts. Otherwise, checks are made to ensure that the request is either to READ or WRITE to the disk in the first two floppy drives or the first two hard drives. Once these parameters are established, the routine decides whether the request is for hard or floppy disk and branches accordingly. If the request is for access to a hard disk, the routine sets a flag and exits. Floppy access, on the other hand, results in the virus checking the disk to determine its layout and whether it is already infected. If the disk is suitable for infection, the trigger counter is incremented and tested for divisibility by 63. If the condition is not met, processing continues with the code randomisation mentioned above.

This consists of swapping the position of certain instructions within the code to be inserted into the Master Boot Sector. This is undoubtedly done to confuse scanning software and make recognition difficult. The effect is to produce six slightly different versions of the virus on a cyclical basis.

Once this modification is complete, a second check is made for the New Zealand virus. This time the test is done properly (using the recognition pattern again) on the existing Master Boot Sector and, if New Zealand is found, it is removed and replaced by the original Master Boot Sector from the relevant sector of the boot track (track 0, head 0, sector 7 for hard disks, sector 3 side 1 for 360K floppies).

The Wrong Bit

At this point, a check is also made to discover whether the target disk was previously infected with V-Sign. It is here that an interesting error occurs - the code which is supposed to recognise the existence of V-Sign on the disk compares a specific location within itself with a similar location on disk. However, one of the addresses is wrong in such a way that the check will fail. V-Sign will thus re-infect disks and in so doing will irreparably damage the boot sequence.

Of course this will not affect floppy disks used only for data, and will only occur on hard disks if the Master Boot Sector is read once the virus is resident. The error is caused by a single incorrect bit in the code. The nature of the mistake makes it unlikely that it was done deliberately. However, it could conceivably be due to 'degeneration' [*see Technical Notes, VB, September 1992, p.4. Ed.*]. It should be noted that this error turns a 'benign' virus into a destructive one.

During the infection process, the virus calculates exactly where to place its code depending upon the format of the disk in accordance with the following table:

Target Disk	Track	Head	Sectors
Hard disk	0	0	4/5
5.25" 360k	0	1	2/3
5.25" 1.2M	0	1	13/14
3.5" 720k	0	1	4/5
3.5" 1.44M	0	1˙	14/15

*Error - should be Head 0.

Apart from the hard disk and the last floppy, these represent the last two sectors allocated for use as directory sectors. This will cause corruption and data loss on disks with files approaching the maximum number within the root directory. The 3.5" 1.44M floppy is an obvious mistake since it results in the virus code being stored in the first data sectors on the disk and these will be the first to contain data!

Trigger Routine

As mentioned above, this occurs every time the counter passes an exact multiple of 63. The display is a simple one of a red 'V' shown on a black background. The 'V' is made up of block characters on a text screen and will therefore display properly even on old monochrome monitors. Once the display is completed, the computer will go into an infinite loop and hang. This will certainly cause data corruption if it occurs during file update procedures.

Disinfection

Disinfection must be undertaken in a clean DOS environment, i.e. having booted from a clean system disk.

On hard disks, the 38 bytes of virus pointer code embedded in the Master Boot Sector (track 0, head 0, sector 1) start at offset 36h. The actual pointer to the sector number where the remainder of the virus code is stored will be found at 4Eh (on hard disks this will be at track 0, head 0, sector 4 which is usually unused). The original 38 bytes of good boot sector code in sector 4 are located at offset 6h, the first byte of which will be EBh which is the very first byte of the Master Boot Sector. The 38 bytes starting at offset 8h are the displaced boot code and should be written to offset 36h in the Master Boot Sector.

Note: If a backup copy of the hard disk boot sector is available, none of this convoluted procedure is necessary. The PC can be restored with the minimum of fuss. Under DOS 5 the virus can be removed from the Master Boot Sector using the straightforward FDISK/MBR syntax.

Files can safely be transferred from diskettes using the DOS COPY command and infected diskettes should then be formatted under clean system conditions.

V-SIGN

Aliases:	Cansu
Type:	Resident boot sector virus.
Infection:	Infects logical sector 0 of diskettes (any density) using the last two sectors of the root directory to store the remainder of its code.

On hard disks the virus inserts 38 bytes of pointer code into the Master Boot Sector (track 0, head 0, sector 1). The remainder of the virus is stored at sectors 4 and 5.

Recognition:

Disk
Value of 9876h at offset 5Ah in the Master Boot Sector.

Hex Pattern

```
1372 FA?? ???? ???? ??B9 0E00 BA00
01CD 1372 EAE9 A601 7698
```

System
9876h value at offset 0D6h into segment pointed to by segment portion of INT 13h vector.

Intercepts:
INT 13h for infection and calculation of trigger conditions.

Trigger:
Displays large 'V' sign in block characters on a text screen. Sign will be red on black on colour monitors.

Whale... A Dinosaur Heading For Extinction

Jim Bates, VB November 1990

By far the largest virus that researchers have yet seen was recently uploaded to a bulletin board in the United States and comprises just under 10K of code.

The virus has been called 'The Whale' since that is the 'title' which appears within the code after the first level of code decryption has been executed. Disassembling this code has proven time-consuming and full analysis is incomplete due to the pressures of other work on the various researchers currently disassembling it. I am indebted to Dr. Peter Lammer of Sophos, and Morgan and Igor of McAfee Associates for access to their work on this - the report which follows collates results from all these sources, although any errors in analysis or interpretation are entirely my own.

The Fidonet Message

Before describing the code in such detail as we have, mention should be made of the 'motherfish' message which was posted anonymously to VIRUS ECHO on Fidonet and reported in full in *VB,* October 1990, p.14.

There are several discrepancies in this message which might suggest that the sender was either not familiar with the code or he was spreading disinformation. Since more than half the virus code is concerned with confusing and misinforming anyone trying to disassemble it, I incline to the latter theory.

The use of 'motherfish' (which does not appear in the code) in preference to 'whale' is strange, and the reference to the virus 'learning' detection methods and being a 'living, breathing entity' is fanciful in the extreme and inaccurate. That 'the virus cannot be detected by present methods' is incorrect, despite concerted attempts on the part of the author(s) to make the virus undetectable. The use of the word 'disavow' is interesting since text within the code suggests that the author comes from Hamburg where such a word seems unlikely to be common parlance. However, the suggestion that the code is modularly constructed is accurate, so unless this was a guess we must assume that the sender has some knowledge of the virus as a whole.

Heavyweight Confusion Coding

Following self-encrypting and 'stealth' viruses, a new term has been coined by a member of the *Computer Crime Unit* at New Scotland Yard. 'Armoured' virus code describes the deliberate disinformation and confusion techniques noted in Fish6 and Whale. It is certainly appropriate in the case of Whale since the 'armour' outweighs the 'stealth'!

The Whale virus is characterised by large sections of code (estimated as at least 50 percent of the total) which involve extremely convoluted processing around and across the debug and single step interrupt handlers and accessing such hardware as the Programmable Interrupt Controller. There is no reason for this other than to confuse researchers trying to disassemble the code.

Paradoxically, the presence of this 'confusion' code has caused the research community to heave a sigh of relief. The reason for this is quite simply that such code is costly in processing time and when a machine becomes infected, processing speed slows by up to 50 percent - Whale is simply carrying so much programming weight (armour) that its very bulk is its giveaway. [*Rather like the dinosaurs, such viruses seem doomed to extinction... Ed.*]

A substantial amount of time and effort has been expended in writing this virus and it could well have been undertaken by more than one author. Program construction is modular and no effort has been spared to make the code difficult for scanning programs to detect.

Encryption Routines

Aside from the now accepted technique of self-encryption, this virus scrambles the order of its subroutines and varies the encryption algorithm used during file infection.

Now also accepted as a 'standard' technique is the decryption/ encryption process which is used to prevent detection of the virus code in memory. This technique consists of maintaining most of the resident virus code in memory in encrypted form and only decrypting it just prior to processing. Once a particular section has been executed, a re-encryption routine is called which collects a new pseudo-random key value and re-encrypts the code just executed before storing the new key and continuing to the next part of the code. The result is that only a small 'window' around the code currently being executed is actually 'in plain view', the remainder is variously and randomly encrypted. This is obviously to forestall the possibility of a recognition pattern being used to identify virus code in memory. The author(s) obviously likes this technique since it is used at least 96 times throughout the code. This is another part of the bulk that this unwieldy virus carries.

As with other recent viruses, there are several 'undocumented' system calls (most of which are now well documented within the technical community) but two have been noted which may relate to specific software packages, possibly of an anti-virus nature.

General Structure

There is still much work to be done in analysing this code. However, we can say that this is a parasitic virus which infects executables with an infection length of around 9416 bytes. The actual appended length varies from infection to infection and this is probably due to the insertion of some random junk and alignment of code on paragraph boundaries.

No simple search pattern is possible because of the multiple encryption techniques and modular scrambling. There are considerable sections of self-modifying, self-checking and self-switching code within WHALE. This last technique consists of laboriously switching individual bytes within a specific subroutine using pre-calculated XOR values. The result is a sort of global XOR effect which can be used to switch between two different routines or as a decryption/encryption process.

The code appears to install itself as resident within the first available Memory Control Block and monitors system activity during normal DOS processing.

Stealth techniques are used to fool DOS into reporting original file sizes rather than the increased ones when files become infected. This is done by intercepting the DOS Get File Size function (23h) and checking whether the target file is infected before returning either a true or modified file size to the calling routine. [*See also VB, November 1990, p.20. Ed.*]

Infection Method

The virus' method of detecting infection is still being analysed but there is some evidence that several checks are made, failure of any one of which will indicate that a file is **not** infected.

The complexity of these checks means that a 'sparse infection' method (i.e. where not all files are infected) may be employed. This makes external detection more difficult, but it does reduce the virulence of the code. This should mean that if this specimen does appear in the wild, it is unlikely to exist for long before detection and would therefore not spread too far.

One of the checks for infection seems to be that the hour field in the file time must be equal to or greater than 16 (i.e. 4pm or later) since the top bit of that field is modified within the Function 57h (Get/Set file Date/Time) handler. This too may limit the number of files suitable for infection.

Programming Style

There are several similarities with the Fish6 and 4K viruses and this might indicate either a distinct development cycle by the author(s) or simply that someone has copied useful code and ideas from the earlier specimens. I incline to the former view, but whatever the truth of the matter, the similarity in file infection techniques provides a useful method of identifying the presence of any of these three viruses. However, it is reported from the United States that some generations of Whale may not display this similarity and might therefore slip through this particular detection net.

The technique itself is discussed in a 4K data infection report [*VB, November 1990, p.4. Ed.*], and with the exception of the differences in infected length (and the as yet unconfirmed U.S. reports), all three viruses show identical repetition of the original host header information.

Generation Code

The external results of running Whale have so far produced at least 27 different 'generations' [*the total number of possible generations equals 30. Ed.*] and each generation appears to be the result of scrambling the order in which subroutines are written to the target file as well as changing both the encryption 'lock' and 'key'.

There is a counting mechanism fairly close to the beginning of the virus code which counts back from 0F0h (240 decimal) on the dissection copy but the significance of this has not yet become clear. Possibly sections of the virus still to be dissected may be invoked when the counter reaches zero.

Infection apparently takes place during a Function 4Bh call to DOS (Load and Execute) and thus affects COM, EXE, OVR and other executable code which is run in this way.

At various times, the interrupt vector addresses for Interrupts 1h, 2h, 3h, 9h, 13h, 24h and 2Fh are accessed and may be modified for use by the virus code.

The main area of code subversion centres around the DOS Interrupt 21h and this is intercepted and passed through a function dispatcher routine. This dispatcher monitors 15 separate DOS functions including both types of FindFirst/Next (11h, 12h, 4Eh and 4Fh), Open and Close file operations (0Fh, 3Dh and 3Eh) and various types of file Read and Seek calls (14h, 21h, 27h and 42h). Other functions handled are Get File Size (23h), Load and Execute (4Bh) and Get/Set Date/Time (57h). As is now expected of this type of code, the DOS Critical Error vector is hooked during virus operation and appears to be correctly restored after use.

Text Strings

As various layers of encryption are peeled back, two areas of plain text are revealed. The first of these is written to a hidden file in the root directory of the C drive on a 1-in-4 random chance. This file is named FISH-9.TBL and contains a copy of the boot sector of the drive, together with the following plain text:

```
FISH VIRUS 9 A Whale is no Fish! Mind her
Mutant Fish and the hidden Fish Eggs for
they are damaging. The sixth Fish mutates
only if the Whale is in her Cave.
```

No other reference is made to this file from within the virus code. The content indicates a juvenile mind at work.

The 'sixth Fish' may refer to the Fish6 virus (and establish another definite link) but this has yet to be established. Since I haven't yet disassembled Fish6, I would be interested to know just how it got its name (why the '6'?). It is also interesting to note that TBL is one of the data file extensions attacked by the 4K virus.

The second plain text section is displayed as a screen message if the system date is between 19th February and 20th March [*consistent with the astrological star sign of Pisces the fish. Ed.*] in any year except 1991. Subsequently the system hangs with a Divide Overflow message, necessitating a power down reboot. This is the only trigger point noted so far but there is a possibility that even these dates may be modified within differing generations, resulting in unpredictable trigger dates.

The message reads:

```
THE WHALE IN SEARCH OF THE 8 FISH I AM
'~knzyvo}' IN HAMBURG
```

This is exactly as the message appears on screen and the characters between the single quotes appear to be a name of some sort.

Elementary cryptanalysis suggests that this name is probably 'TADPOLES' (which ties in with the ichthyological theme) since this results from simply subtracting a value of 42 (decimal) from each character value. Whether the authors actually do come from Hamburg [*Chaos Computer Club? Ed.*] is not certain: since they are capable of producing this ludicrously silly code, it is quite probable that they are pathological liars as well.

Many researchers have conjectured that Whale might be designed to interact with other viruses (notably Fish6) but to date, no evidence of this has been found either within the virus code or by live testing with both viruses active on the same processor.

Possible Motives for the Virus

As knowledge currently stands on this virus, it may well be an extremely childish and malicious attempt to waste the time of virus researchers across the world. In rather the same way that the fire brigade can never ignore false alarms, the research community cannot ignore even the simplest virus code.

Any virus code is potentially destructive and the perpetrators should be aware that the *Computer Crime Unit* at New Scotland Yard is now building a dossier of computer virus incidents in the UK and will seek the extradition and prosecution of any virus writer who causes damage to data, programs or processing equipment within the United Kingdom. Under current legislation, conviction could carry a maximum five year prison sentence*. If 'TADPOLES' reads this, he/they might like to reflect on such a sentence.

The arrival of this virus caused initial consternation among knowledgeable researchers but preliminary examination has dispelled most of this concern. It is interesting to speculate that in Whale, virus writers have at last reached a predicted point where their code has to carry so much protection that the original parameters of invisibility and mobility can no longer be maintained with any reliability. Such bulky and processor intensive code will generally reveal itself long before any payload can be delivered.

*Under the provisions of the United Kingdom Computer Misuse Act, 29th August, 1990. Ed.

ADDENDUM - *VB* November 1990

The parasitic virus Whale is not only the bulkiest but also the most convoluted specimen seen to date. Whale uses several techniques to make itself not only difficult to find using anti-virus software, but also difficult to disassemble and analyse. However, disassembly is still a relatively straightforward process using DEBUG and the virus has now been disassembled in full.

Whale includes several different anti-tamper measures. The 'active' obstacles range from disabling of the keyboard to exercising the single-step and breakpoint interrupts as an integral part of the code. The 'passive' traps include deeply buried routines which use checksums on the ROM BIOS data area and on Whale's own code to detect any use of debuggers and breakpoints. If any sign of interference is found, Whale attempts to erase itself from memory: a demure virus, which would die rather than be molested.

After removing some outer layers of active protection, one can disassemble the entire contents of the virus with relative ease, by invoking Whale's own decryption routines in a controlled manner from DEBUG.

Many of the rumours regarding this virus are unfounded, including the claim that the virus was undetectable using conventional methods. While Whale is distinctly slippery to detect in memory, due to the constant application of random-key decryption/encryption methods, it is relatively straightforward to find in executable files.

When Whale infects a file, it first makes a 1-in-2 random choice whether or not to mutate and if appropriate then chooses one of its 30 possible mutations at random. Otherwise the virus replicates without mutating. Even when Whale does not mutate, the virus constantly changes in appearance due to decryption/encryption routines in its code.

On disassembling Whale's file infection routine one is reminded irresistibly of the legendary bird of paradise which, when attacked, flies in ever-decreasing circles until it disappears up its own fundament - from which position of safe refuge it is said to bombard its pursuers with abuse and excrement. Whale performs a similar contortionist's act in memory in order to append itself to a COM or EXE file on the disk; it re-modifies all of its self-modifying code, mutates itself in memory and re-applies all of its various layers of encryption until, poised in an impossibly precarious position, it carries out a prearranged INT 21h function call to infect the target file. It then has to use its new mutated code to decrypt itself before it can return to its own depths and continue processing the file infection subroutine.

Whale does not appear at present to do anything more significant than replicate, occasionally displaying fish-related messages. In addition to the Piscean activation dates reported above, currently available copies contain a trigger date of 1st April 1991, after which no replication will take place. One of Whale's confusion tactics is that on approximately one in ten infections, it appends a randomly chosen amount of garbage, up to 4 kilobytes, to the target file. Due to the way the virus is written, it is possible for files with extensions other than EXE and COM to become 'infected', exactly as described for 4K. This means that Whale could inadvertently have damaging effects on certain data or text files.

Another sign of sloppy programming is that when the virus 'forges' the lengths and time-stamps of files, it fails to distinguish between those which are genuinely infected and those which happened by chance to have a time-stamp 'hours' value larger than 15. If any file has a time-stamp hours value of 16 or more, Whale will subtract 16 from this value (for example when a DIR command is processed), regardless even of whether the file is a program, let alone whether it is genuinely infected. If the file is of type COM or EXE, Whale also subtracts 9216 from the reported length, again regardless of whether the file genuinely has been infected. On infecting a file, furthermore, Whale sets the top bit of the hours field high without checking whether this would set the value to greater than 23 hours.

An interesting aspect of Whale's programming is that one piece of self-modifying code makes the execution flow of identical copies of the virus vary from one processor to another. This depends on the length of the instruction queue. The sequence is shown here in simplified form as:

```
mov       bx, offset retpt
mov       al,c3              ;opcode for 'ret'
mov       cs:[bx],al
add       ax,020C
retpt:    int  3
```

It does not follow the same execution path on an 8088-based PC as on an 8086 based one; the 8088 chip has a 4-byte instruction queue, whereas the 8086 has a 6-byte queue. On an 8086 the 'INT 3h' instruction will already be in the queue before it is modified to read 'RET', and will therefore execute as 'INT 3h'. On an 8088, by contrast, the instruction will be modified before entering the queue and will therefore execute as 'RET'. It is unlikely that the author of the virus was aware of this particular feature of his code.

All in all, it is improbable that Whale will pose a practical threat as a virus; it is too large and slows down performance of any PC much too noticeably to spread undetected. It is also relatively easy to detect using normal methods.

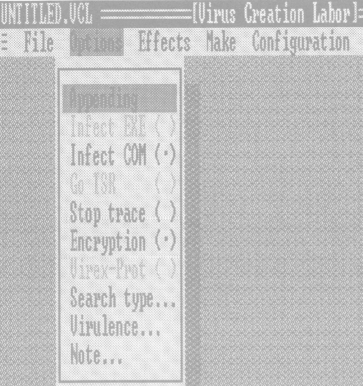

Virus construction toolkits

Tim Twaits

O holy simplicity!

Jan Hus

What is a Virus Construction Kit?

A virus construction kit is a collection of automated tools designed to assist in the production of viruses. In addition to complete software kits, there have been a number of books, such as Burger's *Computer Viruses: A High-Tech Disease*, as well as published virus code from a number of other sources, which could be considered to be tools for the prospective virus writer. This chapter discusses construction kits containing software tools which provide the user with the ability to produce a fully functional virus.

What is available?

A number of toolkits have been appeared since 1990. Detailed information about individual construction kits is provided at the end of the chapter:

- The Virus Construction Set (VCS)   1990

- The Virus Creation Laboratory (VCL)   1992

- The Phalcon/Skism Mass Produced Code generator
  (PS-MPC)   1992

- The Instant Virus Production kit (IVP)   1992

- The Second Generation in Virus Creation (G^2)   1993

Although these programs differ significantly both in the level of sophistication of the interface and the variety of virus code produced, they all allow a person with very little technical knowledge to produce a working virus with relative ease.

Who produces them and why?

These construction kits have all been written by individuals involved in virus writing groups. The most significant contributions have originated from one group: the Phalcon/Skism group based in California. The group has been connected with the three most sophisticated kits (VCL, PS-MPC and G^2). The only other recent entry, the Instant Virus Production kit, is an obvious copy of the earlier PS-MPC.

The most common reason supplied by the authors for producing a construction kit is to teach people how to write viruses. One cannot help being cynical about such altruistic motives. It seems far more likely that notoriety is their aim, for it would appear that, in the circles these people frequent, producing sophisticated code is one way of gaining appreciation.

Do they work?

The construction kits examined here all work; some much better than others. Selecting the basic options in any of the kits will produce a fully functional virus. However, selecting more obscure options often causes problems, both when building the virus and when the virus code is executed.

More importantly, the viruses produced are very simple. They will work, but the chances of them becoming widespread in the wild, without significant modification, are negligible. For a start, without modifications they will immediately be detected by most of the commercially available virus-scanning packages.

Where does one get a construction kit ?

A key question is how readily available the virus construction kits are. One could try asking any of the many groups involved in virus research for the programs, but in most cases this will not produce the goods. The more normal source is a bulletin board. There are a fair number that deal extensively with viruses. Finding and gaining access to one of these bulletin boards is a non-trivial task unless one knows the right people. However, with determination and enough money to pay the phone bill it can be done.

Success in the wild ?

It is difficult to say how many viruses seen in the wild have been produced with the construction kits. Collections held by virus researchers at the moment contain more than 100 samples. A large proportion of these viruses, however, have not been modified from the basic code produced by the construction kit, and are very easily detected. It seems likely that many of these may have been produced just to see how the construction kits would work, rather than with any intention of spreading a virus maliciously. A small number of the samples have obviously been deliberately modified to improve the operation of the virus and avoid detection.

A simple measure of a virus' success in the wild is the number of reported infections. On this basis, construction kit viruses score very low. *VB* has never received a report of a real infection caused by a virus produced by, or based on, code from a construction kit. All the samples seem to have been detected before they could spread in the wild and cause any significant damage.

Future development

The development of virus construction kits will continue as long as it is perceived to be clever to do so. One should expect to see features such as stealth and support for boot sector viruses in new construction kits. It will also become more difficult for the manufacturers of virus scanning programs to ensure they can detect all the viruses produced with a particular construction kit. It is possible to imagine a situation where construction kits have become so complex that it is virtually impossible to produce a reliable generic detection routine. This would represent a much more significant threat than the current kits do. Fortunately, because of the effort required to produce a reliable program of this complexity, the situation is unlikely to occur.

Conclusion

The conclusion must be that there is no great cause for concern arising from the virus construction kits seen to date, except that they are part of an increasingly widespread distribution of information about viruses. A virus only becomes a significant threat if it remains undetected after it has been released and the chance of a virus produced with the current construction kits remaining undetected is extremely low. This, of course, does not apply to construction kit viruses which are subsequently modified, but this is not a new problem; the availability of source listings for complex viruses is a much greater potential threat.

Some Virus Construction Kits

The Virus Construction Set (VCS)

The Virus Construction Set (VCS) was written in Germany in 1990 by VDV (Verband Deutcher Virenliebhaber): the association of German virus lovers. VCS was the first virus construction kit for the PC. Interestingly, an earlier construction kit for the Atari also originated in Germany.

VCS is a very simple program which produces ready-to-execute virus code. Within a few minutes (assuming your can understand some German) you can produce your own virus. There is no need to have any technical knowledge or to understand assembler program development; all you have to do is to provide the answers to two questions. The main drawback of this simplicity is that all the viruses produced are virtually identical.

```
          V i r u s   C o n s t r u c t i o n   S e t
          (c) 1991 by VDV - Verband Deutscher Virenliebhaber

 VDV international präsentiert: Virus Construction Set V1.0

 Für einen Virus benötigen Sie ein Textfile von maximal 512 Bytes Länge.
 Dieser Text wird dann nach einer vorgegebenen Anzahl von Generationen aus-
 gegeben. Außerdem werden AUTOEXEC.BAT und CONFIG.SYS gelöscht. Ansonsten
 wird kein Schaden angerichtet, die größeren Gemeinheiten hebe ich mir für
 meine eigenen Viren auf (hehe...)

 Dateiname der Text-Datei ? test.txt

 Erste aktive Generation (1..100) ? 100

 Es wurde jetzt eine Datei VIRUS.COM erstellt, die Ihren Virus enthält.
 Um ein Programm (nur .COM-Dateien) zu infizieren, gehen Sie wie folgt vor:

 1) Kopieren Sie das zu infizierende Programm auf eine leere Diskette:
       C:\>copy programm.com a:
 2) Wechseln Sie auf das Diskettenlaufwerk:
       C:\>a:
 3) Starten Sie VIRUS.COM:
       A:\>c:virus
 Das infizierte Programm ist dann 1077 Bytes länger als vorher und kann
 an Bekannte, Freunde oder Feinde weitergegeben werden.

 Taste drücken, um zum DOS zurückzukehren
```

Typical screen output from VCS

The viruses produced are all 1077 bytes long, infect COM files and use simple encryption. They are not memory-resident, or polymorphic, and can be detected using a single search pattern. The viruses are triggered after a specified number of generations and will overwrite the CONFIG.SYS and AUTOEXEC.BAT files before displaying a text message. The only differences between any two viruses produced by VCS are the number of generations before the virus is triggered and the text message displayed. Both are selected at the time of virus creation.

Time has shown that VCS viruses have not been successful in the wild.

The Virus Creation Laboratory (VCL)

The Virus Creation Laboratory was first circulated in May 1992. It was produced by somebody calling himself Nowhere Man, who is apparently part of a Californian virus writing group called NuKE and who has strong connections with the Hell Pit virus exchange BBS.

Windows icon supplied with VCL

A custom installation program is supplied which, when the correct password is provided, will automatically decompress all the components of the tool kit and install them on the hard disk. Once installed, VCL consists of:

- The VCL program and configuration files

- 15 pages of documentation

- 8 example viruses

Substantial effort was obviously required to produce the kit which works despite containing a number of faults.

The interface to the VCL program has been modelled on Borland's Turbo Languages IDE (Integrated Development Environment). Context-sensitive help is available and this, taken in conjunction with the written information supplied with the program, makes the system very simple to use. The following steps will produce a working virus:

1. Select the type of virus on the Options Menu

2. Select the trigger condition and action on the Effects Menu

3. Select Make to build the virus

VCL does not produce executable code directly but creates assembler code which is subsequently assembled and automatically linked by the VCL program. The net result so far as the user is concerned is the same: a ready-to-run virus program.

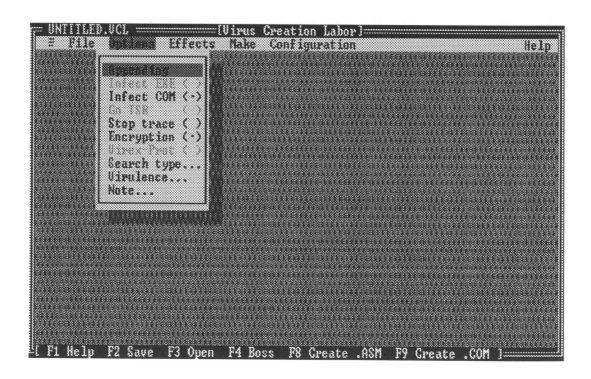

VCL main menu

The trigger conditions can be selected from a list of about 20 options, including the date, time, DOS version etc. The trigger action can also be selected from a list of 25 different effects, ranging from clearing the screen to completely destroying data on all disks. The conditions and the effects can be used in combination to produce fairly complex results. In addition, instructions are provided to allow custom effects to be easily incorporated.

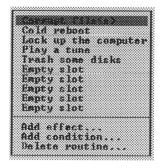

Selecting the virus trigger action

VCL currently produces only non-memory-resident COM infectors, each of which can be detected by most commercial virus-scanning software. An option is available to introduce encryption, which is slightly polymorphic, but this is also easily detectable.

There a number of problems with the construction kit and a proportion of the viruses produced will not operate correctly. This appears to have contributed to the lack of VCL viruses in the wild.

The Phalcon/Skism Mass Produced Code generator (PS-MPC)

The Phalcon/Skism Mass Produced Code generator (PS-MPC) was produced by 'Dark Angel' of the self-styled Phalcon/Skism group which runs the Hell Pit virus exchange BBS in California. The same group was known to the author of the VCL program who was apparently the inspiration behind the Mass Produced Code generator.

The program differs significantly from VCL. The most noticeable change is that there is no menu-driven interface. All the configuration options are selected by editing a text-based configuration file, such as the following:

```
; VirusName= <string>
; The only limitation to the string is that you may not use both
; the single and double quotes together in the string, i.e. the
; string B'li"p is not legal
VirusName=[TESTER]
```

Another major difference between PS-MPC and VCL is the form of the output. VCL is capable of producing a fully functional ready-to-execute virus. This is not the case with PS-MPC, where only assembler source files are produced. These must then be assembled and linked to create the executable code (instructions are provided). Furthermore, the program does not include any trigger routines; these must be added by the user. Thus, the sequence of events required to create a virus is as follows:

1. Edit the configuration file to select the type of virus to be produced

2. Run the PS-MPC program to produce assembler source code

3. Modify the source code to include a trigger routine (optional)

4. Assemble and link

There have been several different versions of the PS-MPC program. The earlier ones did not support the creation of memory-resident viruses. The latest version can create simple, memory-resident viruses which infect all programs executed. There is no stealth capability. The basic options for the type of virus that can be produced are:

*   Program type infected (COM and/or EXE)

*   Encryption (ON or OFF)

*   Memory-resident (YES or NO)

There is no variation in the code produced for a given set of options, so it is very simple for a scanner to detect all the viruses produced by the program. The encryption routine, although polymorphic, is also easily detectable. It is based on the V2P6 virus, where one decryption algorithm uses randomly chosen registers. However, to produce an effective virus, the output from PS-MPC must be modified to include a trigger routine; at this point the virus code can easily be modified to avoid detection as an PS-MPC virus. In the current *VB* collection, 12 viruses were produced with the PS-MPC program but then modified in such a way as to avoid standard detection. There are a further 40 samples which are detected as standard PS-MPC.

The Instant Virus Production kit (IVP)

The Instant Virus Product kit (IVP) very closely resembles PS-MPC and works in a very similar manner. Virtually the same options are available, except the generation of memory-resident viruses, and they are selected by editing a configuration file. No trigger routines are included and the output is in the form of assembler source code. The group responsible for this program calls itself Youngsters Against McAfee (YAM) and has been behind the production of a number of viruses. Unlike the PS-MPC authors, they could not resist producing a pretty screen display for the program.

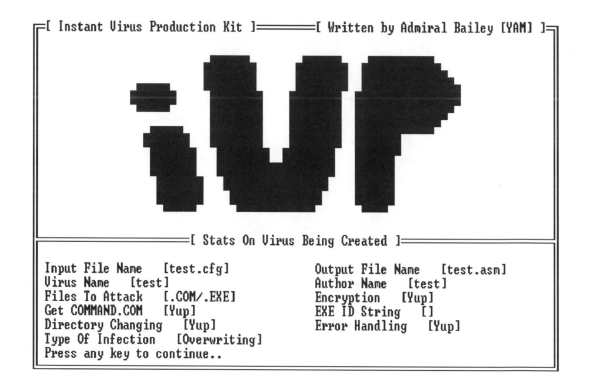

```
┌─[ Instant Virus Production Kit ]═══════[ Written by Admiral Bailey [YAM] ]─┐
│                                                                            │
│                                                                            │
│                                                                            │
│                                                                            │
│                                                                            │
│                                                                            │
│                                                                            │
│                                                                            │
│                                                                            │
│                                                                            │
│                                                                            │
│                                                                            │
│═══════════════════[ Stats On Virus Being Created ]═════════════════════════│
│                                                                            │
│ Input File Name    [test.cfg]      Output File Name    [test.asm]          │
│ Virus Name    [test]               Author Name    [test]                   │
│ Files To Attack   [.COM/.EXE]      Encryption    [Yup]                      │
│ Get COMMAND.COM   [Yup]            EXE ID String   []                       │
│ Directory Changing   [Yup]         Error Handling   [Yup]                   │
│ Type Of Infection   [Overwriting]                                          │
│ Press any key to continue..                                                │
└────────────────────────────────────────────────────────────────────────────┘
```

IVP sign-on Screen

The only improvement over PS-MPC is the addition of random NOP instructions to the virus code to try (unsuccessfully) to avoid detection by virus scanners.

G^2 Virus Code Generator

G^2 was released in January 1993 and is the successor of PS-MPC. It was written by the same person, who claims it heralds a second generation of virus production tools. In reality, the program is very similar to PS-MPC. The method of operation is identical, as is the format of the configuration file. The only major addition is the ability to order the instructions within the virus code randomly so that two consecutive viruses produced with the same configuration file will be different. This obvious attempt to defeat scanning programs has undoubtedly failed. All good virus scanning programs will be capable of detecting all the progeny of G^2.

```
C:\G2>g2 g2.dat
Welcome to G², the second generation virus creator.
Brought to you by Phalcon/Skism, the innovators in modern virus creation.
Written by Dark Angel of said group.
Version 0.70β

G² using data file [G2.DAT]
Thank you for using G² version 0.70β
```

Using the G^2 code generator

The interesting facet of G^2 is the reason behind the authors claim that this is a second generation product. The idea is due to a modification to the design of the program. There are two parts to the generator: the program and an associated data file. The program itself is described as a generic code generator with no specific knowledge of virus operation. The nature of the code produced is determined by the contents of the data file.

So far *VB* has not encountered any 'real' viruses in the wild produced by the G^2 program.

NEWZE2.BIN	FORM.BIN	CASC1701.CO	CASC1704.COM	TEQUILA.EXE
TEQUILA.BIN	JOSHI.BIN	JOSHI1.BIN	EDDIE.COM	EDDIE2.COM
EDDIE2.EXE	DARKAVEN.EXE	DARKAVEN.COM	JERUSAL1.COM	JERUSAL1.EXE
4K.COM	4K.EXE	SPANTELE.COM	SPANTROJ.BIN	SPANTEL2.COM
NOMENKLA.EXE	NOMENKLA.COM	YANKEE1.EXE	YANKEE2.EXE	VACSINA.COM
MICHELAN.BIN	1575.COM	ITALIAN.BIN	2100.COM	2100.EXE
SYSLOCK.COM	FLIP.COM	VSIGN-5.BIN	VSIGN-6.BIN	PENZA.EXE
NOINT.BIN	CAPTRIP.COM	CAPTRIP.EXE	W13_A.COM	W13_B.COM
DARTH1.COM	DARTH2.COM	DARTH4.COM	MACHO.COM	MACHO.EXE
BE452.BIN	BEIJING1.BIN	LIBERTY.COM	LIBERTYE.EXE	SBC.COM
FATHER.COM	FATHER.EXE	WARRIER.COM	WARRIOR.EXE	TESTSET.TXT
CMOS1-T2.EXE	CMOS1.BIN	CMOS1-T1.EXE	FLIP.EXE	SLOW.EXE
SLOW.COM	KEYPRESS.COM			
AIRCOP.BIN	SPANZ.COM			
VIRDEM.COM	VZP6.COM	777.COM		
PCVRSDS.COM	MUSICBUG.BIN	DISKKILL.BIN	ANTICAD.COM	ANTICAD.EXE
VIENNA2A.COM	VIENNA2B.COM	YALE.BIN	NOTHING.COM	WHALE.COM
DIR-II.COM	VSIGN-1.BIN	VSIGN-2.BIN	VSIGN-3.BIN	VSIGN-4.BIN
DATALOCK.COM	DATALOCK.EXE	HELLOWEE.COM	HELLOWEE.EXE	LIBERTY.COM
LIBERTY.EXE	NECROS.COM	NECROS.EXE	LOREN.EXE	LOREN.COM
WINVIR14.EXE	BEIJING.BIN	DOSHUNT.COM	NECROPOL.EXE	PITCH.COM

Viruses in the wild

Be fruitful and multiply.
Genesis

In August 1993 there were between 2700 and 2800 viruses known to the research community, of which only about 50 were causing real problems in the wild.

The following statistics are those reported to *Virus Bulletin* between 1st January 1991 and 20th June 1993. The wide spread of a particular virus seems to be linked to the capability to infect the boot sector (in the first six months of 1993 about 67% of reports were due to pure boot sector viruses and 17% to multi-partite viruses). Of all known viruses only 5% are boot sector viruses and 4% multi-partite. The age of a virus can also contribute to its wide distribution. Cascade (a comparatively old parasitic virus) accounted for 4.8% of the infections in the first six months of 1993. The older the virus, the more chance it has to spread. The wide spread of boot sector viruses is probably due to the fact that floppy disks are exchanged on a large scale, with PC users being unaware that non-system disks can carry a virus.

A disproportionate increase in the stealth, multi-partite viruses Tequila and Spanish Telecom should also be noted.

These reports indicate that currently just 8 viruses, on average, are responsible for about 75% of all infections. Almost all of the reported cases involved a few PCs, but a number of large-scale attacks (100+ PCs) were also reported. These usually involved file servers and were in the majority of cases attributable to poor use of network security features.

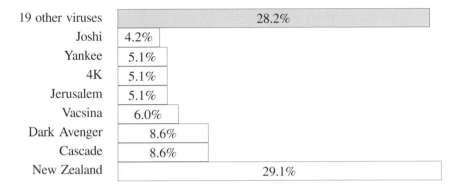

Virus reports from 1st January 1991 to 30th June 1991 (117 reports)

19 other viruses ── 26.6%
Jerusalem ── 3.9%
Michelangelo ── 4.4%
Spanish Telecom ── 4.4%
Joshi ── 5.5%
Cascade ── 5.5%
Tequila ── 8.8%
Form ── 16.6%
New Zealand ── 24.3%

Virus reports from 1st July 1991 to 31st December 1991 (181 reports)

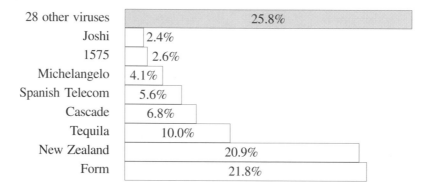

Virus reports from 1st January 1992 to 30th June 1992 (340 reports)

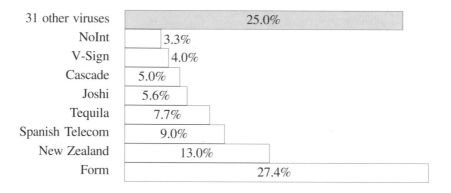

Virus reports from 1st July 1992 to 31st December 1992 (299 reports)

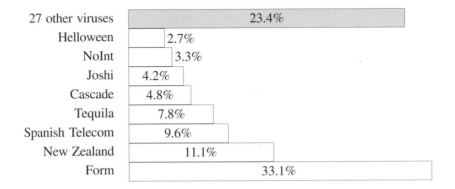

Virus reports from 1st January 1993 to 30th June 1993 (332 reports)

Filename	Ext	Size	Time HH:MM:SS	Date DD-MM-YY	Starting Cluster	Attributes Arc	Dir	Vol	Sys	Hid	R/O
BATES	CPI	720	11:20:50	04-08-93	867	Arc	.	.	.	.	.
BONCZOSO	CPI	23395	06:34:54	24-08-93	868	Arc	.	.	.	.	.
BONTCHEV	EXE	10774	01:34:10	31-08-93	869	Arc	.	.	.	.	.
CASE	COM	6399	16:30:02	24-08-93	875	Arc	.	.	.	.	.
COHEN	EXE	15796	12:12:03	14-08-93	879	Arc	.	.	.	.	.
FERBRACH	EXE	16092	18:15:00	07-08-93	887	Arc	.	.	.	.	.
FISCHER	EXE	16200	14:43:44	04-08-93	905	Arc	.	.	.	.	.
FORD	EXE	14282	03:41:45	12-08-93	913	Arc	.	.	.	.	.
GREENBER	COM	10652	05:19:03	13-08-93	920	Arc	.	.	.	.	.
HIGHLAND	COM	11793	18:30:31	17-08-93	926	Arc	.	.	.	.	.
HOFFMAN	SYS										
HRUSKA	EXE	18650	23:13:69	09-08-93	935	Arc	.	.	.	.	.
JOHNSON	EXE	6770	13:04:54	11-08-93		Arc	.	.	.	.	.
KASPERSK	COM	11205	23:04:62	15-08-93	949	Arc	.	.	.	.	.
MCAFEE	COM	19694	22:23:12	08-08-93	955	Arc	.	.	.	.	.
RADAI	PRO	21232	03:36:30	01-08-93	965	Arc	.	.	.	.	.

Who's Who in virus research

There is only one thing in the world worse than being talked about
and that is not being talked about.

Oscar Wilde

Cluster 866 byte 0 dec (0 hex) (byte 0 in sector 3,571)

This chapter lists some of the more prominent individuals engaged in the anti-virus field. The inclusion (or exclusion) of any particular individual does not imply an endorsement by *VB* (or the withdrawal of the endorsement). We apologise to all who feel aggrieved by their omission from this list.

Jim Bates

Jim Bates has been involved in electronics all his working life: he was an Air Radar Engineer in the RAF before embarking on writing special system software for third party manufacturers. When the first computer viruses appeared, he began disassembling them to find out how they could be detected and removed - this has now become a full time occupation. In 1989 Bates broke the code encryption and analysed the infamous AIDS Information Disk. This marked the start of his connection with the Computer Crime Unit at New Scotland Yard; he is now regularly consulted by them and other national law enforcement agencies on matters involving computer crime. He is a long-standing contributor to *Virus Bulletin* and was elected a Fellow of the Institution of Analysts and Programmers in 1987.

Noel Bonczoszek

Noel Bonczoszek works for the Computer Crime Unit (CCU) as a Scotland Yard Detective. His particular field includes the investigation and prosecution of hackers, computer virus authors and distributors, and those who write malignant code. Bonczoszek has been closely involved in almost all computer crime investigations of the category described above in the UK since 1988. As a result, he has developed unique skills in dealing with and interviewing computer criminals. He has extensive contacts within the computer fraternity worldwide, and often acts as a contact point for victims and specialists alike. He also lectures on various computer related topics.

Vesselin Bontchev

Vesselin Bontchev graduated from the Technical University of Sofia in 1985 with an MSc in Computer Science. He worked for the Institute of Industrial Cybernetics and Robotics in the Bulgarian Academy of Science (BAS) for five years, building expert systems. It was in 1988 that he began to develop a serious interest in computer viruses. Two years later, he was made Director of the Laboratory of Computer Virology at BAS - a laboratory created mainly due to his own efforts. Bontchev is currently working on his PhD at the Virus Test Center in the University of Hamburg, under the leadership of Professor Klaus Brunnstein. His main fields of interest include computer security, encryption and data protection.

Tori Case

Tori Case joined Central Point Software in September 1990 as Marketing Manager for *Central Point Anti-Virus*. From 1987 to 1990, she was Product Manager for Symantec Corporation. Ms Case represents Central Point Software as a charter member of the National Computer Security Association's Anti-Virus Developers Consortium. This organization was developed to establish industry-wide standards in the counting and classification of viruses, educate the market with regard to computer viruses and virus prevalence, help prevent the spread of computer viruses and reduce their impact on both individual users and organizations. Ms Case holds a BA in Biology from Scripps College in Claremont, California.

Fred Cohen

Fred Cohen, President of Management Analytics (formerly Advanced Software Protection), is a leading expert on computer viruses. He has been remarkably prolific as a writer, with over 60 professional publications on various aspects of computer security. He is best known for his pioneering work on computer viruses and automation of protection management functions. His invention of high integrity operating system mechanisms is now used by over 80% of current PC-protection products. Cohen regularly lectures and provides consulting services for top management worldwide.

David Ferbrache

David Ferbrache graduated with a BSc from Heriot-Watt University in 1986. He has been active in promoting the UK's response to malicious software through research, infrastructure and organisation of anti-virus seminars. He is the author of *Pathology of Computer Viruses* and co-author of *UNIX installation security and integrity* and *Computer Viruses: dealing with electronic vandalism and programmed threats*. Ferbrache is a member of the UK Government working group which examines proposals for ITSEC evaluation of anti-virus products. Since 1991, he has been working as a senior scientific officer at the Defence Research Agency in Malvern, advising the MOD on the security implications of its growing use of commercial IT systems, with particular emphasis on UNIX security and countermeasures to malicious software.

Christoph Fischer

Christoph Fischer graduated from the University of Karlsruhe with a degree in Electronics and Engineering. His first contact with computer security was in a computer centre during his time in the German Airforce as a draftee. After his studies, he joined the staff at the computer department at Karlsruhe University. Cooperation with IBM led to the foundation of a support group, Micro-BIT Virus

Center (MVC), which is now under Fischer's direction. Fischer is an active member of a number of research groups in this field of computer security, such as FIRST (Forum for Incident Response and Security Teams), CARO (Computer Anti-virus Research Organisation) and EICAR (European Institute for Computer Anti-virus Research). His current research activities deal with semi-automatic virus analysis and categorization. He also runs a consultancy firm in Karlsruhe which specializes in computers and communication.

Richard Ford

Richard Ford obtained a BA in physics from The Queen's College, Oxford in 1989, and went on to study for a DPhil in semiconductor physics. His interest in computer viruses began during the course of his research, when the computer he was using became infected with the Spanish Telecom virus. The virus triggered, nearly destroying six months' worth of results. Rather than turning to anti-virus software for the answer, Ford analysed the virus himself. In the following year he wrote various articles for *Virus Bulletin* and became Editor in January 1993. Since then he has lectured and talked worldwide on the problems posed by malicious software.

Ross Greenberg

Ross Greenberg was the author of the first anti-virus program, *FluShot*. Initially distributed as freeware, it later evolved into shareware, and then into a commercial product now known as *Virex PC*. Greenberg studied Physics, Mathematics and Philosophy. He has done extensive writing for many of the trade journals, including *Byte*, *PC Magazine* and *Microsoft System Journal*, and was the Technology Editor of *Unix Today*. Greenberg has spoken at many of the virus-related conferences. He is currently working on the final stages of a new communications program. Greenberg is the Sysop of GEnie's Computer Virus & Security Round Table.

Harold Joseph Highland

Dr Highland is one of the most long-standing figures in the anti-virus industry, and is known particularly for his pioneering research. In 1982 he started the international journal *Computers & Security* of which he was editor until 1990. His first article about computer viruses appeared in February 1987, eight months before the appearance of the Brain virus. Now retired, Dr Highland continues to lecture at universities and international conferences and serves on many international computer security committees - he is Managing Director of Compulit's Microcomputer Security Laboratory and President of the Virus Security Institute. Highland is a prolific author and has written 26 books in the past 35 years, including *The Computer Virus Handbook*.

Patricia Hoffman

Patricia Hoffman was educated at San Jose State University, where she gained a BS in Business Administration in 1978. She went on to become a programmer and analyst for a division of Westinghouse. In a later appointment, when working as manager of a data security database administration group, she was called in to help a user whose machine was infected with a virus. It was at this time that she realised the lack of information on computer viruses and decided to create a database of all known viruses which would be understandable to the non-technical user - thus VSUM was born. The VSUM database is now one of the most widespread virus databases in existence, reaching an estimated 5-7 million people.

Jan Hruska

Dr. Jan Hruska is the Technical Director of Sophos Plc, one of the first UK companies to address the virus problem. A graduate of Downing College, Cambridge, he gained his doctorate at Magdalen College, Oxford. He regularly speaks at computer security conferences and consults on a number of security aspects, including virus outbreaks. He is a co-author of *The PC Security Guide*, *Computer Security Solutions*, and *Computer Security Reference Book*. He is also the author of *Computer Viruses and Anti-Virus Warfare*.

Eugene Kaspersky

Eugene Kaspersky's anti-virus career developed from a hobby when a program of his detected and removed the virus Cascade-1704 in September 1989. It was only in 1990, when his first article on computer viruses was published, that he set up his program as freeware, having previously distributed it to friends only. In 1991 he began work for KAMI, and his anti-virus product was launched commercially. His programming team has increased considerably in numbers, with continued emphasis on the importance of anti-virus research. Kaspersky's product is popular in Russia, and accompanies each PC sold by KAMI. He has written a book about viruses, as well as many articles for *Virus Bulletin*.

John McAfee

John McAfee has 23 years' experience in software engineering with companies such as Xerox, General Electric, Siemens and Lockheed. He designed and developed one of the world's first anti-virus products and is currently Chief Technical Officer of McAfee Associates, a public company focused on anti-virus products and electronic software distribution. He was founder of the Computer Virus Industry Association and has authored a book as well as numerous articles on computer viruses.

Yisrael Radai

Yisrael Radai has worked in the Computation Center in the Hebrew University of Jerusalem since 1972, and in the Microcomputer Group for the last seven years. He became active in the fight against computer viruses at the time of the PC virus outbreak in Jerusalem in January 1988. Since then he has devoted a major portion of his time to combating them, specializing in integrity checking techniques. He was involved in the foundation of the Virus Security Institute, is a member of CARO and is on the committee of the Virus Test Center at the University of Hamburg. He regularly speaks at virus and security related conferences, and is a frequent contributor to the electronic forum VIRUS-L.

Roger Riordan

Roger Riordan, Technical Manager of CYBEC Pty Ltd, and veteran electronics engineer, became involved with viruses in 1989, when the New Zealand virus invaded the PC labs at the University where he lectured. The program he wrote to remove it, named *VET*, was immediately successful worldwide. Today *VET* is installed on over 60,000 PCs around the world. Riordan has analysed and named a number of viruses, including the infamous Michelangelo virus, and is well known as an inventor, author and computer virologist.

Fridrik Skulason

Fridrik Skulason received a BSc from the University of Iceland. In 1987 he started his own software company in Reykjavik, specialising in programs tailored for Icelandic needs. Skulason became involved in computer viruses in early 1989, when they first appeared in Iceland. He is the author of the popular *F-Prot* anti-virus software, and has been the Technical Editor of *Virus Bulletin* since February 1990.

Alan Solomon

Alan Solomon began research in the anti-virus field in 1988, after experience in a variety of areas including defence systems, forecasting, corporate planning and stockbroking. In 1988 he designed the first version of his *Anti-Virus Toolkit*, which was launched early in 1989. Now chairman of S&S International, he continues to work closely with the programming team on the *Toolkit*. Much of his time is spent lecturing around the world on security issues; he is also a regular contributor to the anti-virus newsletter *Virus News International*. Solomon is a founder member of CARO, Technical Director of EICAR, chairman of the IBM PC User Group and one of the consultants to the Computer Crime Unit.

David Stang

David Stang has a long-standing interest in viruses. He founded the National Computer Security Association (NCSA) in the US to assist users with viruses, and is both founder and chairman of the International Computer Security Association. He has conducted virus seminars in a dozen countries over the past four years, and has written a collection of virus analysis tools. Stang is now President of Norman Data Defense Systems Inc., a firm that develops and markets anti-virus products for DOS, *Windows*, *OS/2*, and *NetWare*, as well as virus information in hypertext.

Peter Tippett

Peter Tippett was the founder (1986) and President of FoundationWare, later to become Certus International which in 1992 merged with the Peter Norton Group of Symantec Corporation. He designed several PC anti-virus and security products including *Vaccine*, *Corporate Vaccine*, *Certus* and *NOVI*. He is the author of *The Kinetics of Computer Virus Replication*, as well as several trade publication articles on corporate virus protection strategies and virus cost analysis. Dr Tippett has done much consultancy work with large organisations and spoken at many trade shows on virus, security and enterprise issues. Dr Tippett is a member of the board of directors of the NCSA and the Computer Ethics Institute.

Joe Wells

Joe Wells received and disassembled his first virus in 1989, at almost the exact time that the *Virus Bulletin* started publication. Virus analysis became his hobby. As research editor at a business magazine, he made contact with several anti-virus developers while planning a product review. In February 1991, he moved to Ohio and became virus specialist at Certus International. There he worked on the *Certus* product and later co-developed *NOVI*, being responsible for virus detection and repair. He is currently part of the *Norton Anti-Virus* development team and, oddly enough, viruses are still his hobby.

Edward Wilding

Edward Wilding is a consultant in Network Security Management Ltd's investigations division, specialising in computer forensics, the submission of computer-related evidence and the use of relational databases and link analysis software to assist asset tracing and recovery operations. Wilding graduated in history and politics in 1986 and worked in newspaper production and scientific publishing prior to joining the software security specialist Sophos Plc. He is the founding Editor of *Virus Bulletin*, and is a former Editor of *Computer Fraud & Security Bulletin*. He has lectured extensively on the subject of computer security and has devised PC and network security policy in a wide range of organisations. He was a contributor to *Computer Security Solutions* and an advisor to *Computer Viruses and Anti-Virus Warfare*, by Dr. Jan Hruska.

Steve White

Steve White received a PhD from UCSD in theoretical physics in 1982, and since then has been at the IBM Thomas J. Watson Research Center. He has had articles published on a variety of subjects, including condensed matter physics; optimization by simulated annealing; software protection; computer security and computer viruses. White holds several patents in security-related fields. He organized and now manages the High Integrity Computing Laboratory at IBM Research where he is responsible for the research and development of IBM anti-virus products. His research interests include the long-term implications of computer viruses and other self-replicating programs in distributed systems.

Righard Zwienenberg

Righard Zwienenberg is the Research Manager of Computer Security Engineers Ltd, and a part-time student of informatics. He started dealing with computer viruses in 1988, when he encountered a virus problem on a system at the Technical University of Delft. His interest thus kindled, he has studied viral behaviour and presented solutions and detection schemes ever since, initially as an independent consultant, and since 1991 as part of CSE.

```c
int level;
static struct{
      unsigned char *vd_start;
      int offset;
      int orig_offset;
      int range;
      unsigned char *cont;
} for_loop[MAX_LEVEL];
int call_level;
static unsigned char *call_stack[MAX_LEVEL];

int check_for_rest_of_virus(ip,offset_vd,offset,pos_in_file,bytes_in_buff)
struct identity *ip;
int offset_vd;
int offset;
long int pos_in_file;
int bytes_in_buff;
{
      unsigned char *vd,*bufp,*original_buffp;
      static unsigned char local_buff[READ_BUFF_BYTES],aux_buff[READ_BUFF_BYTES];
      register int i,j,k,n,number_instr,jj;
      static int bytes_in_local_buff;
      unsigned long checksum;
      int in_repair,identity_reported;

      original_buffp=buff;
      bufp=buff; /* initially */
      level=call_level=(-1);
      in_repair=identity_reported=FALSE;

      for(vd=(unsigned char *)ip+sizeof(struct identity)+offset_vd,number_instr=0;;number_instr++){
            switch(*vd){
            case CHECKSUM_N_BYTES:
                  n= *(vd+1);
                  if(offset<0 || offset>bytes_in_buff-n) break;
                  checksum=combine_bytes_into_long(vd+2);
                  if(pos_in_file+offset+n>file_len) continue;
                  if(checksum!=checksum_array(bufp+offset,n)) continue;
                  vd+=6;
                  offset+=n;
                  continue;
            case NON_FATAL_CHECKSUM_N_BYTES:
                  n= *(vd+1);
                  if(offset<0 || offset>bytes_in_buff-n) break;
                  checksum=combine_bytes_into_long(vd+2);
                  if(pos_in_file+offset+n>file_len) jj=TRUE;
                  else jj=(checksum!=checksum_array(bufp+offset,n));
                  stack[tos=(tos+1)&MAX_STACK_MASK]=(jj?0:1);
                  vd+=6;
```

Anti-virus vendors

To be poor and independent is very nearly an impossibility.

W. Cobbett

Bangkok Security Associates, PO Box 5-121, Bangkok 10500, Thailand. Tel +66 2 251 2574, Fax +66 2 253 6868

Bates Associates, The Old Barn, Wistow Hall, Leicestershire, LE8 0QF, UK. Tel +44 533 593 010, Fax +44 533 593 878

Brightwork Development International, 766 Shrewsbury Avenue, Jerral Centre West, Tinton Falls, NJ 07724, USA. Tel +1 908 530 0440, Fax +1 908 530 0622

BRM Technologies Ltd, 67 Dereh Hahoresh, Ranot, Jerusalem, Israel. Tel +972 2 861092, Fax +972 2 867503

Central Point Software Inc., 15220 NW Greenbrier Parkway, Suite 200, Beaverton, OR 97006, USA. Tel +1 503 690 8090, Fax +1 503 690 8083/5157

Central Point Software Ltd, 3 Furzeground Way, Stockley Park, Uxbridge, Middlesex, UB11 1DA, UK. Tel +44 81 848 1414, Fax +44 81 569 1017

Cheyenne Software Inc., 3 Express Plaza, Roslyn Heights, NY 11577, USA. Tel +1 516 484 5110, Fax +1 516 484 3446

Clurwin Pty Ltd, 73 Kensington Road, South Yarra, Victoria 3141, Australia. Tel +61 3 827 8002, Fax +61 3 826 2514

Commcrypt Inc., 10000 Virginia Manor Road, Suite 300, Beltsville, MD 20705, USA. Tel +1 301 470 2500, Fax +1 301 470 2507

Computer Security Engineers Ltd, St James House,
New St James Place, St Helier, Jersey, JE4 8WH, UK.
Tel +44 534 500 400, Fax +44 534 500 450

Cybec Pty Ltd, PO Box 205, Hampton, Victoria 3188, Australia.
Tel +61 3 521 0655, Fax +61 3 521 0727

Cybersoft, 210 West 12th Avenue, Conshohocken, PA 19428-1464,
USA. Tel +1 215 825 4748, Fax +1 215 825 6785

Datawatch Inc., PO Box 51489, Durham, NC 27717, USA.
Tel +1 919 490 1277, Fax +1 919 490 6672.

Digital Despatch Inc. (DDI), 55 Lakeland, MN 55043, USA.
Tel +1 612 436 1000, Fax +1 218 436 2085

Distributed Management Systems, Stockclough Lane, Feniscowles,
Blackburn, DB2 5JR, UK. Tel +44 254 208 419,
Fax +44 254 208 418

EliaShim Microcomputers Ltd, 5 Haganim Street, Haifa 31086,
Israel. Tel +972 4 516111, Fax +972 4 528613

Enigma Logic Inc., 2151 Salvio Street, Suite 301, Concord,
CA 94520, USA. Tel +1 510 827 5707, Fax +1 510 827 2593

ESaSS BV, PO Box 1380, 6501 BJ Nijmegen, The Netherlands.
Tel +31 80 78788, Fax +31 80 789186

Fifth Generation Systems Inc., 10049 North Reiger Road,
Baton Rouge, LA 70809-4112, USA. Tel +1 504 291 7221,
Fax +1 504 295 3268

Firefox Communications Ltd, Cranmore House, Cranmore Blvd,
Solihull, B90 4RX, UK. Tel +44 21 609 6090, Fax +44 21 609 6060

Frisk Software International, PO Box 7180, 127 Reykjavik, Iceland.
Tel +354 1 617 273, Fax +354 1 617 274

Frisk Software UK Ltd, 138 Tenby Road, Mosley, Birmingham, B13 9LT, UK. Tel +44 21 777 2142, Fax +44 21 778 2979

H+BEDV, Datentechnik GmbH, Olgastasse 4, D-88069 Tettnang, Germany. Tel +49 7542 6353/93040, Fax +49 7542 52510

Hilgraeve Inc., Genesis Centre, 111 Conant Avenue, Suite A, Monroe, MI 48161, USA. Tel +1 313 243 0576, Fax +1 313 243 0645

IBM, T J Watson Research Center, PO Box 218, Route 134, Yorktown Heights, NY 10598, USA. Tel +1 914 945 3000, Fax +1 914 945 2141

IMSI, 1938 Fourth St, San Rafael, CA 94901, USA. Tel +1 415 454 7101, Fax +1 415 454 8901

Intel Corp., 5200 N E Elam Young Parkway, Hillsborough, OR 97124, USA. Tel +1 503 629 7354, Fax +1 503 629 7580

Intel Corp. UK Ltd, Pipers Way, Swindon, Wiltshire, SN3 1RJ, UK. Tel +44 793 696 000, Fax +44 793 641 440

Iris Software, 6 Hamavo Street, Givataim 53303, Israel. Tel +972 3 571 5319, Fax +972 3 318 731

Jerry Fitzgerald and Associates, 506 Barkentine Lane, Redwood City, CA 94065-1128, USA. Tel +1 415 591 5676, Fax +1 415 593 9316

Leprechaun Software Pty Ltd, PO Box 184, Holland Park, Queensland 4121, Australia. Tel +61 7 343 8866, Fax +61 7 343 8733

Management Analytics, PO Box 1480, Hudson, OH 44236, USA. Tel +1 216 655 9770, Fax +1 216 655 9776

McAfee Associates, 2710 Walsh Avenue, Suite 200, Santa Clara, CA 95051, USA. Tel +1 408 988 3832, Fax +1 408 970 9727

National Semiconductor, Industriestrasse 10,
D-82256 Fuerstenfeldbruck, Germany. Tel +49 8141 103 325,
Fax +49 8141 103 506

Panda Systems, 801 Wilson Road, Wilmington, DE 19803, USA.
Tel +1 302 764 4722, Fax +1 302 764 6186

PC Enhancements Ltd, The Acorn Suite, 15 Greenleaf House,
Darkes Lane, Potters Bar, Hertfordshire EN6 1AE, UK.
Tel +44 707 659016, Fax +44 707 655523

PC Guardian, 1133 East Francisco Blvd, Suite D, San Rafael,
CA 94901, USA. Tel +1 415 459 0190, Fax +1 415 459 1162

PC Security Ltd, The Old Courthouse, Trinity Road, Marlow,
Buckinghamshire SL7 3AN, UK. Tel +44 628 890 390,
Fax +44 628 890 116

Peter Hoffman Service GmbH, Friedrichsplatz 12,
68165 Mannheim, Germany. Tel +49 621 431 1901,
Fax +49 621 444 273

Ports of Trade, 6 Alcis Street, Newlands, Cape Town 7700,
South Africa. Tel +27 21 686 8215, Fax +27 21 685 1807

Prime Factors Inc., 1832 Orchard Street, Eugene, OR 97403, USA.
Tel +1 503 345 4334, Fax +1 503 345 6818

Quaid Software Ltd, RR5 Orangeville, Ontario L9W 2Z2, Canada.
Tel +1 519 942 0832, Fax +1 519 942 3532

Reflex Magnetics Ltd, 31-33 Priory Park Road, Kilburn, London
NW6 7UP, UK. Tel +44 71 372 6666, Fax +44 71 372 2507

Remarkable Products, 245 Pegasus Avenue, Northvale, NJ 07647,
USA. Tel +1 201 784 0900, Fax +1 201 767 7463

RG Software Systems, 6900 East Camelback, Suite 630, Scottsdale, AZ 85251, USA. Tel +1 602 423 8000, Fax +1 602 423 8389

RSA Data Security Inc., 100 Marine Parkway, Suite 500, Redwood City, CA 94065, USA. Tel +1 415 595 8782, Fax +1 415 595 1873

Safetynet Inc., 55 Bleeker Street, Millburn, NJ 07041, USA. Tel +1 908 851 0188, Fax +1 908 276 6575

SA Software, 28 Denbigh Road, London, W13 8NH, UK. Tel +44 81 998 2351, Fax +44 81 998 7507

S&S International Ltd, Berkley Court, Mill Street, Berkhamsted, Hertfordshire HP4 2HB, UK. Tel +44 442 877877, Fax +44 442 877882

Sikkerheds Radgiverne, Gassehaven 52, Holte, DK-2840, Denmark. Tel +45 33 323 537, Fax +45 33 323 547

Softcraft AG, Niederwiesstrasse 8, CH-5417 Untersiggenthal, Switzerland. Tel +41 56 281 116, Fax +41 56 281 116

Software Concepts Design, Virus Acres, New Kingston, NY 12459, USA. Tel +1 914 586 2023, Fax +1 914 586 2025

Sophco Inc., 5890 Woodurne Hollow, Boulder, CO 80301, USA. Tel +1 303 530 7759, Fax +1 303 530 7745

Sophos Plc, 21 The Quadrant, Abingdon Science Park, Abingdon, Oxfordshire OX14 3YS, UK. Tel +44 235 559933, Fax +44 235 559935

Symantec Corporation, 10201 Torre Avenue, Cupertino, CA 95014, USA. Tel +1 408 725 2762, Fax +1 408 253 4992

Symantec Peter Norton Group, 2500 Broadway, Suite 200, Santa Monica, CA 90404, USA. Tel +1 310 453 4600, Fax +1 310 453 0636

Symantec UK, Sygnus Court, Market St, Maidenhead, Berkshire, SL6 8AD, UK. Tel +44 628 592 222, Fax +44 628 592 393

Tekware Ltd, The Barclay Centre, 127A Worcester Road, Hagley, West Midlands, DY9 0NW, UK. Tel +44 562 882 125, Fax +44 562 884 855

The Davidson Group, 20 Exchange Place, 27th Floor, New York, NY 10005, USA. Tel +1 212 422 4100, Fax +1 212 422 1953

Total Control, Unit 3, Station Yard, Hungerford, RG17 0DY, UK. Tel +44 488 685299, Fax +44 488 683288

Trend Micro Devices Inc., 2421 W. 205th Street, Suite D-100, Torrance, CA 90501, USA. Tel +1 310 782 8190, Fax +1 310 328 5892

V Communications Inc., 4320 Stevens Creek Blvd, Suite 275, San Jose, CA 95129, USA. Tel +1 408 296 4224, Fax +1 408 296 4441

Visionsoft, Unit C7, Enterprise Way, Five Lane Ends, Idle, Bradford, West Yorkshire BD10 8EW, UK. Tel +44 274 610503, Fax +44 274 616010

Further information

It is a great nuisance that knowledge can only be acquired by hard work. It would be fine if we could swallow the powder of profitable information made palatable by the jam of fiction.

W. Somerset Maugham

Books on Viruses

A Pathology of Computer Viruses, Ferbrache, D., *Springer-Verlag,* 1992

A Short Course on Computer Viruses, Cohen, F., *ASP Press,* 1991

Computer Security Reference Book, Jackson, K., Hruska, J., Parker, D., *Butterworth-Heinemann,* 1992

Computer Viruses, Peers, E., Ennis, C., *Deloitte Haskins & Sells*

Computer Viruses, a High Tech Disease, Burger, R., *Abacus,* 1988

Computer Viruses and Anti-virus Warfare, Hruska, J., *Ellis Horwood,* 1990, 1992

Computer Viruses and Data Protection, Burger, R., *Abacus,* 1991

Computer Viruses, What They Are, How They Work, and How to Avoid Them, Mayo, J. L., *Windcrest,* 1989

Data Security Reference Guide 1991/92, *Sophos Ltd.,* 1993

Dataquest Virus Survey, *NCSA,* 1991

LAN Desktop Guide to Security NetWare Edition, Sawicki, E., *SAMS,* 1992

PC Viruses, Detection, Analysis and Cure, Solomon, A., *Springer-Verlag,* 1991

The Complete Computer Virus Handbook, Frost, D., Beale, I., Frost, C., *Price Waterhouse and Pitman,* 1989

The Computer Virus Crisis, Fites, P., Johnston, P., Kratz, M., *Van Nostrand Reinhold,* 1989

The Computer Virus Handbook, Levin, R., *Osborne/McGraw-Hill,* 1990

The Computer Virus Handbook, Highland, H. J., *Elsevier Advanced Technology,* 1990

The Little Black Book of Computer Viruses, Ludwig, M., *American Eagle Publications Inc.,* 1992

Virus Bulletin 1991 International Conference Proceedings, *Virus Bulletin*, 1991

Virus Bulletin 1992 International Conference Proceedings, *Virus Bulletin*, 1992

Virus Bulletin 1993 International Conference Proceedings, *Virus Bulletin*, 1993

Periodicals on Viruses

Virus Bulletin, 21 The Quadrant, Abingdon Science Park, Abingdon, Oxfordshire OX14 3YS, UK. Tel +44 235 555139, Fax +44 235 559935

Virus News International, William Knox House, Brittanic Way, Llandarcy, Swansea SA10 6NL, UK. Tel +44 792 324000, Fax +44 792 324001

Bulletin Boards Carrying Virus-related Discussions

BIX is a bulletin board run by Byte magazine in the US. On-line subscription is possible on +1 617 861 9767 (full duplex, 8 bits, no parity, 1 stop bit or 7 bits, even parity, 1 stop bit). Hit the Return key, on *login* prompt enter *bix* and on *Name?* prompt enter *bix.flatfee*. Credit cards are accepted. The Packet Switch Stream (PSS) address is 310690157800. A number of virus-related conferences are going on; try *law/virus* and *security/critters*.

CIX is a London-based bulletin board which carries regular discussions on a number of security-related topics, including viruses. To register, telephone +44 81 390 1255 (any modem speed up to 14.4 Kbaud). Payment by credit card is accepted.

Virus Bulletin can be contacted via CIX (username *virus_bulletin*).

Virus-L is an archived moderated bulletin board system which carries virus-related information. It is available from a number of sites including **cert.sei.cmu.edu** (maintained by Ken Van Wyk) and **pdsoft.lancs.ac.uk** (maintained by Steve Jenkins and also available by direct dialup on +44 524 63414). For a complete list of sites, see *A Pathology of Computer Viruses* by David Ferbrache.

Virus Information on Disk

Virus information summary list (VSUM), monthly from Patricia Hoffman, USA. Tel +1 408 988 3733, Fax +1 408 246 3915

Virus Training Videos

Computer Security - Who's Solving the Problem, Positive Image, UK. Tel 071 407 0265, Fax 081 403 2355

PC's Under Attack, Mediamix, USA. Tel +1 908 277 0058, Fax +1 908 277 0119

The Computer Virus and How to Control It, 23 min, James C. Shaeffer & Associates, USA. Tel +1 800 968 9527, Fax +1 313 741 9528

Virus Video, S&S International Ltd, Berkley Court, Mill Street, Berkhamsted, Hertfordshire HP4 2HB, UK. Tel +44 442 877877, Fax +44 442 877882

Viruses on Personal Computers training video, 30 min, Sophos Plc, 21 The Quadrant, Abingdon Science Park, Abingdon, Oxfordshire OX14 3YS, UK. Tel +44 235 559933, Fax +44 235 559935

Other Useful Books

Peter Norton Programmer's Guide to IBM PC & PS/2, Norton, P., and Wilton, R., *Microsoft Press,* 1985

Technical Reference for IBM Personal Computer AT, *IBM*, No. 6280070, 1985

Technical Reference for IBM Personal Computer XT, *IBM*, No. 6280089, 1986

The MS-DOS Encyclopedia, Duncan, R., *Microsoft Press,* 1988

Glossary

> Proper words in proper places make the true definition of a style.
>
> *Jonathan Swift*

Access control:	The process of ensuring that systems are only accessed by those authorised to do so, and only in a manner for which they have been authorised.
Active attack:	An attack on a system which either injects false information into the system, or corrupts information already present on the system. See passive attack.
Algorithm:	An algorithm is a set of rules which specifies a method of carrying out a task (e.g. an encryption algorithm).
ANSI:	American National Standards Institute is the organisation which issues standards in the US.
ASCII:	American Standard Code for Information Interchange is the standard system for representing letters and symbols. Each letter or symbol is assigned a unique number between 0 and 127.
Asymmetric encryption:	Encryption which permits the key used for encryption to be different for the key used for decryption. RSA is the most widely used asymmetric encryption algorithm.
Audit log:	See audit trail.
Audit trail:	Audit trails provide a date and time stamped record of the usage of a system. They record what a computer was used for, allowing a security manager to monitor the actions of every user, and can help in establishing an alleged fraud or security violation.
Authentication:	The process of assuring that data has come from its claimed source, or of corroborating the claimed identity of a communicating party.
Authorisation:	Determining whether a subject is trusted for a given purpose.
Availability:	The prevention of unauthorised withholding of information or resources.
Back door:	An undocumented means of bypassing the normal access control procedures of a computer system.

Background operation: The name applied to a program running in a multitasking environment over which the user has no direct control.

Backup: A copy of computer data that is used to recreate data that has been lost, mislaid, corrupted or erased.

Bad sectors: During formatting of MS-DOS disks, all sectors are checked for usability. Unusable sectors are labelled as bad and are not used by DOS. The remaining areas can then still be used. Viruses sometimes label good sectors as bad to store their code outside the reach of users and the operating system.

BAT: The extension given to 'batch' file names in MS-DOS. A batch file contains a series of MS-DOS commands, which can be executed by using the name of the file as a command. AUTOEXEC.BAT is a special batch file which is executed whenever a PC is switched on, and can be used to configure the PC to a user's requirements.

BBS: Bulletin Board System, a computer with one or more modems attached which can be accessed by telephone. Most bulletin boards act as repositories for downloadable software, and have electronic mail systems.

Bell-LaPadula model: An access security model couched in terms of subjects and objects. Information shall not flow to a lesser or non-comparable classification.

Biba model: An integrity model in which there can be no contamination by a less trusted or non-comparable subject or object.

Binary: A number system with base 2. The binary digits (bits) are 0 and 1. Binary arithmetic is used by today's computers since the two digits can be represented with two electrical or magnetic states, for example the presence and absence of a current.

Biometrics: A technique for identifying a person by one of his personal characteristics e.g. retina pattern, fingerprint.

BIOS: The Basic Input/Output System of a PC which constitutes the lowest level of software which interfaces directly with the hardware of the microcomputer. The BIOS is usually stored in a ROM chip.

Bit: The smallest unit of information. It can only have the value 0 or 1. The word 'bit' is derived from the initial and final letters of the phrase 'Binary digIT'.

Bit copying: A technique for making a copy of a disk by reading all of the individual bits on each track of the disk, and making a direct copy of each track onto a new disk. A bit copying program has no knowledge of the file structure being used on a disk.

Block cipher: A cipher which provides encryption and decryption by operating on a specified size of data block, e.g. 64 bits.

Boot protection: Method used to prevent bypassing security measures installed on a hard disk by bootstrapping a microcomputer from a floppy disk.

Boot sector virus: A type of computer virus which subverts the initial stages of the bootstrapping process. A boot sector virus attacks either the master bootstrap sector or the DOS bootstrap sector of a disk.

Booting-up: A process carried out when a computer is first switched on or reset, where the operating system software is loaded from disk.

Bootstrap sector: Part of the operating system which is first read into memory from disk when a PC is switched on (booted). The program stored in the bootstrap sector is then executed, which in turn loads the rest of the operating system into memory from the system files on disk.

Bootstrapping: See booting-up.

Bug: A small electronic device used for covert eavesdropping. Different types are available to listen to voice conversations, data being transmitted across a network, or telephone lines. A fault in a computer program is also called a bug. The two meanings are entirely separate.

Bulletin board   See BBS.

Byte: A set of 8 bits which is the amount of information sufficient to store one character. It is usually the smallest individual unit that can be read from or written to memory.

Cache: High-speed data storage used to hold data retrieved from a slow device. Using a cache normally increases the overall performance of a system.

CBC: Cipher Block Chaining, a mode of use of a block cipher.

CCC: Chaos Computer Club, an infamous group of German hackers based in Hamburg, Germany.

CCTA: Central Computer and Telecommunications Agency, the UK Government agency responsible for government computer purchases (amongst other duties).

CESG: Communications-Electronics Security Group, a UK government COMPUSEC agency (CCTA is another).

CFB: Cipher Feedback, a mode of use of a block cipher.

Checksum:	A value calculated from item(s) of data which can be used by a recipient of the data to verify that the received data has not been altered. Usually 32 or 64 bits long.
Cipher:	Encryption algorithm.
Ciphertext:	A term used to describe text (or data) that has previously been encrypted. See encryption.
CMOS:	Complementary Metal-Oxide Semiconductor is a technology used to manufacture chips which have very low power consumption. CMOS chips are used in battery-backed applications such as the time-of-day clock and for the non-volatile storage of parameters in IBM-ATs.
COM:	The extension given to a type of executable files in MS-DOS. They are similar to EXE files, but can only contain up to 64K of code and data. In other operating systems, the extension COM can have a different significance.
Companion virus:	A virus which 'infects' EXE files by creating a COM file with the same name and containing the virus code. They exploit the MS-DOS property that if two programs with the same name exist, the operating system will execute a COM file in preference to an EXE file.
Compiler:	A computer program which translates programs written in a high-level language that can be readily understood by humans into low level instructions that can be executed by a computer's CPU.
COMPSEC, COMPUSEC:	Often used abbreviations for COMPuter SECurity.
Computer crime:	This phrase has two meanings: Any crime mediated by a computer; or any crime that attacks a computer system as part of the process of committing the crime. The meaning used in any particular situation is context dependent, and not always clear.
Confidentiality:	The process of ensuring that data is not disclosed to those not authorised to see it. Also known as secrecy.
Conventional memory:	The bytes of PC memory addressable by the 8086 instruction set.
Co-processor:	Specialised computer hardware used in conjunction with a CPU to perform a specific task very efficiently, e.g. floating point arithmetic, matrix multiplication.
Copy protection:	A method which makes it difficult (if not impossible) to make copies of a computer program. Copy protection tries to prevent software theft.

CPU: Central Processing Unit, the heart of every PC, the device which takes instructions from memory and executes them. In most PCs the CPU is a single microprocessor.

CRC: Cyclic Redundancy Check, a mathematical method for verifying the integrity of data. It is a form of checksum, based on the theory of maximum length polynomials. While more secure than a simple checksum, CRCs do not offer true cryptographic security. See cryptographic checksum.

Cryptanalysis: The study of an encryption system, often with the intention of detecting any weakness in the encryption algorithm.

Cryptographic checksum: A checksum calculated using a cryptographically based algorithm. It is impossible to 'engineer' changes to data in such a way as to leave a cryptographic checksum unchanged.

Data protection: A group of techniques used to preserve three desirable aspects of data: confidentiality, integrity and availability. Also a legal term with specific meaning (somewhat different to the above definition).

Deciphering: See decryption.

Decryption: Decryption is the process of transforming ciphertext back into plaintext. It is the reverse of encryption.

Decryption key: See key.

DES: Data Encryption Standard, an algorithm for encrypting or decrypting 64 bits of data using a 56 bit key. DES is widely used in the financial world.

Device driver: A program used to 'handle' a hardware device such as a screen, disk, keyboard etc. This allows the operating system to use the device without knowing specifically how the device performs a particular task.

Digital signature: A means of protecting a message from denial of origination by the sender, usually involving the use of asymmetric encryption to produce an encrypted message or a cryptographic checkfunction.

Diskless node: See diskless workstation.

Diskless workstation: A PC which does not contain a floppy disk drive and is connected to a network.

Dongle: A hardware security product which must be plugged into a computer system before a particular application program will execute. A dongle aims to prevent illegal copying of a computer program.

DOS: Disk Operating System. See MS-DOS.

DOS bootstrap sector: The bootstrap sector which loads DOS into PC RAM and starts its execution. Common point of attack by boot sector viruses.

Downloading: A process where data is transferred electronically from a 'host' computer to an intelligent terminal or PC.

EAROM: Electrically Alterable Read Only Memory, a particular type of EEPROM, in which individual bytes can be altered by electrical pulses.

ECB: Electronic Codebook, a mode of use of a block cipher.

EEPROM: Electrically Erasable Programmable Read Only Memory, a non-volatile memory which can be written to and read from many times. It is erased by an electrical pulse. EPROMs are used for storing data which does not change frequently e.g. setup parameters.

Electronic mail: Messages exchanged over a computer communications network.

Enciphering: Means the same as encrypting. See encryption.

Encryption: A process of disguising information so that it cannot be understood by an unauthorised person.

Encryption key: See key.

EPROM: Electrically Programmable Read Only Memory, a non-volatile memory which can be programmed (written to) once, and read from many times. Most types of EPROM can be erased by exposure to ultra-violet light. EPROMs are used for storing data which is unlikely to be changed.

EXE: The extension given to executable files in MS-DOS.

Exhaustive key search: Finding out which key was actually used by an encryption system by testing all possible keys in turn.

Expanded memory: PC memory which conforms to the industry standard specification EMS (Expanded Memory Specification), and enables DOS to access more than 640K of memory.

Extended memory: Memory in PCs which lies above 1 MByte in a 80286 (or above)-machine.

False negative: An existent event reported as non-existent, e.g. a virus failing to be detected.

False positive: A non-existent event reported as existent, e.g. a virus being reported when no virus is present.

FAT: File Allocation Table, a mnemonic term used by the MS-DOS operating system (and others) to describe the part of a disk which contains information describing the physical location of files on the disk.

File compression: The compacting of a file through the process of recoding its bit structure into a shorter form. File compression must be reversible.

File encryption: The transformation of a file's contents (in plain text) into an unintelligible form by means of some form of cryptographic system or manipulation.

File integrity: Techniques used to provide 'safe' backup files for recovery purposes in the event that critical files have become contaminated through some accidental or intentional mechanism (e.g. computer virus attack).

File labelling: The classifying of the sensitivity level of a file either by external (visible outside marking) or internal (magnetic coding of the header label) coding, or by a combination of these two methods.

File server: A central data repository for a computer network, which may provide other centralised services such as shared printer control.

Firmware: Jargon for a computer program stored in a non-volatile memory, such as an EPROM or an EEPROM.

Floppy disks: Interchangeable magnetic disks which are used to store computer data. Usual formats are 3.5" and 5.25" disks, and capacities of the order of 1 Mbyte.

Hacker: An individual whose interests, motivated for benign or malicious reasons, concern 'breaking into' computer systems. The word hacker is also used to denote someone who produces prodigious amounts of software. The two meanings are completely distinct, and often confused.

Hard disk: A hermetically sealed magnetic disk, generally fixed within a computer, which is used to store data. Hard disk capacity is of the order of 10 Mbytes to 1 Gbyte.

Hardware: Any component of a computer system that has physical form. It is a term used to draw a distinction between the computer itself (hardware), and the programs which are executed on the computer (software).

Hash function: A function which maps a set of variable size data into objects of a single size. Widely used for fast searching.

Hashing: The process of calculating a hash function.

Hexadecimal:	A system of counting using number base 16. The numbers 10 to 15 are represented by the characters 'A' through 'F' respectively. Hexadecimal is often abbreviated to hex. Each hex digit is equivalent to four bits (half a byte) of information.
IC:	Integrated Circuit, an electronic device containing many discrete electronic components such as transistors, resistors and the wire links which interconnect them. ICs are usually made in very large numbers and in miniaturised form, on a common base or substrate of silicon.
ID:	An identification code, username, identification card or identification token.
Integrity:	A security protection aimed at ensuring that data cannot be deleted, modified, duplicated or forged without detection.
Internet:	One of the largest world-wide networks for the transmission of electronic mail messages.
Interrupt:	A mechanism by which a process can attract the immediate attention of the CPU, usually in order to serve an urgent request from an external device. The interrupt table on 8086 microprocessors occupies the bottom 1K of RAM.
I/O port:	A computer communicates with the outside world through Input/Output (I/O) ports. Examples are the RS-232 serial port and printer ports on a PC.
ISO:	International Organisation for Standardisation, the worldwide federation of international standards bodies.
IV:	Initialisation Variable, a value used to initialise modes of use of certain block ciphers.
K:	Shorthand for a thousand (1000), but in computing it is often used to mean 1024 (2^{10}, approximately 1000). For example, 64K or 64 Kbytes refers to 64*1024 = 65536 bytes.
Key:	When used in the context of encryption, a series of numbers which are used by an encryption algorithm to transform plaintext data into encrypted (ciphertext) data, and vice versa. Confusingly, key can also refer to a physical token which gives access to a system.
Key management:	The process of securely generating, transporting, storing and destroying encryption keys.

LAN: Local Area Network, a data communications network covering a limited area (up to several kilometres in radius) with moderate to high data transmission speeds.

Letter bomb: A logic bomb contained in electronic mail, which will trigger when the mail is read.

Link virus: A virus which subverts directory entries to point to the virus code.

Logic bomb: A program modification which causes damage when triggered by some condition such as the date, or the presence or absence of data e.g. a name.

M: Shorthand for a million (1000000), but in computing it is often used to mean 1048576 (2^{20}, approximately one million). For example, 1M or 1 Mbyte refers to 1048576 bytes.

MAC: Message Authentication Code, a cryptographic checksum for a message. Unlike a digital signature, a MAC requires knowledge of a secret key for verification.

Mainframe: Large computer systems, often occupying purpose-built facilities, used for IT applications requiring extremely fast processing speeds or large quantities of data. Typical processing speeds are of the order of 100 MIPS.

Master bootstrap sector: The first physical sector on the hard disk (sector 1, head 0, track 0) which is loaded and executed when the PC is bootstrapped. It contains the partition table as well as the code to load and execute the bootstrap sector of the 'active' partition. Common point of attack by boot sector viruses.

Menu-driven: Software which presents the user with a fixed 'menu' of command choices, often requiring only a single key or mouse button depression to select the required option.

Message authentication: The process of calculating and then subsequently verifying a message authentication code.

Message digest: See hash function.

Microprocessor: An integrated circuit which condense the essential elements of a computer's CPU into a single device.

Minicomputer: A fixed, generally multi-user, computer designed for use as a communal information processing system. Typical processing speeds are between 10 and 100 MIPS.

MIPS: Millions of Instructions Per Second.

Mirroring: A technique where data is written to two (or more) disks simultaneously, with the intention of enabling data retrieval if one of the disks fails.

Modem: A MOdulator/DEModulator is a device which translates digital computer data into a form suitable for transmission over an analogue telecommunications path such as a telephone line, radio channel or satellite link.

Mouse: A data input device which, when moved by hand on the surface of a desk, conveys the direction and amount of movement to a computer. A mouse is commonly equipped with one, two or three press-buttons to actuate commands on the computer.

MS-DOS: The Disk Operating System sold by Microsoft. It is the most common microcomputer system in the world, and operates on the IBM PC. See PC-DOS and compatibles.

Multi-partite virus: A virus which infects both boot sectors and executable files, thus exhibiting the characteristics of both boot sector and parasitic viruses.

Multitasking: The ability of a computer to divide its processing time amongst several different tasks. Although most computers contain only one CPU, they can switch between operations so quickly that several processes appear to run simultaneously.

Nibble: A set of 4 bits.

Non-volatile memory: Integrated circuits which retain their content when their normal power source is switched off. The main types are ROM, EPROM, EEPROM and battery backed CMOS RAM.

OFB: Output FeedBack, a mode of use of a block cipher.

Off-site backup: A backup stored at a geographically remote location.

One-way function: A function that can readily be calculated, but whose inverse is very difficult to calculate.

Operating system: The computer program which performs basic housekeeping functions such as maintaining lists of files, running programs etc. PC operating systems include MS-DOS and OS/2, while minicomputer and mainframe operating systems include Unix, VMS and MVS.

Optical disk: A storage device using a laser to record and read data from a rotating disk.

OS/2: An operating system for 80286+ based IBM compatibles. It allows true multitasking.

OSI: Open Systems Interconnection, a set of standards defining the protocols for communication between open (non-proprietary) systems.

OVL: The extension commonly given to overlay files in MS-DOS. Overlay files are used with large programs which cannot fit into RAM: parts of the program are loaded as and when needed. Overlay files can have any extension, not just OVL.

Parasitic virus: A computer virus which attaches itself to another computer program, and is activated when that program is executed. A parasitic virus can append itself to either the beginning or the end of a program, or it can overwrite part of the program.

Partition table: A 64-bit table found inside the master bootstrap sector on hard disks which contains information about the size and position of up to four partitions on the hard disk. The partition table also contains information on the type of the partitions, e.g. DOS partition, UNIX partition.

Passive attack: An attack on a system which extracts information and makes use of it, but never injects false information or corrupts any information (which would be an active attack).

Password: Sequence of characters which allows users access to a system. Although they are supposed to be unique, experience has shown that most people's choices are highly insecure. Humans tend to choose short words, such as names, which are easy to guess.

PC: Personal Computer, a desktop or portable single-user computer usually comprising a CPU, memory, screen, keyboard and disk drive(s). PC has become synonymous with IBM compatible computer, even though this definition is not strictly correct.

PC-DOS: Microcomputer operating system originally used by IBM for its PCs. It is functionally identical to MS-DOS.

Peripheral: External device connected to a computer. Examples include printers, plotters, disk drives, external modems and a mouse.

Peripheral access control: Technique to restrict the use of certain computer peripherals to authorised users.

Pest program: A collective term for programs with deleterious and generally unanticipated side effects e.g. trojan horses, logic bombs, viruses and malicious worms.

Plaintext: Data before it has been enciphered. The opposite of ciphertext.

Polymorphic virus:	Self-modifying encrypting virus.
Port access control:	Restricting the use of computer data ports to authorised users only.
Processor:	A unit of hardware that is capable of executing instructions contained in a computer program.
Program:	A precise sequence of instructions that specifies what action a computer should perform. 'Software' is often used to describe a computer program.
Proprietary encryption algorithm:	An encryption algorithm designed to a proprietary (and usually secret) specification.
PS/2:	A series of computers from IBM designed to replace the PC/XT/AT range. All models, except model 30, support the 'microchannel architecture'. Expansion cards designed for the IBM PC/XT/AT are not compatible with PS/2 machines.
Public domain:	Two totally distinct meanings exist: the area which is outside government security arrangements; or something which is neither subject to copyright nor a trademark.
RAM:	Random Access Memory, volatile memory which can be written to, and read from, at high speed. It is normal to load programs from disk into RAM, and then to execute them. The operating system takes care of the allocation of RAM to executing programs.
Reverse-engineering:	The process of deducing how something works without having access to the design details.
ROM:	Read Only Memory, a form of non-volatile memory in a computer. Data is embedded into a ROM during manufacture. A ROM is usually used to store the startup software which is executed by a PC on power up. See bootstrapping.
RS-232:	The most widely used standard for serial data communication. The speed of communication is measured in baud.
Scrambling:	See encryption.
Secret key:	Encryption key that must not be disclosed. If it is revealed, the security offered by the encryption algorithm is compromised. Not all encryption keys have to be kept secret, e.g. public keys in asymmetric encryption.
Security:	Protection against unwanted behaviour. The most widely used definition of (computer) security is *security = confidentiality + integrity + availability*.

Security policy: A security policy is the set of rules, principles and practices that determine how security is implemented in an organisation. It must maintain the principles of the organisation's general security policy.

Security server: A special LAN station which runs software that monitors LAN usage, and controls access independently of the LAN operating system.

Server: See file server and security server.

Smart disk: A device in the shape of a 3.5" floppy disk which contains a microprocessor and memory. It can be read from and written to in a standard floppy disk drive.

Software: See program.

Spoofing: Pretending to be someone or something else (e.g. entering someone else's password).

Stealth virus: A virus which hides its presence from the PC user and anti-virus programs, usually by trapping interrupt services.

Stream cipher: A cipher which provides encryption and decryption by operating on continuous stream of data, without imposing limits on the length of the data.

Symmetric Algorithm: An algorithm in which the key used for encryption is identical to the key used for decryption. DES is the best known symmetric encryption algorithm.

SYS: The extension given to system file names in MS-DOS. An example is the file CONFIG.SYS which sets up various configuration parameters for the operating system on power-up.

Terminal: A device which consists of a VDU and keyboard. It allows a user to interact with a computer.

Time bomb: A logic bomb set to trigger at a particular time.

Timeout: A logical access control feature which automatically logs off users of terminals which do not exhibit signs of activity for a certain duration of time.

Token: A physical object, sometimes containing sophisticated electronics, which is required to gain access to a system. Some tokens contain a microprocessor and are called intelligent tokens, or smart cards.

Trapdoor: A hidden flaw in a system mechanism that can be triggered to circumvent the system's security.

Trojan horse: A computer program whose execution would result in undesired side effects, generally unanticipated by the user. The trojan horse program may otherwise give the appearance of providing normal functionality.

TSR: Terminate and Stay Resident, a term used to describe an MS-DOS program which remains in memory after being executed. A TSR can be re-activated either by a specific sequence of keystrokes, at some specific time, or by some specific signal from an I/O port.

UNIX: UNIX is a multi-user operating system, developed by AT&T. Several versions of UNIX exist, which do not all achieve compatibility with each other.

Uploading: The process of transferring data from a remote computer to a central host.

UPS: Uninterruptible Power Supply, a device which detects mains failure and provides power from an internal battery supply for a limited period.

VDU: Visual Display Unit, a computer peripheral which displays text and/or graphics on a television screen.

Virus: Sometimes explicitly referred to as a computer virus, a program which makes copies of itself in such a way as to 'infect' parts of the operating system and/or application programs. See boot sector virus and parasitic virus.

Virus signature: An identifier recognised by the virus as meaning 'this item is already infected, do not reinfect'. It can take different forms such as the text 'sURIV' at the beginning of the file, the size of the file divisible by a number or the number of seconds in the date stamp set to 62. Some viruses do not recognise their signatures correctly.

WAN: Wide Area Network, a set of computers that communicate with each other over long distances.

Workstation: An ill-defined term used to describe a powerful single user, high performance, minicomputer or microcomputer, which is used by individuals for tasks involving intensive processing, perhaps CAD or simulation.

Worm: A program that distributes multiple copies of itself within a system or across a distributed system.

Worm Attack: Interference by a program that is acting beyond normally expected behaviour, perhaps exploiting security vulnerabilities or causing denials of service. See worm.

XOR: An abbreviation of the logical operation known as Exclusive-or. An exclusive-or function is defined as having the value true when either of the input conditions (but not both) is true.

Index

EOF	▶EOF	866	4	5	6	7	8	9	10	11	12	13
14	15	16	17	18	19	▶EOF	21	22	23	24	25	26
27	28	29	30	31	32	33	34	35	36	37	38	▶EOF
40	41	42	43	44	45	46	47	48	49	50	51	52
53	54	55	56	57	58	59	60	61	62	▶EOF	64	65
66	67	68	69	70	71	▶EOF	73	74	▶EOF	76	77	78
79	80	81	82	83	84	85	86	87	88	89	90	91
▶EOF	93	94	95	96	97	98	99	▶EOF	101	102	103	104
105	106	107	108	109	110	111	112	113	114	115	116	▶EOF
118	119	120	121	122	▶EOF	124	125	126	127	128	129	130
131	132	133	134	▶EOF	136	137	138	139	140	▶EOF	142	143
144	145	▶EOF	147	148	149	150	151	152	153	154	155	156
▶EOF	158	159	160	161	162	163	164	165	166	167	168	169
170	171	172	173	174	175	176	177	178	179	180	181	182
183	184	▶EOF	186	187	188	189	190	191	192	193	▶EOF	195
196	▶EOF	198	199	200	201	202	▶EOF	204	205	206	207	208
209	▶EOF	211	212	213	214	215	216	▶EOF	218	219	220	221
222	223	224	225	226	▶EOF	228	229	230	231	232	233	234
▶EOF	▶EOF	▶EOF	238	239	240	241	242	243	244	245	246	247
248	249	250	▶EOF	252	253	254	▶EOF	▶EOF				

Unavailable cluster in large FAT

Logical sector 1 (First copy of FAT) byte 0 (0 hex)

Computer virus update....

If you found this book of interest and would like regular access to current information on the computer virus threat, *Virus Bulletin* also publishes a technical monthly magazine. Each issue contains industry news, detailed product reviews and analyses of the latest malicious programs, providing an invaluable aid to computer security professionals in over 30 countries worldwide.

As a special offer, the purchase price of this book can be reclaimed against the cost of your first year's subscription. To place your order, simply photocopy and complete the form below.

❏ Please enter my subscription to *Virus Bulletin* (ISSN 0956-9979) for 1 year (12 issues), including a free binder, at the discounted price of:

❏ UK £175.00 ❏ Europe £205.00 ❏ International £225.00

Name: _____ Position: _____

Company: _____

Address: _____

_____

Tel: _____ Fax: _____

Company VAT Reg. No. (EC only): _____

❏ Payment enclosed

❏ Please invoice my company (Purchase Order No._____)

❏ Please charge my credit card ❏ Visa/Mastercard/Eurocard/Access
                               ❏ American Express

Card Number: _____ Card Holder: _____

Expiry date: _____ Signature: _____

Fax this order to +44 (0)235 559935 or send it to
Virus Bulletin Ltd, 21 The Quadrant, Abingdon, Oxon OX14 3YS, UK